The Cruel Dilemmas
of Development:
Twentieth-Century
Brazil

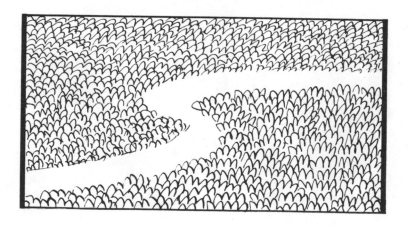

THE CRUEL DILEMMAS OF DEVELOPMENT: TWENTIETH-CENTURY BRAZIL

C. 1

SYLVIA ANN HEWLETT

Basic Books, Inc., Publishers

NEW YORK

Library of Congress Cataloging in Publication Data

Hewlett, Sylvia Ann, 1946–
   The cruel dilemmas of development.

   Includes index.
   1. Brazil—Economic conditions—1945–
2. Brazil—Social conditions—1945–   3. Brazil—
Politics and government—1954–   I. Title.
HC187.H48   330.981'06   79–5198
ISBN:0–465–01497–6

To my parents Vernon and Jean Hewlett,

for their love and encouragement

CONTENTS

LIST OF TABLES

(following page 221)

ACKNOWLEDGMENTS

IN THE FIVE YEARS it took me to write this book, I have received generous institutional, collegial, and personal support which it is my pleasure to acknowledge.

The field research in Brazil was supported by grants from the Nuffield and Spencer Foundations. Girton College, Cambridge University, and Queen Elizabeth House, Oxford University, gave me the time and the research facilities with which to develop the initial ideas for this study. An appointment as a Research Fellow at the Lehrman Institute in New York City during 1976–77 provided me with the rare opportunity to present several chapters of my book to critical but constructive colleagues. Albert O. Hirschman, Edward Nell, Robert Heilbroner, Emma Rothschild, Alfred Stepan, Abraham Lowenthal, Peter Winn, Charles Perrow, Peter Leslie, Louis Goodman, and Nicholas Rizopoulos were particularly helpful during this year.

My greatest intellectual debt is to Joan Robinson and Celso Furtado, both of whom encouraged me to tackle the large issues and examine the human consequences of contemporary growth strategies. Without their support and their example, I would not have found the courage to attempt this study.

During the last five years, I have incurred heavy debts of gratitude to Brazilians and to "Brazilianists." Edmar Bacha, Fernando Henrique Cardoso, Sergio Corrêa da Costa, Paulo Singer, Pedro Paulo Poppovic, Fernando Gasparian, Ronald Levinsohn, Elio Gaspari, Luciano Martins, Thomas Skidmore, Joel Bergsman, Douglas Graham, and John Wells have been particularly generous in sharing their time and their knowledge.

I am extremely grateful to Richard Fagen and Albert Fishlow for many valuable discussions and for thoughtful comments on earlier versions of this study. My thanks are also due to Deborah Milenkovitch, Duncan Foley, Annette Baxter, Douglas Chalmers, Louis Henkin, Kenneth Maxwell, and Alex Erlich, colleagues at Barnard College and Columbia University, and to Martin Kessler, my editor at Basic Books, who have lent me continuing encouragement and support.

I feel an immense intellectual and personal gratitude to my husband, Richard Weinert. At critical stages of the writing process he devoted his best energies to my book. His penetrating and detailed criticisms and his loving encouragement often made it possible for me to rethink and re-write important segments of the manuscript. And over the last three years he has spent many weekends cooking, shopping, and looking after the children so that I could work. Would that every author had such a spouse!

A final word of thanks is due to my stepdaughter Shira and my daughter Lisa, for putting up with my absences and for restoring a sense of perspective to scholastic pursuits.

SYLVIA ANN HEWLETT
New York City, December 1979

Introduction

CHAPTER

1

Tragic Trade-offs

In the economic policies of government one finds not only
the explanation for its repressive crimes, but also a greater
atrocity which punishes millions of human beings with carefully planned misery. . . .

Open letter by Rodolfo Walsh
to the Argentinian Junta

PUBLIC DISCUSSION on the issue of human rights in the Third World
is floundering in a sea of platitudes and good intentions. Lofty sentiments and admirable aspirations have hit us from all sides. The United
Nations has committed itself to "work urgently for the establishment of
a new international economic order . . . which shall correct inequalities
and redress existing injustices . . . and ensure steadily accelerating economic and social development and peace for present and future generations." [1] While President Carter in his enthusiastic pursuit of human
rights has promised to dedicate himself "to the dignity and well-being
of people throughout the world." [2]

Fine-sounding, noble ideas, but scratch the surface and one finds little
consensus as to what causes misery and brutality in today's underdeveloped world, and an extremely confused sense of which policies, if any,
are capable of ameliorating these conditions. For the concerned citizen,
appalled by reports of starvation in India, torture in Chile, and mass
murder in the Amazonian jungle, it is easy to heap the blame on the
shoulders of some "bad guy." This scapegoat syndrome leads to some
rather simple-minded recommendations. If only the world could rid itself of the Shah, or of Pinochet, or of the CIA, or of the multinationals,

the human rights problem would disappear, and we would all live happily ever after! A seductive line of reasoning since it enables most of us to feel self-righteous while neatly evading any direct responsibility. However, despite the attractions of this approach, it is far from being an adequate answer to the issues in hand.

It is a basic contention of this book that poverty and repression are grounded in the harsh realities of economic development. Most human rights violations, far from being the idiosyncratic preference of some evil ruler are integral parts of the development struggle. Not that underdeveloped countries, or their leaders, deliberately set out to "grind the poor under," or design growth strategies with the expressed intention of killing students or torturing labor leaders; but the fact of the matter is that industrial takeoff in the mid-twentieth century has some supremely painful human consequences. In concrete terms, the impressive economic performance of Brazil (Turkey or the Philippines) in the modern period has depended upon massive poverty and political repression, and it would not have been possible under democratic governments pursuing egalitarian economic policies.

The Optimistic Perspective

This is a sobering thesis, and it runs counter to the progressive assumptions of much postwar social science, which has tended to assume a smooth and linear progression from various states of economic and political backwardness to an age of high mass consumption and representational democracy for all.[3] In the 1950s, it is true, there was some concern over the ability of underdeveloped countries to improve their economic performance. But it was taken for granted that if actions were taken to speed up a country's rate of economic growth, "increased popular participation in the political process and a more equitable distribution of income would eventually follow."[4] Walt Rostow, Seymour Martin Lipset, David Lerner, and Karl Deutsch were just some of the luminaries who taught us how societies evolve from economic underdevelopment to economic maturity, from tradition to modernity, from

reduced to expanded political participation, and from national isola-
tionism to international integration.[5] A similar euphoria spread over
to the policy sphere. In Latin America, for example, the Alliance for
Progress was built on the premise that "All good things go together;" [6]
and that the combination of economic aid and institutional reform was
capable of guaranteeing growth, freedom, and social justice in the future.

Such optimism about the benign and progressive consequences of
economic growth owed much to the conviction that it is "the history of
advanced or established industrial countries which traces out the road
of development for the more backward countries." [7] Theorists and policy
makers alike looked at the histories of Western Europe and North
America and assumed that economic growth was the means whereby
the underdeveloped nations, too, would become well-behaved representational democracies with the normal menu of social and political
rights for their citizenry.

This belief in across-the-board progress did not survive into the present decade. Underdeveloped countries did manage dramatically to improve their economic performance in the years following World War II.
Between 1950 and 1970, for example, income levels in the Third World
rose by 75 percent, which is more growth in real income per person
than in the previous twenty centuries.[8] But this rapid growth was accompanied by ugly social and political trends. By the 1970s it was no
longer possible to ignore the evidence of deepening poverty and increased repression in the newly dynamic economies of the Third World.[9]
Increasing inequality, high rates of malnutrition and infant mortality,
coups d'état, torture, and arbitrary imprisonment have been some of
the grim accompaniments of modern development processes. On the
face of this evidence economists and others have been compelled to
consider the idea that there might be an organic link between contemporary growth processes and social and political oppression, that
"economic growth itself not only tends to be accompanied by actual
declines in political participation but is one of the prime causes of income inequality." [10]

Despite this new awareness, there has been little systematic examination of the nature or the depth of the trade-offs at work. In crude terms,
what price is being paid for each percentage point of economic growth,
and how many generations will have to shoulder this burden? This book
begins to answer these momentous questions.

The Costs of Growth

Economic development is usually defined as a significant increase in the real per capita income of a nation. Its ultimate purpose is the achievement of better nourishment, better health, better education, better living conditions, and an expanded range of opportunities in work and leisure for the people of that nation. In essence, development means the transformation of the economic structures of society in order to achieve a new level of productive capability. This, in turn, requires unprecedented levels of savings and investment. Rostow, in his famous work on the stages of economic growth, stated that "the main feature of take-off is an increase in the ratio of savings and investment to national income from 5% to 10% or more." [11] While many economists have disputed the details of his theory, there is no disagreement over the general principle that takeoff into sustained development needs high levels of savings and investment.[12] This brings us to the crux of the matter. Extracting a surplus large enough to propel society to a new level of productive capability often means the forced restriction of consumption for the mass of the people.[13] The resulting oppression takes two forms—social injustice (severe and deepening poverty) and political repression (authoritarian rule and the loss of political and civil liberties). The former is a direct ressult of the capital accumulation process; the latter is the apparatus of control necessary to prevent effective revolt on the part of the oppressed.

It is true that historically a handful of nations have managed to avoid paying the full costs of economic development. From the sixteenth century until the middle of the twentieth century, various European nations used their military superiority to build empires and extract a trading surplus from Asia, Africa, and Latin America. Such a transfer of resources from the colonies was an important component in the financing of early industrialization, and it did serve to lighten the burden on the people of Europe.

Take the example of Britain and India. The East India Company had its origins in privateering. The booty brought back by Drake in the *Golden Hind* . . .

may fairly be considered the fountain and origin of British foreign investments. Elizabeth paid off out of the proceeds the whole of her foreign debt and invested a part of the balance (about £42,000) in the Levant Company; largely out of the profits of the Levant Company there formed the East India Company, the profits of which . . . were the main foundations of England's foreign connections.[14]

By the nineteenth century, India was financing more than two-fifths of Britain's trade deficit. The flow was as follows: British India had a large trading surplus with China and the rest of Asia. These surpluses were siphoned off to England "through the (politically established and maintained) Indian trading deficit with Britain, through the 'home Charges'—India's payments for the privilege of being administered by Britain—and through the increasingly large interest payments on the Indian Public Debt." [15]

This surplus from the colonies did lighten the load carried by the British population. While it would be wrong to ignore domestic sources of capital accumulation, such as the starvation wages of workers and the high rates of saving within the entrepreneurial class, there can be no question but that the transfer of resources from colonial territories was an important element in the financing of the original industrial revolution.

Nations which began their development in the twentieth century, however, could not take advantage of a colonial subsidy. The Soviet Union, for instance, was forced to rely on its own people to produce the wherewithal to industrialize. By destroying the propertied classes and depressing the standard of living of agricultural workers to a subsistence minimum, the Soviet authorities succeeded in extracting a surplus large enough to maintain extremely high levels of industrial investment. In the absence of transfers from outside, the Soviet Union became an advanced industrial nation by leaning particularly heavily on those classes that were politically dispensable. The cost in terms of human suffering was enormous.

These historical antecedents underline the fact that economic development is a costly and disruptive business. Extracting a surplus large enough to push society to a new level of productive capability has involved colonial exploitation, war, revolution, and the elimination of entire social classes. Some nations have managed to shift the burden so that some of the costs are borne by a subjugated territory; other nations have laid the entire load on the shoulders of their less important—and less fortunate—citizens. In no case has growth been cost-free.

When we move into the contemporary Third World, we find that the costs of growth are particularly severe. Many of these countries are former colonies and still suffer from being part of unequal trading relationships. For example, India and Brazil, far from being able to appropriate the surplus of other countries, are continually having their own savings depleted by more powerful economic entities (corporations and nations), while their ability to exploit more backward and poorer territories is limited.[16] This places a particularly heavy burden on their own populations.

The difficulty is compounded by a whole gamut of problems which surround late development and serve to increase the constraints on growth and magnify the social and political costs associated with modernization. Unlike early developers, the developing countries of the mid-twentieth century must industrialize in the face of a fiercely competitive and protectionist international environment that makes it extremely difficult to become successful exporters of manufactured goods. Another set of problems revolves around the technological gap faced by late developers. In many Third World countries the transfer of capital-intensive technologies from advanced nations means a low rate of labor absorption in the modern sector and the exclusion of the mass of the people from industrial employment, a state of affairs that is exacerbated by demographic trends. As death rates decline in response to newly imported medical techniques from advanced countries, there is an explosive increase in the rate of population growth that simply cannot be matched by the creation of new employment opportunities. Nor does the contemporary Third World have a population safety valve in the form of mass emigration such as was available to early developers. During the nineteenth century, for example, thirteen million people emigrated from the British Isles seeking better lives in the New World.[17] Without this mass exodus, Britain (and many other European nations) would have been unable to absorb her surplus labor force into high-productivity employment, and standards of living would have remained low for the majority of the people.

Unlike early developers who were partially cushioned by favorable historical circumstances, late developers are having to pay the full social and political costs of economic takeoff.

My main purpose in this book is to analyze the critical structural characteristics of late development and to demonstrate why these characteristics have such dire implications for political freedom and social justice in the Third World, specifically in the national setting of Brazil. My approach to these issues is not deterministic in any simple sense; while regarding economic factors as fundamental, I do not see a mechanistic causal link between growth and equity. The story is much more complicated. The characteristics and the consequences of late development can be understood only if due weight is given to the complex legacy of the past, to the ongoing interaction between internal and external factors, and to the presence of political constraints on the economic growth process.[18]

The ingredients and the results of Brazilian development place it in the mainstream of capitalist Third World nations. Like Brazil, most countries that have attempted to industrialize in the mid-twentieth century have had to contend with colonial social structures, extremely fast rates of population expansion, the massive presence of foreign capital, and the transfer of capital-intensive industrial techniques from the advanced world. And, like Brazil, many of these nations have achieved rapid rates of economic growth while at the same time sacrificing an array of social and political rights. (See table 1 which details a number of Third World countries that have followed similar development paths in the modern period.)

I make no claim that the Brazilian experience can be extrapolated in its entirety to other underdeveloped nations, but I do feel that Brazil's route to the modern world exemplifies many of the constraints and the options involved in capitalist growth. This is not to imply that socialist development strategies do not also entail painful choices. As we shall see in the concluding chapter where I compare and contrast the development of Brazil and China, all contemporary growth processes involve considerable sacrifice.

In this book I shall focus on two key categories of human rights, social justice and political freedom, because they are the most important aspects of human welfare, and because they demonstrate significantly different interactions with the growth process.

Social justice in underdeveloped nations must involve the elimination of the desperate forms of poverty in these countries. Few Americans have ever seen this kind of poverty:

it does not exist in the United States, not even in the depths of Appalachia or in the wastes of the South Bronx. Real poverty leads parents to cripple children they love in the hope that they will be able to stay alive through charity. Real poverty is destitution, pauperism. Life becomes a war to survive and like war it consists of terrifying stretches of boredom, punctuated unexpectedly by tragedy.[19]

Social justice for the citizens of these nations, as for those of any nation, must ensure that everyone has access to "minimally acceptable life-sustaining and life-enhancing support systems involving food, shelter, health, work and culture"[20]—in short, the essentials of a decent life. Social justice also implies a reduction in the gap between the rich and the poor, a gap that is extremely wide in many Third World nations and exacerbates the suffering of the poor.

In the political sphere, three types of rights are crucial to individual freedom. First, the right to enjoy certain civil liberties such as "freedom of thought, of religion, of assembly, freedom of speech, freedom of the press; and, freedom of movement both within and outside one's own country."[21] Second, the right to be "free from governmental violations of the integrity of the person. Such violations include torture; cruel, inhuman, or degrading treatment or punishment; and arbitrary arrest or imprisonment."[22] And, finally, there is the right to political participation. Most important in this respect are the right to vote, to form political parties, to organize independent trade unions, and to take part in government.

Social justice and political freedom are prominent goals of European-based civilization and hinge on such values as Christian doctrines of brotherly love, and the eighteenth-century humanistic doctrines of the natural rights of man. Both categories of human rights have been given a certain international legal status through such declaratory acts as the Universal Declaration of Human Rights and the Three Human Rights Covenants passed by the United Nations General Assembly in 1946 and 1966 respectively.[23]

As we shall find out in later chapters of this book, social injustice is much more deeply embedded and intractable than political repression in the capitalist Third World. In the Brazilian case, uneven and unequal development became entrenched during the colonial primary commodity exporting era. It was built upon and exaggerated by the industrialization strategies of the modern period. Of particular relevance were policies of import substitution, which encouraged multinational corporations to produce sophisticated consumer goods for the Brazilian elite.

This type of industrialization triggered rapid growth but absorbed little labor and resulted in a situation where the bulk of the population became excluded from the modernization process, both as consumers and producers. Succeeding cycles of industrial growth have exaggerated this pattern, as the imperatives of maintaining the growth conditions (in particular inflation and balance-of-payments difficulties) have required that segments of the industrial work force, as well as the rural population, be excluded from the fruits of economic progress.

Massive poverty and increasing inequality are thus firmly embedded in the historical evolution of Brazil; successive stages of economic growth have divided the country into a privileged few and an impoverished many. Solving these huge and deeply rooted social problems would have to involve a profound restructuring of the economy and of society. In short, it would require revolutionary change.

In the sphere of political freedom, the scope for marginal improvements is greater. The recent history of Brazil illustrates that for considerable periods of time it has proved possible to award the normal menu of political rights to the elite classes. This was particularly true in the 1946–64 period, before severe economic constraints (primarily inflation and balance-of-payments problems) and the threat from a militant Left made democratic politics an unaffordable luxury. Effective stabilization means suppression of wages, budget cutting, credit restrictions, and high taxation. All these measures are unpopular, and in the Brazilian context could only be carried out by a repressive authoritarian regime that was both willing and able to suspend many political rights and civil liberties. The elite classes rallied behind these repressive measures, because they saw them as the only method of avoiding a much more painful turn to the Left in domestic politics.

However, the need for the more extreme types of political repression has proved to be rather temporary. In the recent past, less serious economic problems, as well as the absence of a radical Left, have muted political reaction to economic crisis. In the late 1970s, the political system is more open than it was a decade ago, and elite groups have regained at least some of their civil and political freedoms. In short, it appears that one can have significantly more political rights within the existing political and economic structures of Brazil.

This book starts with a brief analysis of the difference between early and late development, in order to destroy the extremely misleading historical analogy with Western Europe and North America. I shall attempt to demonstrate that the trade-offs involved in contemporary development processes are different and more pervasive than those which characterized the original industrial revolution. I then take up my case study of Brazil.

Part One traces the historical evolution of the Brazilian economy. The aim of chapters 3 and 4 is to show how the distinctive economic and political frameworks of this nation have interacted and built upon one another through time so as to produce rapid growth, massive poverty, and political repression in the modern period. Marx once said that "Men make their own history, but they do not make it just as they please; they do not make it under circumstances chosen by themselves, but under circumstances directly found, given and transmitted from the past." [24] This statement is particularly apt in Brazil where contemporary growth strategies are firmly embedded in and conditioned by the historical evolution of this late-developing country.

Part Two singles out inflation, the state, and the multinational corporation for detailed analysis. Inflationary distortions grew out of the structural conditions of late industrialization and have served to deepen the social and political costs of economic development. For example, inflation was the major economic catalyst of the 1964 military coup, and in the recent period, stabilization policies have been directly responsible for increased inequality and heightened repression.

The state and the multinational corporation have been (and are) the most important actors in the industrialization of Brazil and have had a critical impact in the equity sphere.

Industrial takeoff in the mid-twentieth century necessitates considerable state intervention. The protection of "infant industries" against foreign competition and the provision of the elaborate infrastructural requirements of modern industry are just two of the areas where state action is essential. However, if state intervention is a necessary part of late industrialization, the goals of such initiative reflect the priorities of ruling classes. In modern Brazil, the state has been part of the ruthless drive to maximize growth rates and can be more accurately seen as an efficient and powerful agent of accumulation than as a source of redistributive or "welfare state" policies. In short, the Brazilian state is profoundly illiberal and has served to bolster the inequitable patterns of contemporary development.

Turning to the role of the multinational corporation, Brazilian industrialization policies have encouraged the production of sophisticated consumer goods for the domestic elite. In all developing nations (and not just Brazil) this means a reliance on the giant international corporations that have critical technological and financial advantages over national firms in the production of consumer durables. With their "rich country" goods and their capital-intensive technologies, multinational corporations trigger rapid rates of industrial growth but generate little employment. In other words, multinational corporations have served to exacerbate the uneven and unequal properties of Brazilian development.

In Part Three I play out the human consequences of the development experience in some detail. Chapter 8 examines the dimensions of poverty and inequality in Brazil. The modern period has seen a widening of the gap between the rich and the poor (by 1976, for example, the top 1 percent of all Brazilians appropriated a larger proportion of national income than the bottom 50 percent) and a continuation of massive poverty (in the 1970s, 30 percent of Brazilian families fell below a subsistence minimum). Chapter 9 traces the ways that successive Brazilian governments have dealt with labor, as this issue illustrates how much and what kinds of political freedom are compatible with the Brazilian development strategy. In the 1940s and 1950s it was possible to accord significant concessions to the industrial working class. In the post-1964 period inflation control and authoritarian politics have meant periodic and severe repression of this class.

In the final chapter I place my analysis in the context of conservative, reformist, and radical approaches to the development of the Third World. The conservative (capitalist) and the radical (socialist) routes to the modern world constitute the starkest alternatives. The former offers rapid growth with at least some political freedom. The latter offers a significant measure of social justice. How one judges these results depends on one's personal value judgments.[25] In particular, it depends on how one rates the fulfillment of basic needs for the majority against political freedom for a minority. One conclusion is unambiguous. There are no easy solutions for those countries attempting to develop in the twentieth century. The choices involved are painful and will pursue policy makers and theorists into the future.

NOTES*

1. Albert Fishlow et al., *Rich and Poor Nations in the World Economy* (New York: McGraw-Hill, 1978), p. 11.

2. President Carter speaking before the United Nations in March 1977; cited in Patricia Weiss Fagen, "The Links between Human Rights and Basic Needs," *Background* (Washington, D.C.: Center for International Policy, Spring 1978), p. 1.

3. This linear evolutionary thinking is deeply embedded in the social sciences. It had its origins in the work of Darwin and Spencer and was introduced into economics by Marshall who invented the maxim that "nature does not willingly make a jump" (Alfred Marshall, *Industry and Trade* [London: Macmillan, 1920], p. 6).

4. Irman Adelman and Cynthia Taft Morris, *Economic Growth and Social Equity in Developing Countries* (Stanford, Calif.: Stanford University Press, 1973), p. 1.

5. Elaborated in Simon Schwartzman, "Back to Weber: Corporatism and Patrimonialism in the Seventies," in James M. Malloy, ed., *Authoritarianism and Corporatism in Latin America* (Pittsburgh: University of Pittsburgh Press, 1977), p. 89.

6. Robert Packenham, *Liberal America and the Third World* (Princeton, N.J.: Princeton University Press, 1973), pp. 123–29.

7. Alexander Gerschenkron, *Economic Backwardness in Historical Perspective* (New York: Praeger, 1965), p. 6.

8. See Michael Lipton, *Why Poor People Stay Poor* (Cambridge, Mass.: Harvard University Press, 1977), p. 29.

9. See, for example, Hollis Chenery et al., *Redistribution with Growth* (Oxford University Press, 1974); and ILO International Labor Office, *Employment, Growth and Basic Needs: A One-World Problem* (New York: Praeger, 1977), p. 3.

10. Adelman and Morris, *Economic Growth* (note 4), p. 2.

11. W. W. Rostow, *The Stages of Economic Growth: A Non-Communist Manifesto* (Cambridge, England: Cambridge University Press, 1961), p. 37.

12. Gerald Meier, for example, is of the opinion that economic takeoff "requires that a country withhold from personal consumption about one-quarter of the national output" (*Leading Issues in Economic Development*, 2nd ed. [New York: Oxford University Press, 1970], p. 173).

13. Marvin Harris, Stanley Diamond, and Simone Weil have all pointed out that the only instances of nonoppressive societies are primitive forms of economic and social organization that do not depend on the extraction of a surplus by a privileged few from the masses. The progression to a vastly more productive and more complex form of economic life has to mean a new dependence on leadership and bureaucracy to administer an unequal division of labor, and the sponsorship of a political system through which a privileged few exert control over the masses. See Richard Falk, "Comparative Protection of Human Rights in Capitalist and Socialist Third World Countries" (paper delivered at the 1978 Annual Meeting of the American Political Science Association [New York: September 1978], p. 3).

14. J. M. Keynes, *A Treatise on Money*, vol. 2, *The Applied Theory of Money* (London: Macmillan, 1930), pp. 156–57.

15. E. J. Hobsbawm, *Industry and Empire* (London: Weidenfeld & Nicolson, 1986), p. 123.

16. See Samir Amin, *Imperialism and Unequal Development* (New York: Monthly Review Press, 1977), for a classic treatment of this theme.

* In each chapter, a reference to a source first cited in the immediately preceding note consists of author's surname plus shortened title. If the original reference occurs in an earlier note, that note is specified in parentheses.

17. Between 1815 and 1899, 13,127,900 people emigrated from the British Isles, according to B. R. Mitchell, *European Historical Statistics, 1750–1970* (New York: Columbia University Press, 1975), pp. 137–40. Statesmen were not unaware of the significance of the mass emigration. See, for example, the following statement by Cecil Rhodes: "In order to save the 40 million inhabitants of the U.K. from a bloody civil war, we colonial statesmen must acquire new lands to settle the surplus population." Quoted in Kenneth Paul Erickson and Patrick V. Peppe, "Dependent Capitalist Development, U.S. Foreign Policy and Repression of the Working Class in Chile and Brazil," *Latin American Perspectives* 3, no. 8 (Winter 1976): 27.

18. A similar concept has been elaborated by Gunnar Myrdal, *Rich Lands and Poor* (New York: Harper & Brothers, 1957), pp. 11–23. Myrdal uses the term "circular and cumulative process" to describe this complex intertwining of factors.

19. Nick Eberstadt, "China: How Much Success?" *New York Review of Books*, 3 May 1979.

20. Richard R. Fagen, "Equity in the South in the Context of North–South Relations," in Albert Fishlow et al., *Rich and Poor Nations in the World Economy* (New York: McGraw-Hill, 1978), p. 175.

21. Cyrus R. Vance, "Human Rights Policy" (speech delivered on Law Day before the University of Georgia Law School, 30 April 1977, Athens, Ga. [Washington, D.C.: Department of State, Bureau of Economic Affairs, PR 194], p. 1).

22. Vance, "Human Rights Policy," p. 2. Such individual political rights are often treated separately in the literature on human rights. I include them in the general category of political freedoms because government violations of the integrity of the person tend to be enmeshed with encroachment on civil liberties and rights of political participation. As Richard Ullman has said, "so long as persons are allowed to speak out freely against governmental authority and to come together with others to organize opposition to that authority, those rights whose violation entails more drastic consequences—rights of the person against summary execution, torture, or unwarranted detention—would perforce be safeguarded" (in Jorge J. Dominguez et al. eds., *Enhancing Global Human Rights* [New York: McGraw-Hill, 1979], p. 5).

23. For texts of the Universal Declaration and the Covenants, see Ian Brownlie, ed., *Basic Documents in International Law*, 2nd ed. (New York: Oxford University Press, 1972), pp. 144–86. The human rights movement in the United States has tended to emphasize political and civil liberties. This is predictable given the intellectual and ideological origins of the American nation. It was not until the fall of 1977 that President Carter accepted the UN Covenant on economic and social rights. See Richard Falk, "Ideological Patterns in the United States Human Rights Debate: 1945–1978," mimeograph (Department of Politics, Princeton University, 1978); and "What Are Human Rights," *Wall Street Journal*, 25 November 1977.

24. Karl Marx "The Eighteenth Brumaire of Louis Bonaparte," in Robert C. Tucker, ed., *The Marx-Engels Reader*, 2nd ed. (New York: W. W. Norton, 1978), p. 595.

25. Modern social scientists have been loathe to incorporate value judgments into their scholarly work; and yet, as Joan Robinson says: "To eliminate value judgments from the subject matter of social science is to eliminate the subject itself, for since it concerns human behavior it must be concerned with the value judgments that people make" (*Freedom and Necessity: An Introduction to the Study of Society* [New York: Vintage Books, 1970], p. 123).

CHAPTER

2

Historical Perspective

The paradigms of "western" social science serve as blinkers
or escape mechanisms preventing scholars and policy makers
from seeing and acting upon strategic fronts.

Paul P. Streeten

THE MASSIVE POVERTY and the political repression that have accompanied rapid economic growth in so many Third World countries,
are repeatedly justified, by theorists and governments alike, as inevitable
and temporary costs of growth, just as they proved to be in the industrialization of Western countries during the nineteenth century.
The implication is that all Third World regimes need to do is concentrate on growing, and that, in the not very long run, the issues of social
equity and political freedom can, and will, be taken care of. This is
a facile and erroneous assumption. For a variety of deeply seated
economic, political, and social reasons, underdeveloped nations are not
about to repeat the "grand dynamics" of the original industrial
revolution.

The Historical Analogy

To begin with, despite the presence of those special conditions described in chapter 1 (for example, transfers from the colonies), early
development in western Europe and North America was a painful

process.[1] (Writers of the period provide us with vivid images of the misery wrought by the industrial revolution. Dickens describes London as being full of "pale and pinched up faces hovering about the windows where there was tempting food; hungry eyes wandering over the profusion guarded by one thin sheet of brittle glass—an iron wall to them." [2] And Engels details "the filth and the stagnant pools in the working class quarters of the great cities" [3] of England and recounts the great typhus epidemic of 1842 which laid low "one sixth of all the poor in Scotland." [4] In a bitter statement he accuses the British government of murder: "if society places hundreds of workers in such a position that they inevitably come to premature ends, their death is as violent as if they had been stabbed or shot." [5])

The lower classes of British society suffered in both absolute and relative terms. The standard of living of the workers (measured in terms of the purchasing power of wages) deteriorated during the last half of the eighteenth century. The trend in the absolute income levels during the first several decades of the nineteenth century is the subject of some dispute, but there is no doubt that throughout this period of industrial takeoff, the gap between the rich and the poor became increasingly extreme.[6] In short, the abysmal living conditions of the poor were rendered even less tolerable by a bourgeois class dripping "with excess capital, to be wildly invested in railways and spent on the bulging opulent household furnishings displayed at the Great Exhibition of 1850." [7]

There is little doubt that the laboring classes paid a heavy price for British industrialization. Yet appalling as these social costs were, they proved to be temporary; after 1850 the workers' standard of living began to improve. The capitalist class was driven toward concessions as the increasingly organized urban proletariat gained both political and economic muscle. During the late nineteenth and early twentieth centuries, increasingly powerful trade unions, periodic labor scarcity, and governmental welfare measures all contributes to enlarging the share of national product going to workers. With some variation in detail, a similar strengthening of working-class economic and political bargaining power followed the early phases of industrial development in most of today's rich countries. Kuznets accurately describes the secular income trends in advanced western countries as constituting a long swing "widening in the early phases of economic growth when the transition from the pre-industrial to the industrial civilization was most rapid; becoming stabilized for a while; and then narrowing in the later phases." [8]

It is interesting to note that Kuznets's third phase of narrowing income differentials has not continued into the second half of the twentieth century. Contrary to general expectations, it is by no means clear that the social and economic policies pursued by most advanced nations in the years since the Second World War have resulted in greater income equality. While in Britain and the United States, for example, the very wealthy have indeed suffered a relative decline in their income shares, the beneficiaries have been the middle rather than the working class.[9] Still, even allowing for these refinements, it is undoubtedly true that the lower-income groups in today's rich nations have enormously increased their absolute living standards and greatly improved their relative living standards over the course of the last two centuries.

But it is unwarranted to infer from this specific historic experience that economic growth will, in all contexts and at all times, enhance earnings opportunities across the board. Kuznets himself has warned of the dangers of simple-minded analogies:

How [he has asked] can either the institutional or political framework of the under-developed societies or the processes of economic growth and industrialization be modified to favor a sustained rise to higher levels of economic performance and yet avoid the fatally simple remedy of an authoritarian regime that would use the population as cannon-fodder in the fight for economic achievement- [10]

An ominous premonition of what was to occur subsequently in so many Third World nations!

Divergences between Early and Late Development

Drawing on the experience of the advanced world, economists have often been willing to tolerate a short-run increase in poverty and inequality in underdeveloped countries on the assumption that extremely unequal distribution of income is needed to generate the savings essential for fast rates of economic growth.[11] According to this argument, a highly unequal distribution of income promotes savings because a large chunk of disposable income is in the hands of an elite group who alone have a high marginal propensity to save. These high rates of savings can then be translated into high rates of investment, which, in turn, are the route to rapid economic growth.

This reasoning simply does not hold water in the contemporary Third World. For one thing, it ignores the tendency of high-income groups in many poor nations to indulge in conspicuous consumption rather than to save. Second, it neglects the growing importance of public sector and corporate savings in modern growth processes.[12] Third, it forgets that private savings may be (and often are) channeled into Swiss bank accounts rather than into domestic investment. And, in fact, the available evidence shows no clear correlation between inequality and high rates of savings and investment in developing countries. Leff, for example, finds that the savings-to-income ratio in less-developed countries averaged 14.2 percent in 1964, while in Western European countries the savings-to-income ratio averaged 25.2 percent—in spite of the fact that income was much more unequally distributed in the less-developed countries in his sample.[13]

It is true that private savings did play an extremely important role in the initial industrialization of Britain and America, and this saving was the result of frugal behavior on the part of entrepreneurs—an elite group within an extremely unequal economy.[14] But this interaction between inequality and a high rate of saving reflected a unique set of historical circumstances. In the contemporary Third World, poverty and inequality contribute to both political stability and economic growth, but—as we shall find out in later chapters of this book—the role they play is quite different from the one they played in nineteenth-century England and America.

Five elements in the economic histories of Western Europe and North America conspired to make the growth/equity trade-off a temporary phenomenon and made long-run economic development compatible with a better deal for the mass of the people. It cannot be emphasized too strongly that *none of these critical factors exist in today's underdeveloped world.*

In the first place, capitalism in the latter half of the twentieth century is an entirely different animal from what it was in the eighteenth and nineteenth centuries when the advanced nations entered their take-off phase. Today, the process of capital accumulation is more highly concentrated, more internationally integrated, and much more technologically advanced.[15] Today underdeveloped nations embarking upon industrialization have few alternatives but to adopt capital-intensive, sophisticated technologies, which have little to do with their own factor endowment. These technologies evolved in rich countries, in contexts of labor scarcity, and they are often ill suited to the conditions of the Third World where labor is abundant and capital scarce. Aggravating the problem of labor surplus posed by this type of capital-intensive industrialization is the transfer of another type of technology from the developed world, that of medical know-how. Within a few years killer diseases are wiped out, death rates fall drastically, and population growth rates assume explosive proportions.[16]

The coincidence of these types of technological transfer has important implications for social welfare in underdeveloped countries. Industrial growth rates are often quite high by any historical standard. But, faced with an imported capital-intensive technology, and with an accelerated rate of population increase, industrial employment often grows at a slower rate than the population. The result is a modern work force that constitutes a constant or even declining proportion of the potential labor pool.[17] Industrial workers become a small privileged minority, a labor aristocracy quite distinct from the mass of the people who remain in a state of miserable poverty.

Note the marked contrast with the early industrialization. In Western Europe and North America during the eighteenth and nineteenth centuries, there was a gradual and mostly indigenous evolution of the technological base of society "from the artisan know-how of the salad days of the industrial revolution and the first half of the nineteenth century to applied science engineering in more recent times." [18] The simple technologies of the original industrial revolution were relatively labor-intensive and absorbed large quantities of unskilled as well as skilled labor.[19] And they were accompanied by a much slower and milder demographic transition. Over the course of a century, first death rates and then birth rates fell, and by the beginning of the twentieth century population growth rates had stabilized in most industrial nations. Moreover, as mentioned in chapter 1, the whole process was facilitated by large-scale migration from Europe to the New World, which acted as a population safety valve. All these trends resulted in the eventual elimination of surplus labor, as the bulk of the labor force was absorbed into more modern, higher-productivity occupations. This elimination of "a reserve army of the unemployed" enhanced the bargaining power and hence the standards of living of the working class.

A second difference revolves around the demand dynamics of early as opposed to late development. Since the middle of the nineteenth century, the advanced nations of Western Europe and North America have relied upon mass production and mass consumption for the maintenance of their growth rates. In these countries recurrent crises of effective demand, caused by the lack of balance between the increased output of a growing economy and the capacity of the mass of consumers to buy this additional output, have posed a major threat to prosperity.

Indeed, this demand constraint on growth has had significant social implications. As the capitalist class came to realize that low wages meant low demand and thus low profits in the long run, business attitudes toward trade unionism and increased money incomes for workers gradually softened. In the late nineteenth century, moreover, the structure of industry was becoming increasingly concentrated, freeing many businesses from the need to pay very low wages in order to remain price competitive. Thus, they could "afford" to play a part in bolstering demand, and they had a collective incentive to do so.

In the contemporary underdeveloped world, this important incentive for wage increases is almost totally lacking. Poverty in underdeveloped nations is generally caused not by surplus production and lack of effective demand but by insufficient production capacity and an inadequate supply of the various factors of production. Under these circumstances, raising wages will only cause inflation because supply—of capital, of skilled labor, of energy—is inelastic. In short, poverty in Latin America, Africa, and Asia is caused by the lack of means to create wealth, not by the superabundance of such means and the absence of demand.[20]

A third distinction between early and late development relates to government intervention. In Western Europe and North America, governments, aware of the link between income levels, effective demand, and the health of advanced industrial economies, have increasingly taken upon themselves the task of regulating demand via social welfare and tax programs. And these programs have, for the most part, reduced poverty and inequality. I do not want to overemphasize the smoothness of this process. Capitalists and governments have not always swallowed the logic of this particular form of enlightened self-interest. Witness the appalling social costs of the Great Depression which were obviously exaggerated by the refusal of governments to reflate via the drastic

and costly method of deficit-financed public works. Even so, there can
be no denying the fairly steady growth of government intervention in
advanced economies from the nineteenth century to the present day.
In setting income floors below which the poor could not fall, governments not only met a conspicuous human need but also dampened the
decline in purchasing power during downturns in the business cycle.
In other words, crisis control, demand management, and income equali-
zation have gone hand in hand. Progressive income taxation, unemployment relief, expanded social security benefits, and a growing public
sector have all tended to reduce the depth of economic crises and, in so
doing, have transferred resources from the rich to the poor.

Almost all these economic reasons for increasing social justice via
welfare state measures are missing in the Third World. In underdeveloped nations, deficit demand is not the prime cause of poverty, nor
is the welfare state a prescription for high profits. Rather, economic
instability is caused by fluctuations in climate and in agricultural production, in foreign demand for exports, and in the external supply
price of industrial inputs—fluctuations that no single government can
control. As to the long-run causes of poverty, these, as already noted,
have far more to do with low productivity and shortages of machines
and human skills than with manipulable deficiencies of domestic demand. Thus, the economic pressures facing governments in the underdeveloped world cannot be met by embarking on social welfare measures,
and governments in these countries are correct to regard growth and
equity as separate issues that cannot be tackled together.

It is now time to turn to the politics of government intervention. In
analyzing the different development paths of underdeveloped and advanced countries, economists (and other social scientists) often ignore
profound differences in value systems. They forget that *all* rich capitalist nations are effective democracies that accord the broad mass of
their population an extremely wide range of political and civil liberties,
and possess an array of public programs which are explicitly geared
toward diminishing inequalities between social classes and between regions. In many countries these "democratic" features are neither novel
nor ephemeral but are firmly rooted in a tradition and a philosophy
that predate the emergence of modern representational democracy; they
go well beyond the requirements of economic strategies.

In the modern evolution of Western Europe and North America,
political freedoms preceded social justice. The eighteenth-century doc-

trines of the natural rights of man hinged on notions of freedom and liberty. Thus, the American Revolution was in essence a struggle against tyranny and oppression (rather than exploitation and poverty) fought in the name of such tangible civil liberties as freedom of movement, of expression, and of assembly, as well as freedom from "taxation without representation."

It was the French Revolution that first turned "the rights of man into the rights of the Sans-Culottes." [21] By the end of the nineteenth century Marx had elevated the welfare of the masses into a key doctrine of the modern age. Life itself became the highest goal, and the "role of the revolution was no longer to liberate men from the oppression of their fellow men, let alone to found freedom, but to liberate the life process of society from the fetters of scarcity so that it could swell into a stream of abundance. Not freedom but abundance now became the aim of revolution." [22]

In essence, the evolution of Western democracies saw successive periods during which three types of rights were conferred on the broad mass of the populace by governments: civil rights (equality in the eyes of the law, freedom of movement, of expression, and of assembly); political rights (universal suffrage, political parties, trade unions); and finally certain social welfare rights (old-age pensions, unemployment benefits, public health facilities).[23]

These successive stages were, of course, related. An initial civil right of assembly greatly strengthened the chances of successful trade unionism, while, in its turn, collective bargaining on the part of workers was an important ingredient in the struggle toward a higher standard of living and enhanced social welfare for the bulk of the population.

This brings us to the fourth major difference between early and late development, which has to do with the political and social attributes of the working class. As I have already noted, an important reason for the gains of the working class in Europe and North America was labor's organizing efforts in trade unions and in political parties. But for such organization to be effective, there had to be an "organizable" working class—that is, a mass of urbanized and substantially literate workers. There are fifteen advanced countries with fairly reliable statistical data on the beginnings of modern economic growth: all except one (Japan) had over 35 percent of the labor force outside agriculture at that time and a greater than 50 percent literacy rate. A vastly different situation prevailed in most underdeveloped nations when they entered their takeoff phases. Generally speaking, only between 10 and 35 percent of workers were outside of agriculture (or were literate), and the gap between the output of these workers and those in the agricultural sector was far greater than was the case in "developing" nineteenth-century Europe or North America.[24] Primarily due to the technological and demographic factors described earlier in this chapter, modern industrialization in underdeveloped countries has confirmed rather than countered existing differences. As a result, the industrial work force has emerged as a labor aristocracy with more to lose than to gain from sharing the benefits of economic growth with the mass of the people, and the trade union movement has grown up as an instrument to protect the interests of this elite group. Thus, "organized labor" in the Third World is likely to fight against equalizing measures: in yesterday's developing nations it spearheaded them

A fifth and final difference between early and late development is grounded in social structures. Many of the traditional props of inequality—feudalism, serfdom, clan and caste—had in most advanced countries been drastically reduced by violence or by legislation before the advent of modern industrialization. Such traditional social structures, resting as they do on ascribed roles rather than on achieved functions, are extremely likely to channel the fruits of progress to a nonproductive elite. But in many underdeveloped countries such traditional social structures still prevail (often as a legacy from the colonial era), and they do much to reinforce the inequitable tendencies within late development. In most poor nations capitalism has never confronted traditional social structures as it did, for example, in Cromwell's England or in late eighteenth-century France. In Europe, the new inequalities of capitalism, to some extent nonhereditary, replaced the relics of feudalism; while in today's underdeveloped world they often reinforce a still thriving, traditional social structure. The landlord class for example, has often been co-opted rather than destroyed, and it survives into the modern period to impede the evolution of a political system that could direct the benefits of development toward the lower classes.

Thus, the Western European and North American analogy fails. There is nothing in the contemporary structure of Third World nations to justify a belief that the "grand dynamics" of the original industrial revolution will repeat itself. The conditions that during the eighteenth and nineteenth centuries in most of Western Europe and North America permitted growth and development to go hand in hand with enhanced civil liberties, increased political participation, and a much higher standard of living for the bulk of the population, were highly special and involved the cumulative interaction of a specific set of economic, political, and social factors. In the modern underdeveloped world the same set of factors is simply not at work in the same way.

Note the coincidence of political and economic incentives for greater equity in the advanced world. The wretchedness and the exploitation of the English, the European, and the immigrant-American working classes in the early and middle nineteenth century stemmed from low wages and permitted high rates of capital formation. But these social costs were short-lived. Not only was there a gradual accumulation of civil and political rights by the laboring classes and increased political activism by and for these classes, but economic imperatives came to the fore. The drying up of the pool of surplus rural labor gave the emerging trade union movement some solid bargaining power; and at the same time, the capitalist class was discovering that it needed a mass market for its products. The result was an increasingly powerful and increasingly prosperous working class. Capitalist self-interest, as much as capitalist humanity, determined the development path of advanced nations.

The contemporary Third World presents a stark contrast. The drift toward one-party states in Africa and the growing prevalence of military governments in Latin America indicate that repressive, autocratic regimes are increasingly dominant. Few of these regimes have avoided that fatally simple remedy of using "the population as cannon fodder in the fight for economic achievement." [25] In addition, the rather elitist trade union movements of many Third World countries have often been taken over by government. A common pattern is for the trade union structure to become a government-sponsored interest group, designed to buy off the industrial work force with material rewards and to ensure that industrial workers do not join with the mass of the population. This pattern tends to complete that differentiation of the lower classes in underdeveloped nations I referred to earlier. The evolution of an official and elitist trade union structure breaks the identification between "the laboring classes" and "the dangerous classes" [26] and, in so doing, prevents the mass from acquiring critical political leadership.

In the economic arena conditions also fail to provide any incentive for egalitarian measures. Almost everywhere in the Third World the growth dynamics of the modern industrial sector have excluded the mass of the people. The capital-intensive nature of industry, which absorbs a small (and often decreasing) proportion of the urban work force, and the composition of production, which normally emphasizes consumer durables or "rich country goods," means it is possible to have rapid industrialization and high average rates of economic growth which bypass a large proportion of the population.

In summary, the distinctive patterns of late capitalist development tend to create a situation where there is no economic incentive for improving social welfare. Indeed, the situation is more extreme: contemporary growth strategies are not merely indifferent to equity considerations; they actually need a less equal and more repressive "solution" to the social question. As I shall explore in later chapters, modern growth processes are grounded in massive poverty and require a significant degree of political repression.

NOTES

1. I use the phrase "early development" to describe the industrial revolutions of the late eighteenth and the early nineteenth centuries. I restrict the phrase "late development" to those countries of the Third World that began industrialization in the 1930s and 1940s. In some rigorous sense these countries should perhaps be called late, late developers (southern Europe and the Soviet Union being the original late developers), but this distinction is irrelevant to my argument.

2. Charles Dickens, *Nicholas Nickleby*, chap. 32; quoted in Steven Marcus, *Engels, Manchester and the Working Class* (New York: Random House, 1974), p. 151.

3. Friedrich Engels, *The Condition of the Working Class in England* (Stanford, Calif.: Stanford University Press, 1968), p. 110.

4. Engels, *The Working Class*, p. 113.

5. Engels, *The Working Class* (note 3), p. 108. For another indictment of the government of the period, see T. Carlyle, *Past and Present* (London: Dent, 1967), chap. 1.

6. Kuznets finds that the years 1780–1850 marked the period of increasing inequality in the United Kingdom. See Simon Kuznets, "Economic Growth and Income Inequality," *American Economic Review* 45, no. 1 (March 1955):18–19.

7. E. J. Hobsbawm, *Industry and Empire: An Economic History of Britain since 1970* (London: Weidenfeld & Nicolson, 1968), p. 72.

8. Kuznets, "Economic Growth" (note 6), p. 18.

9. See A. B. Atkinson, *The Economics of Inequality* (Oxford: Clarendon Press, 1975), pp. 50–121, for the British data; and Lester C. Thurow, *Generating Inequality* (New York: Basic Books, 1975), pp. 20–51, for the American data.

10. Kuznets, "Economic Growth" (note 6), p. 25.

11. As Harry G. Johnson puts it, "there is likely to be a conflict between rapid growth and an equitable distribution of income; and a poor country anxious to develop would probably be well advised not to worry too much about the distribution of income" (*Money, Trade and Economic Growth* [London: George Allen & Unwin, 1962], p. 153).

12. Kuznets finds that only 7 to 12 percent of savings come from private individuals in low-income countries as opposed to 32 percent in high-income countries. The rest of domestic gross savings comes from governments, public and government enterprises, and private corporations. See Simon Kuznets, "Quantitative Aspects of the Economic Growth of Nations," *Economic Development and Cultural Change* 8, no. 4, pt. 2 (July 1960):73.

13. See Nathaniel H. Leff, "Dependency Rates and Savings Rates," *American Economic Review* 59, no. 5 (December 1968): 886–96. For further evidence see H. S. Houtakker, "On Some Determinants of Saving in Developed and Under-Developed Countries," in E. A. G. Robinson, ed., *Problems in Economic Development* (London: Macmillan, 1975), chap. 10.

14. See J. P. Marquand, *The Late George Apley* (Boston: Little, Brown, & Co., 1938), for a vivid illustration of the frugal habits of the New England bourgeoisie during the eighteenth and nineteenth centuries.

15. See, for example, David Felix, "Technological Dualism in Latin American Industrializers: On Theory, History and Policy," *Journal of Economic History* 34 (March 1974): 194–238.

16. One is reminded of the gloomy predictions of T. R. Malthus who saw the population increasing at a geometric rate and the food supply at an arithmetic one. In 1798, in his famous essay on population, Malthus pointed to "the constant tendency in all animated life to increase beyond the nourishment prepared for it" (*An Essay on the Principle of Population*, vol. I [London: J. M. Dent, 1914], p. 5).

17. Paul Prebisch finds that in the postwar period in many Latin American nations "the proportion of the economically active population working in industry steadily declines" (*Change and Development: Latin America's Great Task* [Washington, D.C.: Inter-American Development Bank, July 1970], p. 3). See also Mario M. Cortes, "Technological Absorption and Unemployment: A Comparative Analysis," Ph.D. dissertation, Washington University, 1973.

18. Felix, "Technological Dualism" (note 15), p. 211.

19. In Europe industrial employment "came to represent half, or more than half of total employment." In contrast, in late-industrializing nations "industrial employment represents one third of urban employment, and often even less." See discussion in Stephen H. Hellinger and Douglas A. Hellinger, *Unemployment and the Multinationals* (London: Kennikat Press, 1976), p. 24.

20. This point is developed extremely effectively by Michael Lipton, *Why People Stay Poor* (Cambridge, Mass.: Harvard University Press, 1977), pp. 38–43.

21. Hannah Arendt, *On Revolution* (New York: Viking Press, 1963), p. 55.

22. Arendt, *On Revolution*, p. 58.

23. A similar sequence has been put forward by T. H. Marshall, *Citizenship and Social Class* (London: Cambridge University Press, 1950).

24. These figures are taken from Lipton, *Why People Stay Poor* (note 20), pp. 39–41.

25. Kuznets, "Economic Growth" (note 6), p. 25.

26. E. J. Hobsbawm, *Laboring Men: Studies in the History of Labor* (Garden City, N.Y.: Doubleday, 1967), p. 272.

PART I

The Brazilian
Growth Experience

CHAPTER

3

Evolution of
Economic Structures

An understanding of the historical characteristics of the Brazilian industrialization process is no idle exercise. In few countries has the interpretation of the past so defined and discriminated among policy options in the present.

Albert Fishlow

THE HALLMARK of contemporary Brazilian development has been the coexistence of great and growing wealth with deepening poverty and political repression. This juxtaposition is not new but is deeply rooted in the economic structures of this late-developing nation.

The historical evolution of the Brazilian economy can be divided into three periods. First came the primary exporting era, which was based on the production of agricultural cash crops and on mining. This period lasted from the sixteenth century until the Great Depression and was characterized by domestic stagnation and a highly unequal social structure. Second was the phase of "easy" import-substituting industrialization, which spanned the years 1930–64. This period was marked by rapid industrial growth, recurrent inflation, and a rigidifying of the highly skewed distributional pattern inherited from the previous period. And finally, there is the period since 1964, an era of stabilization and export-led growth, which has resulted in both vigorous economic development and deepening poverty. The second and third phases together constitute the era of modern industrial growth, often simply referred to as the modern period.

An appreciation of the critical economic characteristics of late development are crucial to understanding how the Brazilian growth experience differs from that of early developers described in chapter 2. Four hundred years of economic domination by Europe and North America served to promote long-run stagnation and a highly polarized social structure in Brazil, which conditioned the timing and the shape of the modernization process. Industrialization in the mid-twentieth century, through policies designed by and for an elite group, meant a concentration on sophisticated consumer goods and a reliance on capital- and skill-intensive technologies. The bulk of the people remained redundant to the production process—both as producers and as consumers—and there was a steady and progressive differentiation of Brazil into a privileged elite and a poverty-stricken mass. In short, the special properties of late development have tended to deepen the trade-off between growth and social equity.

A word on my choice of time periods: they represent three distinct economic phases that are associated with specific political and ideological systems. Despite the extremely different time spans, there is an odd sense in which they are equally important. Brazil tripled its population between 1940 and 1977 and tripled its national product between 1960 and 1977. Thus the rate of change has speeded up to such an extent that a modern decade encapsulates much more growth, and many more additional people, than does the entire era of colonial rule.

The Primary Export Economy

From the sixteenth to well into the twentieth century, the economic life of Brazil was dominated by the production of primary commodities for export.[1] Sugar was the major product of the sixteenth and seventeenth centuries; mining was the leading activity of the eighteenth; and coffee was the most important product of Brazil from the mid-nineteenth century to the 1930s. In addition, peripheral enclaves were associated with cocoa, rubber, hides, and leather.

In essence, the domestic economy was integrated into an international market system where it functioned as an exporter of primary commodities and as an importer of manufactured goods. The raw-material needs of the advanced "central" economies of Europe and North America were met by the production of agricultural commodities and minerals at the "periphery." The whole system was enforced through the establishment of trading monopolies and by empire. When Brazil was ruled by the Portuguese, manufacturing activity within the colony was explicitly forbidden; but even after 1821, when the colonial era came to an end, free-trade policies, plus special trading concessions to the British, kept the economy concentrated on primary production and export. What did this mean for economic growth and for social equity within the Brazilian nation?

There can be no question that commercial agriculture and mining did result in the creation of wealth in Brazil, but the structure of the economic system and the balance of political power prevented this new wealth from promoting either domestic growth or equity.

In the first place, the sporadic prosperity associated with sugar production or gold mining did not depend upon technological advance or capital accumulation; it merely reflected a comparative advantage in international trade. The resultant increase in income was partially appropriated by the dominant trading power (Portugal, England, or the United States, depending on the period) and partially by the local elite—that is, Brazilian landowners and commercial intermediaries who used it to finance their increasingly varied and sophisticated consumption habits. In practice, this meant that the wealth remaining in Brazilian hands was largely used to buy goods manufactured in Europe and America, and thus channeled an even bigger proportion of the newly created wealth back to the advanced countries.

This economic situation did not encourage domestic growth or serve to increase the standard of living for the majority of the Brazilian people. The primary exporter economy, with its static technological base, could only absorb "raw" labor, which for three centuries, we must remember, was primarily slave labor. There simply was no incentive to develop a skilled, educated work force of the type that began to emerge in Europe prior to large-scale industrialization.

I can illustrate these points by describing some key characteristics of the sugar economy. According to Furtado's classic account, the sugar colony in northeastern Brazil was exceptionally rich. By the end of the sixteenth century the per capita income of the free population was far higher than that prevailing in Europe during the same period. Income was strongly concentrated in the hands of sugar mill and plantation owners, and the payments made to other groups in the population (mostly food and clothing to a slave labor force) did not amount to much more than 3 percent of total income. What did the planter elite do with this income? The proportion spent on imported luxury items was truly impressive. In 1639, for example, a quarter of the import earnings from the sugar crop was spent on French wines! [2]

The evolution of the sugar economy in the Brazilian northeast shows how the development and exploitation of a primary commodity can bring with it a great wave of prosperity which then recedes, leaving few permanent positive imprints on the domestic scene. In the first place, since the considerable wealth generated by the sugar economy was appropriated by the sugar mill and plantation owners and spent abroad, it was not used to improve or diversify domestic productive capacity. In any case, the possibility of continued prosperity depended upon external factors (foreign competitors and the absorption capacity of world markets) over which the Brazilian nation had no control. When the West Indies began to compete successfully with Brazil in the last quarter of the seventeenth century, the sugar economy of the northeast underwent a slow process of atrophy, and the real income of the population declined steadily until the nineteenth century. As there had been little domestic reinvestment and no diversification into other economic activities, the glittering wealth of the sixteenth and seventeenth centuries proved to be ephemeral. The sugar economy settled into a long slow decline, and the Brazilian northeast gradually assumed its contemporary image of stagnation and miserable poverty.

A similar boom-and-bust scenario accompanied the exploitation of the other major primary commodities in Brazil. Unlike European and North American countries where economic development was associated with the growth of manufacturing activities, domestic reinvestment, and a growing internal market, Brazil, which produced primary commodities for export, was dependent upon external stimuli, and her economic evolution had little internal cohesion or momentum. Brazilian economic structures did not grow smoothly, but rather in spasmodic, isolated whirlpools of new-found wealth which pulled labor, capital, and power from earlier eddies of prosperity, and had no internal momentum.

Not only did the primary exporter economy produce erratic prosperity and long-run stagnation in Brazil, it also led to distinctive patterns of income distribution within the domestic economy. The dichotomy between a planter elite and an undifferentiated mass of agricultural workers resulted in the formation of two quite distinct markets or demand profiles.[3] The demand profile of the planter class largely comprised sophisticated consumer goods manufactured in Europe and North America. Although the size of this upper-class population did not increase significantly over time, its incomes did, particularly at the height of a boom period. As a result, demand (which was highly income-elastic) grew through a process of intensification and diversification, with the upper classes consuming an ever-widening range of imported goods.

The demand profile of the Brazilian masses, on the other hand, was quite different: it comprised a limited range of wage goods (textiles, footwear, processed food, utensils) which, by the end of the nineteenth century, were supplied by domestic manufacturers. Income levels among the working classes did not rise substantially over time, although the absolute size of the Brazilian masses did increase. Here demand grew through a process of extension and dispersion to a growing population.

This profound discontinuity in the Brazilian demand profile during the primary exporter period was paralleled by a corresponding discontinuity in the structure of supply. Luxury consumer goods, relying on advanced technology and a high level of capital accumulation, were imported from Europe and North America. At the same time, wage goods for the masses, which required only a low level of capital formation and little technological sophistication, came to be manufactured in Brazil by national capitalists.

At this stage a word needs to be said about Brazilian manufacturing during this early period. The latter part of the nineteenth century saw the emergence of small-scale manufacturing firms in São Paulo that supplied textiles and other wage goods to the Brazilian lower classes. This development was in response to the abolition of slavery in 1888, to the boom in coffee production, and to the wave of European immigration; these factors boosted the level of effective demand among agricultural workers and enlarged the domestic market for wage goods. However, one should not overestimate the importance of manufacturing in Brazil during this early period. Primary production in general, and coffee in particular, remained the chief source of wealth; and in an essential sense, Brazilian manufacturing remained a convenient supplier of wage goods for the masses.[4] Working with out-of-date equipment and an unskilled labor force, it could not compete with the sophisticated products of foreign manufacturers. Western Europe and North America continued to supply the elite market.

In summary, the economic structures of the primary exporter phase of Brazilian development served to promote long-run stagnation, a highly differentiated social structure, and an extremely skewed distribution of income within Brazil. Many of the structures established during this phase, which after all lasted four centuries, survive in a modified form to the present day and have conditioned the terms and the format of modern industrialization.

Import-Substituting Industrialization: 1930–64

The year 1929 is an important watershed in the economic history of Brazil and of most Latin American nations. The world depression hit the region with particular ferocity "bowling over the props of the area's export-based economies and causing widespread internal dislocation."[5] In Brazil the value of exports fell from US$445.9 million in 1929 to US$180.6 million in 1932.[6] This collapse of the primary commodity market precipitated a major developmental crisis. It provoked a regrouping of political actors and a change in economic strategy, this time toward internal growth and large-scale industrialization. Tentatively in the 1930s and more thoroughly in the forties and fifties, domestic manufacturing was encouraged through protection and subsidy, so that by the early 1960s Brazil was the most significant industrial power in Latin America.[7] This first cycle of industrialization (1930–64) has been described as the era of "easy" import substitution:[8] its attributes had important consequences for the pattern of economic growth and for possibilities of social justice and political freedom within the Brazilian nation.

Three components of the import substitution process are particularly relevant to our analysis: the fact that industrialization was dependent upon spontaneous as well as deliberate government incentives and upon private as well as public investment and was largely unplanned; the fact that import substitution became import reproduction and internalized the existing pattern of demand; and the fact that import-substituting industrialization produced cumulative inflationary distortions and balance-of-payments difficulties that contributed greatly to the economic and political crises of the early 1960s.

Incentive Structures and Investment Patterns

This first phase of modern industrialization in Brazil depended on both direct and indirect government stimuli. Slowly in the 1930s and more rapidly in the late forties and fifties, domestic manufacturing grew through a variety of government initiatives. Some of this encouragement took the form of self-conscious state policy, but some support was indirect, a by-product of programs primarily designed to bolster the coffee sector or ease a balance-of-payments constraint.

In the early years of industrialization much of governmental support was indirect or unself-conscious. For example, the first few years of Getulio Vargas's first term of office were marked by a rather desperate attempt to compensate the coffee growers for the disastrous fall in prices, and industrialization was a somewhat inadvertent, though welcome by-product of these policies. The purchase of coffee surpluses by the state created a major source of spending power among coffee producers and thus prevented Brazil from experiencing the grave collapse in domestic demand which a loss in export earnings generally implies. The resulting maintenance of internal demand, coupled with exchange controls and a progressive currency devaluation, proved to be a powerful stimulant to the growth of domestic manufacturing. Consumers, unable to satisfy their needs through imports, turned to Brazilian manufacturers; and domestic investment that before had gone into the export sector was now attracted by the higher profits to be made in industrial production.[9]

This type of spontaneous industrialization was aided and abetted by considerable and self-conscious state intervention. For Vargas completely repudiated the doctrine of economic liberalism that had held sway in the previous era of primary production. During his first term in office the state expanded its authority to direct the economy in two major

ways. First, through the manipulation of fiscal measures, exchange controls, import quotas, and credit controls, the state acquired the ability
to protect and subsidize private domestic manufacturing. Second,
through direct participation in areas such as railroads, shipping, public
utilities, and basic industrial goods, it acquired considerable productive
capability.

World War II saw a further increase in the state's role in the Brazilian economy. Brazil's formal entry into the war in 1942 provided the
occasion for a full-scale economic mobilization effort; in particular, the
obvious need for raw materials and manufactured goods vital to the war
effort gave new urgency to the Vargas program of state-financed enterprises. The war also provoked greater American involvement in Brazilian economic development. Since the Brazilians were providing vital
bases for the Allied cause, the United States government was anxious
to aid Vargas's mobilization effort (thereby realizing its long-standing
ambitions for greater commercial penetration in Latin America). Examples of this new American involvement included a $20 million loan
for the new National Steel Company (through the Export-Import Bank),
and the work of the Cooke mission, which produced the first systematic
survey of Brazilian resources and initiated a close planning relationship between the respective governments.

But despite progressive industrialization during the 1930s (when
production rose 60 percent), it was not until 1943 that Vargas committed himself unequivocally to systematic industrial development. In
that year he proudly announced that, on the strength of its iron and
steel plants, Brazil was forging "the basic elements for the transformation of a vast and scattered agrarian community into a nation capable
of providing its fundamental necessities." [10] A year later, in a speech
to the military, he stressed that "our first lesson from the present war
was that . . . the only countries that can really be considered military
powers are those that are sufficiently industrialized and able to produce
within their own frontiers the war materials they need." [11]

As we shall see in chapter 4, this linking of national security matters
with the economic development of the nation was to become a dominant
theme in the ideology of subsequent Brazilian regimes. In the post-1964
period it is heavily associated with the ESG (Escola Superior de Guerra)
and the military establishment.

In the postwar years successive Brazilian governments continued this mix of direct and indirect stimulation of industry. There was a brief return to free trade and economic liberalism under Eurico Dutra (1946–47), but this policy was shaken by the rapid exhaustion of Brazil's foreign exchange reserves. In 1947 exchange controls were set up, together with an elaborate import licensing system that discriminated against consumer goods in favor of raw materials and machinery. These measures obviously created a powerful incentive for Brazilian industry to expand. Furthermore, given a high official exchange rate, there was no incentive to export, and investment was channeled into production for the home market.

Not that either the exchange controls of 1947, which were the product of a balance-of-payments crisis, or the coffee support policy in the 1930s were intended primarily to promote industrialization, although both had that effect. These programs underline the fact that much of this early phase of Brazilian industrialization was haphazard or "devoid of any plan."

In Vargas's second term in office (1951–54) and, even more dramatically, in Kubitschek's term (1956–61) there was much more explicit and forceful state control and encouragement of domestic industrialization. Deliberate attempts were made to eliminate the structural bottlenecks (inadequate transportation, insufficient electricity), the sectoral lags (in chemicals and in metalworking industries), and regional disequilibriums (between the northeast and the centersouth and between the hinterland and the coast) from the Brazilian economy by means of state control and public investment. Steps to solve these problems included the creation of a National Bank for Economic Development (BNDE), which was intended to eliminate or reduce the infrastructure deficiencies that impeded the rapid development of the Brazilian economy; the setting up of Eletrobrás and Petrobrás (the state monopolies in electricity and petroleum); and the building of the new capital, Brasilia.

However, it would be wrong to characterize the 1950s as an era dominated by public investment. Both Vargas and Kubitschek made direct appeals to private investors, domestic and foreign. The state offered Brazilian businessmen liberal credit, secured high levels of domestic demand, and gave foreign firms special incentives to invest in Brazilian industry. For example, the Kubitschek government made liberal use of SUMOC (the Brazilian monetary authority) Directive No.

113, issued in 1955. This regulation encouraged foreign firms to bring into Brazil much needed industrial equipment by waiving the need to provide foreign exchange "cover" for imported machinery.

In short, both the Vargas and the Kubitschek administrations demonstrated a pragmatic approach to an already mixed economy. The overriding aim was to achieve the most rapid rate of growth possible by encouraging expansion in both the private and the public sectors and by taking advantage of both spontaneous and deliberate industrial incentives. The effect was to deepen the import substitution process. During these years, Brazil became self-sufficient in an increasingly wide range of sophisticated consumer goods. Kubitschek promised fifty years of progress in five years; and there is little doubt that between 1956 and 1961 Brazil did record remarkable real economic growth (8 percent per year, or three times the Latin American average).

Import Reproduction

The state's protective policies during the 1930–64 period had important effects on the type of industrial structure that developed in Brazil. Successive Brazilian government threw up barriers to trade (tariffs, import licenses) which tended to give the greatest degree of protection to goods that had previously been imported. After all, there was an assured market for those luxury items demanded by the Brazilian elite. This indiscriminate and expedient approach to protectionism had a twofold and cumulative effect. In the first place, import substitution became import reproduction, as products identical to those previously imported (sophisticated consumer goods) came to be made in Brazil.[12] Second, as the production, managerial, and marketing techniques required to manufacture these identical products were effectively monopolized by the giant international oligopolies, this strategy led to a situation where the dynamic sectors of final goods manufacturing in Brazil were increasingly dominated by multinational corporations, with consequences I shall elaborate on in chapter 7.

The cumulative effect of these policies was to rigidify and exacerbate the previous distribution of income in Brazil, which was, as we have seen, extremely unequal. The multinational firms with their capital- and skill-intensive technologies absorbed little labor; individuals who did find employment within this dynamic sector constituted a well-paid minority group—a labor aristocracy that had little in common with the mass of the Brazilian population in either economic or political terms. These characteristics of production obviously fed through to the structure of demand. The industrial work force, along with other members of the Brazilian elite, was able to appropriate an increasing proportion of national income; and this concentration of spending power in the hands of privileged groups provided a significant and expanding market for the products of the multinational corporations. In essence, a "vicious circle of wealth" enabled Brazil to adopt prematurely the goods and the consumption habits of the advanced affluent nations.

Although many economists have recognized the harmful effects of import-substituting industrialization, much of their criticism has confused the specifics of a particular strategy with the issue of protection. Now, some degree of protection is probably both inevitable and advisable if an underdeveloped country is to survive intense international competition in the initial phases of late industrialization. However, it is at least theoretically possible to internalize domestic demand without importing multinational corporations with their "rich country" technology and product mix (for example, American automobiles and hi-fi equipment made with the most advanced labor-saving equipment). From a social welfare vantage point, there is nothing wrong with a policy of import-substituting industrialization if the underdeveloped country concerned substitutes a generalized demand for industrial goods rather than a specific set of luxury products. It should be possible to create a domestic manufacturing capability that is geared to the local factor endowment and caters to the needs of the mass of the population.

Unfortunately theoretical feasibility has little to do with the likelihood of adopting a particular economic policy: as usual one has to recognize the constraints imposed by the realities of political power; and in Brazil these constraints ensured that import substitution emerged as a development strategy designed by and for an elite. To change the emphasis of production away from the multinational corporation and sophisticated consumer goods would have meant, in the first instance, a restructuring of demand via income redistribution. Given the historical roots of inequality in Brazil, which encompassed four centuries of plantation-style agriculture, this would have taken a much more radical regime than that of Vargas.

Inflation Control and Balance-of-Payments Difficulties

A recurrent feature of Brazilian economic policy making during
the import-substituting period was the repeated but largely unsuccessful
attempts to stabilize inflation (in 1953–54, 1955–56, 1959, and
1963–64). Until the 1960s these failures did not prevent a resumption
of growth, but the inflationary distortions increased, and by 1964 it
was doubtful that any elected regime could carry out the draconian
stabilization program needed to move the economy into a phase of renewed growth. Where did these inflationary pressures come from, and
why was it so difficult to control them?

As we shall see in chapter 5, many of the critical inflation-producing
conditions in Brazil were a legacy from that long period based on the
production of primary commodities for export. For example, an inadequate and inappropriate infrastructure provided an important inflationary
pressure. At the onset of modern industrialization, Brazilian roads, railways, electricity supplies, and telephones, insofar as they existed, were
geared to primary exporting activities; and shortfalls and bottlenecks in
these areas served to aggravate inefficiency and to increase costs in the
Brazilian industrial sector throughout the import-substituting period.

These structural tendencies toward inflationary pressures inherited
from the primary exporting economy were exacerbated by the choice
of industrial strategy employed by modern Brazilian regimes. Import
substitution had many inflationary aspects. Tariffs and other barriers to
entry provided a captive home market which tended to generate above-
normal profit margins for those firms (both national and multinational)
that operated within it. The comprehensive Brazilian tariff law of 1957
erected a protective wall that, for certain categories of final goods, was
over 200 percent. This made imports prohibitive, and Brazilian producers, facing no external competition and little internal competition
(for the domestic market structure was thoroughly oligopolistic),
could literally charge "what the traffic would bear" and collect abnormally high rates of return. As import substitution widened, and supply shifted from imports to higher-priced domestic production, there was
a progressive buildup of inflationary pressures.

The distortions of import-substituting industrialization were not limited to inflation but also had a balance-of-payments dimension. The

import-substituting industrialization strategies of Third World nations in the forties and fifties were often justified on the grounds that they alleviated the chronic balance-of-payments pressures of primary production, which revolved around deteriorating terms of trade and unpredictable price levels. At first glance this may seem to be true. After all, such a strategy substituted for industrial imports in an attempt to acquire the domestic capacity to satisfy national needs for manufactured goods. What actually happened, however, is that the import requirements of the domestic economy were not reduced but changed. Often, indeed, the industrializing country ended up becoming more vulnerable to a balance-of-payments constraint than it had been before the industrialization process started.

In simple terms, this is what happened. Since it is impossible to create all stages of the production process overnight, Brazil or any other underdeveloped country is bound to begin the process of import substitution in a partial rather than a complete manner. Generally speaking, countries begin with assembly plants and aim to progress "upstream" to intermediate products and capital goods, until they achieve a vertically integrated industrial structure (that is, one that includes all stages of production). Many of the steps in this process are difficult to take; for example, capital goods production often requires a level of technological sophistication and a depth to the local market that are extremely difficult for an underdeveloped country to conjure up.

Thus for several decades the import requirements of any import-substituting strategy remain large. In the initial years all intermediate as well as capital goods have to be imported; and even if a country succeeds in achieving some vertical integration, there will always remain a hard core of basic products that resist substitution. In addition to the technological and market-size factors mentioned earlier, one must remember that few nations are self-sufficient in such industrial raw materials as ferrous metals or energy resources; and these physical constraints are likely to ensure a permanent reliance on imported industrial inputs.

In short, import substitution merely shifts demand from imported final consumer goods to a variety of imported industrial inputs. But this new set of import needs has several dangerous features.

First, any decline in a country's capacity to import is now likely to have serious effects on domestic levels of production and employment. In the pre-industrial economy a decline in imports meant, essentially, a decline in the availability of sophisticated consumption goods. Although this situation was tough for elite groups, forced to cut back on their consumption of Scotch whisky or American automobiles, it had few effects beyond the consumption habits of the rich. But after the onset of import-substituting industrialization, the impact of an import constraint is quite different. A decline in a country's capacity to import intermediate and basic industrial goods affects the health of domestic industry, slows down production and reduces employment levels: in short, such a constraint is capable of a huge multiplier effect within the national economy.

A further repercussion of import substitution on the balance-of-payments situation is that it pushes the economy away from solving the import constraint via export expansion or diversification. Import-substituting industrialization is, after all, a strategy directed toward domestic growth and is based on internal demand; it tends to create a high-cost manufacturing sector that is, at least in the initial phases, incapable of competing in international markets. The postindustrialization scenario is therefore one in which underdeveloped countries struggle with a new and more urgent need to import and yet continue to rely on the old sources of export earnings (that is, primary commodities with their familiar problems of declining terms of trade and unpredictability).

Exchange rate policy often exaggerates this structural tendency for import-substituting industrialization to be associated with a worsening of the balance-of-payments problem. As we shall see in chapter 5, the Brazilian *cruzeiro* was substantially overvalued throughout the import-substituting cycle of industrial growth (for the purpose of subsidizing the capital imports needed for industrialization). This discouraged exports, especially in the sphere of manufactured goods.

Thus, while easy import substitution in Brazil did produce rapid growth (between 1930 and the early 1960s the manufacturing capability of Brazil quadrupled) and considerable structural transformation (see, for example, the dramatic population shift from the countryside to the cities), it also served to rigidify a highly differentiated social structure and a highly inequitable distribution of income inherited from the colonial period. The specifics of the import-substitution strategy, particularly its expedient and indiscriminate approach to economic planning and its import reproduction attributes, meant that the fruits of industrial development were appropriated by an elite group.

Furthermore, these policies tended to produce cumulative inflationary and balance-of-payments pressures, which during the 1950s and early 1960s were to become increasingly acute, culminating in the crisis of 1964. By this date inflationary and balance-of-payments distortions were so severe that a much more ruthless set of economic and political solutions were called for if Brazil was to get back on the growth path. This brings us to the third stage in the evolution of Brazil's economy —a stage that was a direct result of the 1964 crisis.

Stabilization and Export-Led Growth: 1964–Present Day

In 1964 the resolution of massive inflationary and balance-of-payments distortions was the outstanding economic policy issue. The stabilization package of the military government included a number of new features. Most important of these was a deliberate policy of letting wage increases lag behind increases in the cost of living, so that by 1967 real wages had fallen by 25 percent. A second item involved an attempt to lower real prices for manufactured goods through a reduction in the level of effective protection and through the elimination of credit subsidies. This measure caused many of the smaller, less efficient (and generally Brazilian) firms to go under. Third, there was an effort to balance the federal budget by increasing the price of public services and stringently enforcing the collection of taxes. Finally, there was a direct attack on the balance-of-payments problem through measures designed to encourage the inflow of foreign capital (for example, the restrictive profit remittance law of 1962 was repealed).[13]

Many of these measures were extremely unpopular and could be carried through only by an authoritarian and repressive government. I shall consider the political and ideological dynamics of this critical period in greater detail in chapter 4. Here I would merely stress that from the economic vantage point successful stabilization was not a discretionary item on the agenda of the new regime; rather, it was an essential prerequisite for a new cycle of capitalist growth within the Brazilian domestic economy.

The inflation-control package was successful, and in 1967 Brazil entered that period of boom often referred to as the "miracle." Annual real growth of GNP, which had averaged 4.1 percent per year between 1964 and 1967, rose to 11.5 percent in the years from 1968 to 1973. As can be seen from table 2, industry was the leading sector, expanding at an average annual rate of 13.2 percent. Within manufacturing, the highest growth rates were achieved in such sectors as transport equipment, machinery, steel, electrical equipment, and chemicals—all sectors which were dominated either by multinational corporations or by the state. Expansion in these sectors was truly dramatic. For example, between 1964 and 1975 production of motor vehicles increased from 184,000 per year to 930,000 per year, while the annual output of steel grew from 2.8 million tons to 8.3 million tons. Traditional sectors remained the preserve of private national capital and grew much more slowly. As can be seen from table 3, textiles, clothing, and food products all grew at modest rates during these years.[14]

This era of rapid growth (1968–73) also saw important structural changes. First, there were changes in the ownership pattern of industrial assets and in the relationship among the various economic factors in the growth process. The division of labor remained roughly the same with multinationals dominant in the production of consumer durables; state enterprises monopolizing the basic inputs sector; and private national firms retaining their control of the smaller-scale, more traditional areas of the economy. However, the balance of power did shift slightly over time. Multinationals increased their hold over the largest firms within the manufacturing sector but declined in their overall relative importance. The state productive sector, on the other hand, became the fastest-growing segment of Brazilian industry.

As far as private national capital was concerned, the years of the "miracle" saw some contradictory developments. While some specific government policies discriminated in favor of private national enterprises (for example, through subsidies to private Brazilian firms in the capital goods sector), overall economic policies (for example, the restrictive credit policies of 1965–67 which triggered many bankruptcies) made it difficult for small private firms to survive. In general, the government sought to protect and subsidize some of the larger and more important private Brazilian firms while allowing the sector as a whole to suffer the consequences of a development strategy that had economic growth as its prime focus. I shall have more to say on this increasingly complex relationship between foreign, state, and private capital in chapters 6 and 7.

A second structural feature of industrial growth during this period was the successful export promotion of manufactured products. In the early 1960s industrial exports composed less than 3 percent of total exports; by 1974 they were approaching 30 percent (see table 4). Indeed, during the "miracle" this growth in exports was an important element in the spectacular growth of the Brazilian manufacturing sector. In 1968, 5 percent of the industrial growth rate was due to the increased exportation of manufactured products; by 1971 this proportion had grown to 18 percent.

Success in the sphere of manufactured exports after 1968 contrasts sharply with the import-substitution period of the late fifties and early sixties and is attributable to both domestic and international circumstances. The outward orientation of post-1968 economic policies was crucial. Comprehensive tax credits (or exemptions) for industrial exports, credit incentives, and the minimization of exchange risks through mini-devaluations all contributed to the rapid increase in industrial exports.

External factors were also important. The middle and late 1960s were marked by a dramatic expansion of international liquidity (for example, world reserves grew at the astounding rate of 22.7 percent per year between 1969 and 1973) and by a huge increase in world trade (which grew at 18 percent per year between 1967 and 1973).[15] Although these dramatic developments primarily benefited the more advanced economies, they also spilled over to underdeveloped countries. In the sphere of trade Brazil benefited disproportionately, because multinational corporations chose it to be a major supplier of other markets. In part, their choice reflected the greater economies of scale and lower costs of production that characterized Brazil's maturing industrial structure, but it was also a result of the high degree of political stability and repressive control over labor activity, and hence labor costs, that Brazil was able to offer multinational firms. In this latter respect Brazil had a significant advantage over such competitive economies as Mexico and Argentina. The net result of these economic and political factors was that by the early 1970s a large proportion of Brazilian manufactured exports—in transport equipment and in electrical, pharmaceutical, and plastic goods—came from the subsidiaries of multinational corporations.

A less positive part of the trade picture was the growth of imports. From 1971 import growth outpaced the remarkable growth of exports.

Indeed, imports as a percentage of the GNP doubled from 7 percent in the middle of the 1960s to over 15 percent by 1973. (This dramatic growth in imports can be seen in table 4.) Capital goods played an important role in this increase. The trade deficit, resulting from this rapid import growth, was more than covered by a massive inflow of foreign capital. For example, the net inflow of direct investment grew from a yearly average of $84 million in the period 1965–69 to $944 million in 1974. Indeed, foreign financing exceeded the deficit in the current account to such an extent that Brazil's foreign exchange reserves grew from an average of $400 million in 1965–69 to $5.3 billion in 1974.

Thus, the "miracle" produced impressively high rates of industrial growth, manageable rates of inflation (which were partially neutralized by widespread indexing), a rapid surge in manufactured exports and in capital goods imports, a massive influx of foreign capital, a buildup of reserves, and an increased role for the state in the productive sphere. In the assessment of these accomplishments, two qualifications are in order.

In the first instance, the "miracle" cannot be attributed to the unaided efforts of Brazilian policy makers. Conditions in the international environment and within the domestic economy were unusually conducive to fast growth rates. I have already noted how the unprecedented growth in international trade and in international liquidity helped the Brazilian external account so as to prevent a balance-of-payments constraint on development. In the domestic sphere it is important to remember that there was substantial idle capacity in the Brazilian industrial sector at the beginning of the boom. In 1965 the degree of utilized capacity was only three-quarters of what it had been in 1961, or of what it would be again in 1972–73. The presence of idle capacity not only made possible the subsequent boom but also made rapid growth relatively costless in its initial years, since present growth could be partially based on the investments of previous years. The expansionary policies of Delfim Netto (finance minister 1967–73) would not have triggered inflation-free growth without these favorable supply conditions.

The second qualification involves the human costs of the Brazilian miracle. As the *Economist* has put it, "The Brazilian economy has grown over the past decade in much the same way as a Brazilian drives his car. That is extremely fast, disregarding everyone else on the road, narrowly avoiding accidents and not stopping to consider whether his passengers have been left behind." [16] Later chapters will detail the facts and figures of poverty and inequality in contemporary Brazil. Suffice it to say at this stage that by 1970 the gap between the "haves" and the "have nots" in Brazilian society had widened to such an extent that the richest 1 percent of the population appropriated the same proportion of national income as the poorest 50 percent. In addition, miserable, wretched poverty continued to afflict one-third of Brazilian families. The economic benefits of stabilization and export-led growth seem to have been spread around extremely unevenly.

The Recent Period

Seven fat years of economic boom based on an outward-oriented growth strategy gave way to lean years in 1974 and (especially) 1975. Increased petroleum import prices were part of the problem. The oil crisis raised Brazil's oil bill from $710 million in 1973 to $2.9 billion in 1974. However, the oil shock on its own would have been manageable because these years saw sharp price increases for Brazil's own commodity exports, which buoyed export earnings and foreign reserves, and there was continued access to credit abroad. But oil was only the tip of the iceberg. Between 1973 and 1974 the overall import bill went from $6 billion to $12.6 billion (F.O.B.), and the extra cost of oil accounted for only one-third of this increase. Three other factors contributed to this dramatic rise in the cost of imports. In the first place, there were higher prices for imported capital and intermediate goods as inflation spread through the advanced industrial world. Second, continued rapid industrial growth within the Brazilian domestic economy greatly increased demand for imported industrial inputs. And finally, the balance-of-payments problem was worsened by the exchange rate lagging behind the pace of the devaluation that was appropriate to the ratio of domestic inflation to international inflation.[17]

The balance-of-payments situation deteriorated further in 1975 as stagnation in the developed world reduced world markets and slowed down the rate of increase in Brazilian manufactured exports. Simultaneously prices for Brazil's primary commodity exports began to back off from their mid-1974 peak. The net result was enormous trade deficits

in 1974 and 1975 which were financed by an increase in the foreign
debt (see tables 5 and 6).

The very success of the earlier import-substitution process meant that
remaining imports were critical industrial inputs, goods that were extremely difficult to eliminate without reducing employment levels and
depressing growth rates within the domestic economy. For example, in
1974 consumer nondurables represented only 1.1 percent of total imports
and consumer durables only 6.1 percent. The bulk of imports were either
intermediate or capital goods, essential ingredients of domestic industry.
The need to limit imports in the wake of the huge balance-of-payments
deficits of the mid-1970s produced a series of restrictive measures that
had to fall on these essential items and undoubtedly contributed to the
deceleration of real growth in 1975.

Economic planning in the Geisel era (1974–79) relied mainly on
policies of import restriction and import substitution to tackle the outstanding problems. Tariffs were increased, and advance deposits became
required for the importation of many goods.[18] This latter policy amounted
to a disguised tariff because of the decline in the real value of monetary
deposits during the time they were held idle. Accompanying this move
to restrict imports was a drive toward a new cycle of import-substituting
industrialization in the capital goods sector, the rationale being that this
was the only way of permanently reducing imports. BNDE (the national
development bank) and other state agencies devoted a considerable
proportion of their resources over these five years to the capital and
basic goods sector, and much of the stimulus was directed to private
national firms. For example, BNDE tripled its investment activity between 1974 and 1976; and this increase was accompanied by a redistribution of investment resources toward the basic and capital goods
sectors (which captured 69 percent of total approved funds in 1976
as opposed to 48 percent in 1974) and toward national private capital
(which appropriated 81 percent of total funds in 1976 as opposed to
66 percent in 1974).[19]

How successful were these policies? Import restrictions and the import substitution program tripled national production of capital goods
(produced by subsidiaries of multinationals operating in Brazil and by
domestic private firms) between 1973 and 1977. A particularly important stimulus was BNDE's special program FINAME which finances the
purchase of nationally produced equipment at highly subsidized rates.[20]
Vigorous growth in the capital goods sphere, has had, of course, a

beneficial effect on the trade balance, as Brazil has reduced its need to import machinery and basic goods. For example, in 1977 Brazil's net deficit in its trade in capital goods fell by US$32 million. Partially as a result of this success story the Brazilian economy was able to grow at an average annual rate of 7.1 percent between 1974 and 1978. A creditable performance for an oil-dependent underdeveloped country!

The new policy of import-substituting industrialization in the capital goods sector has been compared with the 1930–64 phase of industrial growth in Brazil. It is as though

the wheel has been brought back to full circle. The soldiers who deposed the civilian government in 1964 wanted to transform a supposedly protected import-substituting Brazil into an open, export-geared world power. The oil crisis and the world recession now appear to be forcing the generals who have succeeded them to think again.[21]

But one can overdramatize this point: on many fronts the Brazilian strategy of growth has remained outwardly oriented. Indeed, successful resolution of the 1974–75 economic problems depended to an important degree on the expansion of Brazilian commodity and manufactured exports and on the continued inflow of considerable amounts of foreign capital.

Brazil achieved a 9 percent increase in export earnings in 1975 and a 17 percent increase in 1976, despite a significant decline in sugar exports and stagnation in manufactures. Coffee (up 140 percent in price and 4 percent in volume) was primarily responsible for the gains in 1976, but soybeans, iron ore, and other primary commodity exports also registered healthy increases. In 1977 continued growth in primary commodity exports was accompanied by vigorous growth in manufactured exports (which grew by 35 percent), and at year end the nation proudly reported a modest trade surplus of $140 million.

In 1978 the balance-of-payments situation looked less rosy, as agricultural exports fell by one-third (hit by droughts, frosts, and cutbacks in agricultural credits). Continued growth in manufactured exports (which grew 20 percent during that year) helped contain the trade deficit. However, relying on growth in manufactured exports as a solution to the balance-of-payments problem in Brazil is a policy fraught with problems.

The success of Brazilian manufactured exports in world markets is crucially dependent upon the welter of incentives and tax breaks provided by the Brazilian government.[22] This incentive structure is now threatened by a new wave of protectionism in the advanced world. To take an example, the Brazilian textile industry sent 15 percent of its total exports to the United States in 1977. In the States these goods were seen as being unfairly subsidized by the Brazilian government, and the United States government threatened to impose punitive countervailing duties of 37.2 percent (calculated by the United States Department of Commerce to be equivalent to the tax credits received by Brazilian textile exporters). In order to avoid these duties imposed by the United States, the Brazilian authorities have agreed to levy their own export tax. This tax, although lower than that threatened by the United States government, is likely to make Brazilian textiles uncompetitive in world markets. In addition, the United States has put pressure on Brazil to impose export taxes on leather, rubber, and plastic goods.

In short, advanced industrialized countries have been afflicted with their own balance-of-payments difficulties in the wake of the oil crisis, and protectionist policies wielded by powerful nations protecting their own home markets can be expected into the future. Brazil has done its best to facilitate export growth by diversifying trading partners. Over the last several years, for instance, the Brazilian government has signed trade agreements with countries as diverse as Poland, China, Iraq, Nigeria, Angola, and Turkey. However, maintaining recent levels of export expansion, particularly in manufactures, is likely to be difficult.

In addition to these developments in the export sphere, the "containment" of the 1974–75 recession in Brazil was heavily reliant upon large inflows of foreign capital. As we have seen, petroleum price increases and lags in the development of domestic basic and capital goods industries pushed Brazil's current account deficit from US$1.3 billion in 1973 to US$7.1 billion in 1974. The effect of this rise was to increase dramatically Brazil's dependence on external funds. By 1975 the total loan inflow required to cover Brazil's needs had increased to US$6.2 billion, and in 1976 it amounted to US$6.9 billion (see table 6). Over this period the international capital market managed to supply these huge amounts of loan funds to Brazil. Indeed, in some years there was an actual inflow of more than was needed, resulting in a substantial increase in Brazil's foreign reserves. However, this dependence on massive inflows of foreign capital circumscribes domestic policy options into the future, as it involves retaining the goodwill of international lending institutions.

The other main problem accompanying the 1974–75 recession in

Brazil was, of course, domestic inflation. As can be seen from table 7, domestic rates of inflation rose significantly in the post-1974 period, and by 1978 inflation was running at an annual rate of more than 40 percent. There were numerous factors behind these price increases, including OPEC and the continuing rise in price of imported oil; generalized inflation in the developed world, which increased the price of key industrial inputs such as imported capital goods; the import deposit requirement, which effectively raised costs for domestic manufacturers; and various "liberalization" measures of the Geisel government, which allowed wage levels to rise in 1975 and again in 1976 (see chapter 8).

Policy responses by the Brazilian government during this period were rather erratic. For example, in the first eight months of 1974, the authorities restricted the growth of the money supply to 14 percent, but in August of that year Geisel decided to take the brakes off, a move that was not unconnected to the fact that the government was trying to win its first relatively free congressional elections in a decade (see discussion in chapter 4). As a result, overall growth in the money supply reached 30 percent for that year, and so did domestic inflation.[23]

Despite these inconsistencies, it is possible to detect distinct policy trends. First, the tightening of credit was a major policy item and adversely affected the smaller Brazilian companies (multinational subsidiaries are able to obtain overseas loans with greater ease). In 1976 and again in 1978 small and medium-sized private national companies suffered in the fight against inflation, "recalling the bad old days of 1964–67."[24]

Second, it seems that inflation repeatedly dampened Geisel's wage liberalization program. A gradual rise in the real value of workers' wages was a goal of *distensão* (the political opening of this period described in chapter 4); it was a declared aim of the government's national development plan, and it figured largely in Geisel's policy speeches during his term in office. However, as inflation mounted during 1976, government wage policies became progressively less liberal. Real wage adjustments in that year were steadily reduced from a January high of 3.7 percent to a December level of −2.2 percent. And in 1977 government wage increases were held to 30 percent, despite the fact that inflation reached a level of almost 40 percent. In 1978 some categories of skilled workers (such as engineering workers in São Paulo) and certain professional groups (such as teachers and junior hospital doctors) took advantage of the political thaw and staged successful strikes for higher pay.[25] However, for most urban workers the combination of wage restraint and industrial recession (both of which are by-products of inflation control) has meant depressed living standards into the late 1970s.

Third, the Geisel government used its control over the public sector to keep expenditures and prices down. For example, the public investment program for 1977 was cut back substantially. "Reflecting the government's concentration on the balance of payments and domestic inflation, all sectors, with the exception of petroleum, raw materials and export goods, will show real public expenditure reductions over 1976 levels." [26] The government also used the considerable powers of the Interministerial Price Council (CIP) to constrain price rises. For example, in October of 1976 the CIP authorized price hikes of 7 percent in the automobile sector for the last quarter of the year; this figure was below the projected (and the realized) rate of inflation and served to put pressure on the industry to increase productivity in order to maintain profit levels.[27] However, there is an obvious limit on the degree to which any Brazilian government can force the multinationally dominated segments of industry to lower prices. Given the vulnerability of the balance-of-payments situation and the necessity of attracting a large inflow of foreign capital, it would seem that the brunt of price restraint has to fall on state and national firms.

In summary, balance of payments difficulties and domestic inflation have always been critical problems in the modern development of Brazil; and the 1974–79 period is no exception. In the main, Geisel and his minister of finance, Mário Henrique Simonsen, sought to contain these problems through cautious programs directed toward increasing national self-sufficiency and containing demand. Import substitution in the capital goods sector served to alleviate the balance-of-payments situation by reducing the import needs of Brazilian industry; and, by cutting down on imported capital goods, it reduced the transmission of inflation from advanced industrial countries. Budget cutting and the restriction of credit are the classic methods of dampening demand, and during these years they were used both to control inflation and to cut back import bills.

Since the coming to power of João Baptista Figueiredo in March of 1979, there has been some change in the direction of economic policy making. At first it seemed as though many of Geisel's programs would remain in place, but the new round of oil price hikes, initiated by the OPEC countries in May of 1979, has produced a dramatic worsening of both the balance of payments and inflation in Brazil. The oil bill is expected to rise from US$4.5 billion in 1978 to at least US$7.0 billion in 1979 as a result of the recent price hikes, pushing the current account deficit to US$9 billion, the foreign debt to US$52 billion, and causing inflation to approach 80 percent for the year as a whole.[28] As a result of these developments, the cautious policies of Simonsen have been abandoned, and Delfim Netto, with a characteristic array of expansionary solutions to the current problems of the Brazilian economy, has been installed in the Ministry of Planning. (Delfim was minister of finance during the years of the "miracle" and is identified with ambitious, pro-growth policies.) The new strategy is based on accelerated growth in all sectors of the economy. Massive investments in agriculture are meant to increase the availability of food and export crops and thus decrease the pressure on the price level and help the trade account. This is to be accompanied by a determined attempt to increase industrial exports in order to eliminate industrial idleness and revitalize the domestic economy.[29] It is too early to tell whether Delfim's policies will work, but it seems clear that the renewed balance of payments and inflationary pressures will severely constrain policy options into the future. Coping with a US$52 billion debt and an inflation rate of 80 percent a year has to mean wage restraint and budget cutting, and these austerity measures will fall most heavily on the lower classes of Brazilian society. In short, no contemporary policy package can significantly improve the social welfare result of the Brazilian style of development.

In this chapter we have covered the broad sweep of Brazilian economic history and can now begin to appreciate the extent to which massive poverty and increasing inequality are embedded in the fabric of this late-developing nation. Uneven and unequal development became entrenched during a colonial, primary exporting past and was built upon by the import-substituting policies of the 1930–64 period, which encouraged multinational corporations to produce rich country goods within the domestic economy. The mass of the people became redundant to the modern industrialization process, both as consumers and as producers; and Brazil assumed its contemporary image of affluence for a minority and of misery for the majority.

The post-1964 period has, in the main, exaggerated this picture, as the imperatives of maintaining growth conditions (in particular coping with inflation and balance-of-payments problems) have required that the living standards of the industrial work force be periodically suppressed. Even during the Geisel era, when official policies stressed the importance of improving social welfare, little progress was made on this front. The broad thrust of the development strategy continued to ignore the Brazilian lower classes (those millions of landless laborers living in the countryside and marginal workers living in the shantytowns of Brazil). And the much-publicized wage liberalization drive for industrial workers was repeatedly stalled by balance-of-payments disequilibriums and accelerating inflation. This pattern seems to be continuing into the Figueiredo administration. Official attempts to ameliorate social welfare conditions are currently being frustrated by a new wave of economic problems triggered by another round of oil price hikes by the OPEC nations. In July 1979, Figueiredo warned that liberalization could be the first victim of the country's deteriorating economic situation.[30] With Brazil currently facing its largest current account deficit in history and its highest inflation rates since the early 1960s, it is unlikely that his government will make long-run and significant concessions to workers.

The economic choices made by successive Brazilian governments in the modern period have been, in the main, consistent. They have promoted rapid economic growth and tolerated the social repercussions of such growth. In chapter 4, I turn to political and ideological factors to explain the values and priorities that underlie these economic choices.

NOTES

1. For accounts of the early history of Brazil, see Celso Furtado, *The Economic Growth of Brazil: A Survey from Colonial to Modern Times* (Berkeley: University of California Press, 1963); Caio Prado Junior, *Colonial Background of Modern Brazil* (Berkeley: University of California Press, 1971); and Roberto Simonsen, *História Econômico do Brasil* (São Paulo: Companhia Editôria Nacional, 1962).

2. Furtado, *Economic Growth of Brazil*, pp. 45–48. See also C. R. Boxer, *The Dutch in Brazil* (London: Oxford University Press, 1957).

3. This type of analysis was first developed by Celso Furtado. See, for example, Celso Furtado, *Análise do "Modelo" Brasileiro* (Rio de Janeiro: Editora Civilização Brasileira, 1972).

4. Warren Dean, *The Industrialization of São Paulo* (Austin, Tex.: University of Texas Press, 1969).

5. James M. Malloy, ed., *Authoritarianism and Corporatism in Latin America* (Pittsburgh: University of Pittsburgh Press, 1977), p. 8.

6. See discussion in Werner Baer, *Industrialization and Economic Development in Brazil* (Homewood, Ill.: Richard D. Irwin, 1965), p. 20.

7. For detailed accounts of this period of import substitution, see Joel Bergsman, *Brazil: Industrialization and Trade Policies* (London: Oxford University Press, 1970); and Nathaniel H. Leff, *Economic Policy-making and Development in Brazil, 1947–1964* (New York: John Wiley, 1968).

8. See discussion in Albert O. Hirschman, "The Turn to Authoritarianism in Latin America and the Search for its Economic Determinants," mimeograph (Institute for Advanced Study, Princeton, N.J.: February 1977). Hirschman identifies the ways in which this first cycle of import substitution adopted the easy or expedient methods of industrialization.

9. As Ruy Maruo Marini has put it, "The crisis in the coffee economy presented domestic industrialists with an economic surplus which it did not need to expropriate since it was spontaneously put at its disposal" ("La Dialectica del Desarrollo Capitalista en Brasil," *Guardernos Americanos* 25, no. 3 [1966]: 137).

10. Getulio Vargas, *A Nova Politica do Brasil* (Rio de Janeiro, 1938), p. 168; quoted in Thomas E. Skidmore, *Politics in Brazil, 1930–1964* (New York: Oxford University Press, 1967), p. 45.

11. Skidmore, *Politics in Brazil*, p. 45.

12. This concept of import reproduction was developed by Frances Stewart, "Technology and Employment in LDC's," in Edgar O. Edwards, ed., *Employment in Developing Nations* (New York: Columbia University Press, 1974), pp. 83–130.

13. For detailed accounts of post-1964 economic policies, see Donald E. Syvrud, *Foundations of Brazilian Economic Growth* (Stanford: Stanford University Press, 1974), pp. 32–59; and Albert Fishlow, "Some Reflections on Post-1964 Brazilian Economic Policy," in Alfred Stepan, ed., *Authoritarian Brazil* (New Haven, Conn.: Yale University Press, 1973), pp. 69–119.

14. An extensive literature exists on the Brazilian economic miracle. See for example: Edmar L. Bacha, "Recent Brazilian Economic Growth and Some of its Main Problems," Textos Para Discussão, no. 25, Departmento de Economia, Universidade de Brasilia (April 1975); Werner Baer, "The Brazilian Boom 1968–72: An Explanation and Interpretation," *World Development* (August 1973), pp. 1–17; Werner Baer, "The Brazilian Economic Miracle: The Issues and the Literature," *Bulletin of the Society for Latin American Studies*, no. 24 (March 1976): 7–28; Eduardo Periera de Carvalho, *Financiamento Externo e Cresimento Economico no Brasil* (Rio de Janeiro: Coleção Relatorios de Pesquisa, IPEA/INPES, 1974); and José Roberto Mendonça de Barros and Douglas H. Graham, "The Brazilian Economic Miracle Revisited: Private and Public Sector Initiative in a Market Economy," *Latin American Research Review* 13 (1978): 5–38.

15. These external factors are emphasized in Pedro S. Malan and Regis Bonelli, "The Brazilian Economy in the Seventies: Old and New Developments," *World Development* 5, nos. 1/2 (1977): 19–45.

16. "A Survey of Brazil," *The Economist*, 31 July 1976, p. 43.

17. This point is elaborated by William R. Cline, "Brazil's Emerging International Economic Role," in Riordan Roett, ed., *Brazil in the Seventies* (Washington, D.C.: American Enterprise Institute for Public Policy Research, 1976), pp. 63–89.

18. Imports subject to duties of 37 percent or more were subject to a prior deposit of 100 percent of the *cruzeiro* equivalent FOB value of the import. This deposit had to be handed over by the importer to the Foreign Trade Board of the Bank of Brazil, CACEX, prior to the issue of an importation certificate. *QER* (*Quarterly Economic Review*. Economist Intelligence Unit, London), Annual Supplement, 1975, p. 13.

19. These figures were obtained from BNDE (Banco Nacional Desenvolvimento Económico), *Report of Activities*, 1974 and 1976.

20. *Latin America Economic Report.* 16 June 1978, p. 181.

21. "A Survey of Brazil," *The Economist.* 31 July 1976, p. 15.

22. The basic measures are exemption from payment of IPI, a tax on the producers of industrialized goods (which goes up to 30 percent) and of ICM, a value-added tax (up to 14 percent). Moreover, the amount that would have been paid in these taxes on exported goods can be deducted from a company's domestic market sales for tax purposes. Tax credits are also available for the purchase of raw materials and inputs used in manufacturing export goods. There are also advantages for company tax. Taxable profits can be reduced by the proportion of a firm's exports to its total sales. (*Latin America Economic Report.* 2 June 1978, p. 166.)

23. See account in Banco Lar, *Trends and Perspectives.* no. 14 (1977) : 4.

24. *Latin America Economic Report.* December 1978, p. 369.

25. *Latin America Economic Report,* 27 October 1978, p. 329; and 1 September 1978, p. 296.

26. Banco Lar, *Trends and Perspectives,* no. 16 (1977) : 2.

27. *Trends and Perspectives,* no. 16 (1977) : 1–3.

28. *Latin America Economic Report.* 1 June 1979, p. 161.

29. *Latin America Economic Report.* 28 September 1979, p. 304.

30. *Latin America Political Report,* 20 July 1979, p. 221.

CHAPTER

4

Political and Ideological Frameworks

Governments rarely indulge casually in egregious violations of human rights. Rather they do so because they feel that they will be deflected from the pursuit of programs that they judge to be in their own interests.

Richard Ullman

WE HAVE SEEN in chapter 3 that the history of Brazilian economic development may be divided broadly into three periods, each of which is characterized by different economic structures and policies, and all of which contributed to the presence of poverty and repression in contemporary Brazil. To understand how and why this happened, it is necessary to consider the different political and ideological contexts in which successive economic structures flourished and decayed.[1]

Colonial and Oligarchic Rule

As we saw in the previous chapter, from the sixteenth to the early twentieth centuries, the Brazilian domestic economy was integrated into an international market system where it functioned as a supplier of raw

materials and as a consumer of manufactured goods—a classic example
of the international division of labor resulting from free trade. Typically, in this era, the raw-material needs of the technologically advanced
central economies of Western Europe and North America were met by
the production of primary commodities at the periphery; and the ar-
rangement was put into effect by the establishment of trading monopolies and by empire. As long as Brazil was ruled by the Portuguese,
manufacturing activity was explicitly forbidden. But even after 1821,
when the colonial era effectively came to an end, free-trade policies,
plus special concessions to the British, kept the economy concentrated
on primary production and export. In essence, colonial domination by
Portugal was followed by a century of economic dependence on Britain,
which wielded military and political might in order to serve its own
special trading interests.

Politically, this long era of primary production can be divided into
three centuries of overt colonial domination by Portugal (1500–1821);
followed by a constitutional monarchy (1822–99) and a republic
(1890–1930) which, although ostensibly democratic, was in practice
rule by a small oligarchy of landlords and commercial intermediaries.
Changes in the formal structures of government should not obscure
the impressive continuity of political power. Throughout this early
period, government was controlled by a wealthy planter-importer elite
who determined economic policy and priorities in accordance with their
economic self-interest and the dictates of international trade.

This political framework was not conducive to either growth or
equity. The economic self-interest of the power-elite was not, at least
in the short run, bound up with domestic capital accumulation. They
cheerfully spent their incomes on imported luxury goods, thereby channeling a great deal of the surplus created by primary production back
to Europe and North America. Without an accumulated surplus available for investment, sustained internal growth was impossible. In the
spheres of political freedom and social welfare, the labor needs of cash
crop agriculture combined with rule by a landed oligarchy to effectively
exclude the majority of the people both from the political arena and
from the fruits of international trade, which was, after all, the major
source of wealth throughout this period.

The ideological orthodoxy of this era revolved around economic
liberalism and laissez faire, although the planter-importer class did not
hesitate to call upon the state to assume a major supportive role when

it suited their own trading interests. For example, by the beginning of the twentieth century the twin evils of overproduction and violent price fluctuations (the chronic problems of primary production) had become acute in Brazil's important coffee sector. In order to maintain foreign exchange earnings and ensure the income levels of the politically powerful planter-exporter elite, the government began to withhold stocks of coffee from the world market. This policy was based on the assumption that world demand for coffee was relatively insensitive to price. A strategy that kept surplus stocks from depressing the market could therefore keep prices high without reducing consumption, and could thus maximize total foreign exchange receipts.

It is interesting to note that these marketing controls or "valorization" programs were bitterly attacked by Brazilian followers of strict laissez faire economics, including some finance ministers. Successive federal governments were torn between the valorization schemes that were vital to the planter-exporter lobby and the counterarguments of Brazilian liberal economists, foreign creditors, and customers. By dint of its virtual control of the government, the landed oligarchy won this battle, and by the 1920s Brazilian governments were effectively committed to this form of state intervention. By skillful manipulation, "the coffee ruling class . . . managed to transfer to the community as a whole the bulk of the burden of the cyclical price fall." [2] The Brazilian state was well on its way to institutionalizing what came to be known as the socialization of losses and the private division of spoils.

For aspiring industrialists, however, economic liberalism held sway. The pre-1930 era saw various unsuccessful attempts by domestic industrialists to gain tariff protection and more liberal credit policies from the Brazilian state. Not only did state intervention on behalf of industry collide with laissez faire liberal concepts of Brazil's "natural" role as a producer of primary commodities, but it also threatened the self-interest of the landed oligarchy, who obviously benefited from free trade. The relatively weak class of domestic industrialists proved to be incapable of galvanizing the state on its behalf.[3] In this case dogma coincided with political expediency and economic liberalism won the day.

The Populist Period

The installation of Getulio Vargas as the president of Brazil in November 1930 brought to a close a four-hundred-year period during which the rural landholding oligarchies controlled domestic politics. Vargas championed "the new urban middle class and industrial sectors against the traditional centrifugal interests of the pre-1930 rural political and economic elite." [4] The hallmark of the new regime was modernization; it was conceived of as industrial growth under the aegis of a centralized, paternalistic state with strong anticommunist, pro-Western overtones. It took several years before a coherent political system emerged. The years 1930–37 witnessed "agitated improvisation, including a regionalist revolt in São Paulo, a new constitution, a popular front movement, a fascist movement, and an attempted Communist coup." [5] In 1937 an exhausted Brazil ended political experimentation and began eight years of authoritarian rule under the *Estado Novo* (a corporatist state organized along lines similar to Mussolini's Italy).

Despite the apparent political turmoil of the 1930s, it is possible to detect the formation of a strong populist coalition that was to dominate the national scene until 1964. Vargas put together an alliance of the landed oligarchy, the urban middle class, and the industrial work force in pursuit of economic growth under the new rules of the development game. In the wake of the 1929 crisis this meant a much more inward-looking development strategy with an emphasis on domestic industrialization. As O'Donnell has put it, "industrialization and nationalism were the ideological glue of the new coalition." [6]

The multiclass alliance involved the absorption and the co-optation of a pre-existing elite group (the landed oligarchy via price supports for coffee) and the manipulation and the co-optation of an emerging class (the industrial work force via various types of material rewards). [7]

Aside from being nationalist and developmentalist, what was the ideological content of Brazilian populism? In Brazil the goals and purposes of a populist state were first articulated by the *Tenentes*, a group of young military officers who gained access to Vargas in the years 1930–32 and were able to set the tone of his thinking on many social and economic questions. Their vision of Brazil included: the assertion of national economic independence, the breaking of semifeudal structures so as to liberate human and material resources for economic development, and the promotion of social harmony.[8] These goals were to be achieved by a strong state supported by a multiclass coalition. Populism was therefore "statist" but not "socialist." Indeed, the political rhetoric of the period rejected both socialism and capitalism and advocated instead a third route to development unique to Brazil. However, despite the veneer of anticapitalism and anti-imperialism, at a practical level, the governments of this era took the position that the conditions of underdevelopment made inadvisable any break with capitalist structures. Rather, the task was to expand state power so as to reform and regulate those structures and to achieve an evolutionary process of controlled economic development. In reality, then, the Brazilian version of populism was nationalistic, capitalistic, statist, and, most important, elitist.

Conventional images to the contrary, the populist era was not a bonanza for the masses. Industrial workers, however, were favored. As we shall see in chapter 9, there was a controlled, limited co-optation of industrial workers who were organized on the basis of functional representation under strict state control. In each *município* (small township) employers and employees set up *sindicatos* (unions) for the various trades and industries. These coalesced into state federations in each field of activity and came together at the national level as confederations that represented workers or employers in such broad spheres as industry and commerce. The system gradually evolved in the 1930s and was codified in 1943 (*O Consolidação das Leis do Trabalho*). State control of the unions took several forms. First, only those unions recognized by the Ministry of Labor were legal. Second, the government placed its own agents in positions of influence, thus excluding militants from the union leadership. Finally, compulsory membership dues (the *imposto sindical,* a tax of one day's wages per year to be deducted from the worker's paycheck) gave the state almost complete control over the labor movement, since these funds were only to be distributed by the Ministry of Labor to government-approved unions for official activities.

Under Vargas, Brazilian labor unions became government-sanctioned interest groups whose main function was the administration of the extensive social services created by the *Estado Novo.* Workers became "objects to be manipulated and controlled. . . . the passive recipients of paternalistic social policies." [9]

This prolonged attempt by Vargas to co-opt the emerging industrial work force had two purposes. It bought worker loyalty for his brand of government, and it pre-empted the Left. The material rewards handed over to this elite segment of the work force were considerable. They included medical services with some hospitalization privileges, subsidies after the first fifteen days of illness, cash payments upon birth or death, old-age pensions, and some limited assistance with purchasing low-income housing. The Vargas legislation included a "tenure" law, which provided that no employee with more than ten years of service in the same firm could be dismissed. It also introduced a minimum wage for some categories of urban workers.

In the 1930s and 1940s this was an impressive list of social security benefits for a country at Brazil's level of development, and it did serve to buy off the industrial work force, the labor aristocracy of the Brazilian lower classes. Vargas accurately saw this segment of the population as increasingly crucial in a country that was entering an era of modern industrialization. As long as industrial workers supported state policy, there was no need to worry about large-scale mobilization and challenges from the Left. The great mass of the population existing at subsistence levels on the *fazendas* and in the *favelas* of Brazil were both illiterate and politically inert. Because of this co-option of the only articulate segment of the lower classes, "the urban mass, the base of the Left in Brazilian politics [remained] . . . a mass rather than a class." [10]

The end of World War II saw the fall of Vargas, the dismantling of the authoritarian structures of the *Estado Novo,* and the resurrection of political parties and free elections. However, despite this much-talked-about rebirth of democratic politics, and despite a change in the formal political structure of the state, the 1946–64 period was in some essential senses a continuation of the 1930s.

In terms of economic policies, industrialization was accelerated, and there was a more explicit emphasis on import-substituting industrialization. But changes were in degree rather than in kind. The dominant ideology of these years remained nationalist and developmentalist. Nationalist sentiment hinged on a vision of a powerful and independent nation. It was Brazil's "destiny" to undertake a massive development drive based on rapid domestic industrialization. Kubitschek (1956–61) made a special point of involving nationalist-minded intellectuals who were attracted by this positive image of the future. He financed the Higher Institute of Brazilian Studies (ISEB), which became a center for research and teaching on Brazil's problems. It published a stream of books and lectures offering a rationale for industrialization and explaining the problems associated with underdevelopment in every sector of the economy. The hundreds of young professionals who attended the one-year course at the institute were profoundly influenced by the "developmentalist" mystique.

It is interesting to note that, despite a great deal of nationalist rhetoric, the 1950s were much more developmentalist than nationalist. For example, there were numerous diatribes against foreign capital by prominent Brazilian politicians; but on the practical level, government policies remained extremely favorable to the establishment of multinational corporations within the Brazilian market. As we shall see in chapter 7, by the end of the decade they dominated the most dynamic sectors of final goods production. In the short run, the national objective *was* fast economic growth. When faced with the choice between greater national control or higher growth rates, both Vargas and Kubitschek chose the latter.

Despite the obvious change in formal appearances in the postwar era (the new constitution of 1946, the re-emergence of political parties, and the institution of elections), the political reality was not significantly altered. The much-enlarged executive created during the *Estado Novo* remained intact, as did many of the policies of the previous regime. And since the electorate was confined to literates, well over half of the adult Brazilian population was excluded from the new democratic processes.[11] There was no reason why the mass of the population should figure in policy calculations any more in 1946 than they had done in the 1930s. A particularly important thread of continuity was the emphasis on populist economic policies.

Kubitschek, like Vargas before him, attempted to reward those segments of the population that were politically important. The state-promoted industrialization program drew enthusiastic support from capitalists, both domestic and foreign. The landed oligarchy was appeased by continued price support for coffee and the assurance that Brazil's archaic and inequitable pattern of land tenure would remain intact. The urban middle class was effectively wooed through more jobs, in the vastly expanded state bureaucracy, in the public enterprises, and in

private industry. Finally, the industrial working class (the only mobilized segment of the lower classes) was co-opted by means of generous wage settlements and extensive fringe benefits.

In the previous chapter I described how inflationary distortions were
part and parcel of the easy import-substitution phase of development
in Brazil. The politics of this period exacerbated this inflationary bias
in ways that ultimately proved incompatible with growth, and produced
a crisis that destroyed the viability of the 1930–64 system.

While inflation usually accompanies import-substituting industrialization, it can also aid growth. Through higher prices and lower real wages,
inflation can penalize consumers and transfer resources to industrial investment. Domestic manufacturers (both national and foreign) charge
higher prices for goods, realize bigger profits, and have both the wherewithal and the incentive to channel new investments into industry. However, such a transfer would not be possible if workers were strong
enough to force an increase in their earnings to compensate for inflation; for such an increase, of course, would raise labor costs and
depress profit margins, thus reducing the incentive for new investments.

In short, a lag in wage adjustment is a necessary condition for making
the inflationary process compatible with economic growth. It was precisely this lag that the governments of Vargas, Kubitschek, and Goulart
were unable to sustain. They failed because their political survival depended upon the goodwill of the urban working class. Time and again
wages were allowed to catch up with, and even surpass, the rate of inflation. When stabilization programs were hatched to deal with the ensuing "stagflation," they failed because it was tantamount to political
suicide to suppress the real wage rate for any length of time. By 1964
the economic situation had become untenable. If Brazil was to resume
growth within the capitalist framework, authentic stabilization was essential and this required tough policies and a repressive regime. Campos
and Bulhões (the planning and finance ministers of the first military
government) succeeded where their predecessors had failed because
they were able to ignore public opinion.

Before moving into the era of authoritarian rule, let me draw together
the important political and ideological dimensions of the populist period. The structural crisis of 1929 was accompanied by a regrouping of political actors in Brazil, and over the succeeding thirty-
five years the formal structure of the state evolved through practically
every political form. However, despite the turmoil of these years and

the dramatic changes in formal political structures, there are some striking continuities, both in the direction of policy and in the consequences of these policies for the Brazilian population. The year 1930 saw a significant break with the traditional landed oligarchy and with the primary exporting model of development. After this date the urban commercial and industrial classes became the dominant groups in Brazilian politics (although the landed oligarchy was still considerably appeased), and internal growth, not international trade, came to be the prime focus of economic planning. The hallmark of the new era was modernization—defined as industrial growth under the aegis of a centralized, interventionist state with strong paternalistic and anticommunistic overtones; and the goal was *grandeza*, which became nothing less than the attainment of world power status.

The political and ideological dynamics of the 1930–64 period had important repercussions in the equity sphere. Roughly speaking, governments of this era were populist coalitions that awarded an array of political, civil, and social rights to the mobilized urban classes. Political rights were obviously more conspicuous in the post-1964 era of democratic structures than they were in the 1937–45 period of authoritarian rule; and yet both periods incorporated the industrial work force into the political arena and made sure that its members benefited from the fruits of economic growth. This contrasts quite markedly with the fate of the rural masses who were bypassed by the new urban-oriented regimes and received little political or social benefit from industrialization.

Military Rule

By the early 1960s, deepening stagflation and populist politics were on a collision course; and it was evident that if Brazil was to get back on the growth path, a drastically revised political and economic strategy was called for.

However, it is by no means obvious that the Brazilian response to economic crisis had to be military dictatorship and violent forms of repression. Cardoso warns us of simple-minded economic determinism: "all too frequently, analysts do not take into account either theoretically or empirically, the dynamic, mutually shaping interrelationship between politics and economics." [12] To understand fully the raison d'être of the 1964 coup and its repressive characteristics, one has to examine the ideological orientation of the Brazilian military in the modern period and to appreciate the extent to which the Brazilian establishment was threatened by a radical Left.

Since 1930 it is possible to see ways in which national security and economic development have been related in the minds of the Brazilian military and other members of the elite. The writings of the *Tenentes* and of Vargas himself point to the inseparable nature of these issues. In the late 1950s and early 1960s this interrelationship took on a new significance. The success of guerrilla warfare techniques against conventional armies (the most dramatic example being, of course, Cuba in 1959) led the military in both the developed and the underdeveloped world to turn more attention toward preventing domestic revolution. An essential ingredient in this new orientation was accelerated development and the consequent containment of economic grievances.

In Brazil the most concrete creator and expression of the new ideology was the Escola Superior de Guerra (ESG), which was set up after the war in order to formulate a more coherent and sophisticated doctrine of national security.

The origins of the ESG are extremely relevant to understanding its modern role. The Brazilian contribution to World War II, the Força Expedicionária Brasileira, had been firmly integrated into the United States Army in Italy. Because of this connection, the Brazilians looked to the United States military for advice in setting up their new war college. A United States advisory mission was invited to Brazil and remained there between 1948 and 1960, with the result that the ESG came to be modeled after the United States's national War College both in organization and in focus. Indeed, some of the distinctive characteristics of post-1964 military governments in Brazil (pro-Americanism, anticommunism, a favorable attitude toward foreign capital, and a distaste for "excessive" nationalism) can be directly traced to this early collaboration between the military establishments of the two countries.

However, it would be wrong to assume that American ideas were adopted en bloc. The Brazilian military very much attempted to shape conventional wisdom to fit the special problems of underdevelopment. As General Golbery do Couto e Silva, chief theoretician of the ESG put it: "The planning of national security is an imperative of the hour in which we live. . . . For us in the underdeveloped countries . . . planning assumes aspects of another order which puts everything else in relief." [13] The chief threats were seen to be "localized conflict, and above all indirect communist aggression, which capitalizes on local discontents, the frustration of hunger and misery, and just nationalist anxieties." [14]

It should be remembered that Latin American fears of communism were very much bound up with the rise of Fidel Castro and of (ultimately unsuccessful) guerrilla movements in Venezuela and elsewhere. The contemporary reality seemed to indicate that conventional military techniques and even counterinsurgent measures were no longer sufficient to contain revolution. For the ESG national security became a matter of "rationally maximizing the output of the economy and minimizing all sources of cleavage and disunity within the country." [15] Thus, "nation-building" and "global development plans" became central ideological themes as the military recognized economic transformation to be a key ingredient in the fight against communism.

Another Brazilian innovation was the determined effort to incorporate civilians into the life of the ESG. Precisely because the military was concerned with all aspects of national development, it was thought appropriate to include government officials and private individuals from such areas as education, industry, communications, and banking in its academic program.

The decision to include civilians as a central part of the ESG proved to be crucial for the development of the school. It brought military officers into systematic close contact with civilian leaders. This gave them civilian allies who shared many of their ideas on development and security, and it also gave the military confidence to discuss problems on terms of equality with civilian specialists.[16]

The participation of civilians proved to be so valuable that by the mid-1960s half of the graduates of the one-year course offered by the ESG were from civilian life, and many of the courses were taught by prominent ministers and technocrats in the government. Given this history of ideological and practical preparation, the military was both able and willing to take over the reigns of government if circumstances warranted. The events of the early 1960s precipitated such a move.

Between 1961 and 1964 the situation of Brazil steadily worsened. The severe economic problems described in chapter 3 were compounded by the lack of firm and effective political leadership. Janio Quadros (1961) swept into power by a huge electoral victory, attempted some reforms and then resigned after a mere eight months in power. He was succeeded by João Goulart who was equally ineffective, due in part to the fact that he was not allowed to exercise full presidential powers. (A notorious labor sympathizer, Goulart was forced to adopt a parliamentary system by his right-wing opponents.) The military became convinced that corruption and ineptitude were encouraging both economic chaos and political subversion, and there were growing doubts about whether any democratically elected president could restore order or carry out the stabilization program that was essential if Brazil was to resume growth within a capitalist framework. As the military saw it, it was either stabilization under an authoritarian government, which at least in the beginning should be controlled by themselves, or social revolution from the Left. They made sure that the crisis was resolved in their favor.

We must remember that by 1964 the military establishment did have the ability to put together an alternative government. It possessed a finely honed, if limited ideology which saw a fundamental connection between internal security and national development, and therefore a narrowing gap between military and political spheres of influence. Through the activities of the ESG there existed a body of military officers and civilian technocrats who held common perceptions of the problems of Brazil and had evolved a coherent program of action. The important role of the ESG in the coup of 1964 is borne out by the fact that of the 102 generals on active duty at that time, those who had attended the ESG were markedly overrepresented among the plotters against Goulart. Indeed, the new president, Castello Branco, had himself been director of the Department of Studies at the ESG between 1956 and 1958, and General Golbery, the "father of the ESG," became director of the important Serviço Nacional de Informações (SNI) under the new government.

Thus, the coup of March 1964 was a predictable response to the circumstances of the day. The link between economic cause and political effect in this context was provided by a military caste with a highly developed, if narrowly conceived, view of the world. The content of this ideology was in tune with the beliefs of earlier incarnations of the Brazilian state and dovetailed with the needs of the contemporary bourgeoisie, but it owed something to the specifics of the modern military establishment. Militant anticommunism and pro-Western rhetoric, intertwined with strong commitments to growth and national destiny, are characteristics of the post-1964 regime that can be understood only in terms of the origins, the loyalties, and the evolution of the Brazilian military.

The ideology developed by the military establishment reflected the attitudes and the needs of the Brazilian bourgeoisie in the mid-1960s. The military coup was initially supported by all segments of the bourgeoisie and was at least tolerated by broad segments of the population at large. Faced with stagflation and an increasingly militant labor movement, the bourgeoisie gladly exchanged the "right to rule for the right to make money." [17] The developmental crisis of 1964 provoked an almost unprecedented degree of elite unity. In Nun's words,

the movement of April 1964 amalgamated all the property owning classes of the society: the agrarian sectors out of fear of reform, the industrial sectors out of fear of the loss of the mechanisms of security, the middle classes out of their panic at seeing the social distance separating them from the masses shortened, and all of these sectors out of the even greater fear . . . [of communism].[18]

Given the choice between military rule or socialist revolution, the Brazilian bourgeoisie opted, quite decidedly, for the former.

There is considerable evidence that Brazilian industrialists were actively involved in planning the coup. For example, in September 1964, *Fortune* magazine published an article entitled "When Executives Turned Revolutionaries," which tells the story of the part São Paulo businessmen played in the coup.[19] It relates how these men reacted to the Goulart government by setting up a right-wing study center, developing contacts with military leaders, stockpiling weapons, and supporting anticommunist political groups.

There was also some external political pressure. The United States government disliked and distrusted Goulart. This was due, in part, to the adverse business conditions produced by the Goulart government. (For example, labor unrest, accelerating inflation, and limitations on foreign capital were all features of the 1962–64 period.) But it was also due to larger geopolitical factors. In the aftermath of the 1959 Cuban revolution, the left-wing rhetoric of Goulart conjured up the specter of socialism spreading through Latin American nations—a prospect that was singularly unattractive to American political leaders. The continuing slide to the Left under Goulart was seen by the Johnson

Administration as "the most serious problem for us in Latin America—
more serious in fact than Cuba since the missile crisis." [20] The recent
declassification of documents at the Lyndon B. Johnson library in Austin,
Texas, demonstrates that the United States was prepared, if necessary,
to intervene with naval and airborne units in support of the military
conspirators who toppled the government of João Goulart.[21] The contingency plan was called "Operation Brother Sam" and involved the
United States Air Force sending six C-135 transports loaded with arms
and ammunition to Brazil. With the success of the 1964 military coup,
this contingency plan was obviously canceled; but an interagency economic task force immediately began work on plans for substantial
financial assistance to the new military government. The International
Monetary Fund (IMF), which had denied loans to Brazil since 1959,
came through with two US$125 million standby credits before the end of
1964 while a "US$50 million loan from AID's emergency fund was ex-
tended within hours after the military had taken over." [22] The Inter-
American Development Bank (IADB) and the World Bank (IBRD)
also dramatically increased their loans. The IADB contribution increased
from an average of US$22 million in 1962–64 to an average of US$97.7
million in the next three years. And the World Bank, which had extended no loans at all to Brazil in 1962–64, loaned an average of US$75.5
million in 1965–67.[23]

The picture is therefore one of considerable national and international support for the 1964 coup. However, once the crisis was over,
and the military ensconced in power, some segments of the domestic
bourgeoisie fared rather better than others.

Since 1964 the state bourgeoisie has, in the main, prospered. This
class comprises key members of the government's bureaucratic and
planning apparatus, and the managerial echelon of the state enterprises.
As we saw in chapter 3, recent governments have dramatically increased
the role of the state in economic affairs, thus promoting the expansion
of these elements in the bourgeoisie. In addition, through the activities
of the ESG, many of the representatives of the "public sector" have
been directly involved in the construction of goals and policies.

The other group that has benefited from military rule is the internationalized bourgeoisie. This class comprises the Brazilian managers
who control the operations of the multinational firms in Brazil. As a
direct beneficiary of the more liberal profit-remittance legislation, and

as a prime target of the export incentives program, this segment of the domestic elite has prospered as a result of the policies of the post–1964 regime.

The national bourgeoisie, on the other hand, has not been favored. As will be discussed more fully in chapter 6, national capital has become progressively less important in the industrial structure of Brazil; consequently, governments have tended to neglect the interests of this sector. By and large, such neglect has not been willful but has been a by-product of the drive for fast growth rates. The efficient or "natural" agents for rapid industrialization in late-developing nations are undoubtedly the state and the multinational corporation, *not* national capital. Domestic entrepreneurs have objected (witness the recent "de-statization" debate discussed in chapter 6); but, given the ultimate alternative (socialism), even this neglected segment of the Brazilian bourgeoisie has accepted the rules of the game as laid down by a military regime.

In summary, the economically powerful international and state elites have given their support to military control of government, while the less important national bourgeoisie has grudgingly accepted military rule as the least of several evils.

The military moved into action in 1964 with "authentic stabilization" as the most crucial issue on its agenda. It was successful. As stated earlier, Campos and Bulhões were able to dampen inflation because the new authoritarian political structures allowed them to ignore public opposition. Time was the essence of the problem. Previous populist regimes had been able to promote unpopular policies for limited periods; but stabilization needs a two- or three-year time span to break the public's well-established inflationary expectations; and the elected politicians shrank from such an extensive and ruthless form of economic therapy. The dramatic success of the 1964–67 stabilization policies directly depended on the absence of elections, which freed economic planners to pursue policies without regard to their short-term practical impact.

The most unpopular component of the anti-inflation package was the deliberate policy of letting wage increases lag behind increases in the cost of living. This reduction in real wages, which amounted to 25 percent by 1967, was justified as the lag effect of lowering inflationary expectation, and it was billed as being "temporary." But, however convincing the explanation, it is difficult to see how such a policy could have been carried out by a government that had to face elections, even under the imperfectly democratic framework of pre-1964 Brazil.

Although the industrial working class was the chief victim of the stabilization policies, it would be wrong to assume that it was the only segment of the Brazilian population forced to pay for lower rates of inflation. The Campos-Bulhões stabilization policies also penalized the interests of domestic capital. In an effort to lower prices within the industrial sector, the government reduced the level of effective protection and put an end to the frequent policy of providing publicly subsidized credit from the central banking system in times of liquidity crisis. As a result, business went through a painful shake-out phase, and during this period multinational corporations were able to acquire Brazilian firms that could not find domestic sources of credit. Again, not the kind of inflation-control that elected governments could pursue for long!

Policies designed to eradicate the federal deficit were also politically unpopular. Previous populist regimes had seen a vast expansion of public spending in state enterprises and in the government bureaucracy. Failure both to increase prices for goods and services and to raise taxes had resulted in large deficits financed by monetary issues. These policies were highly inflationary, and the Castello Branco government moved quickly on both fronts. By increasing the price of services (a step that directly increased the cost of living in the short run), the huge deficits in public transportation, in shipping, and in the oil industry were wiped out. Covering costs meant that long-deferred investments could now be made in these public enterprises, thus increasing productivity and lowering costs for the future. However, whatever the economic rationale, it is doubtful that any elected regime could have withstood the storm of protest over costlier bus fares and other public services.

Even more important in eliminating the deficit were the taxation policies of the new regime. In the crisis year of 1964 government receipts fell short of government spending by one-third; by 1968–69 there was a budgetary surplus mainly as a result of increased tax collections. The military regime was, and is, extremely proud that it has imposed, and stringently enforced, collection of taxes on income. As Schmitter has observed: "The specter of fearful middle- and upper-class citizens paying direct taxes for the first time has been used by the regime to enhance its socially neutral technocratically efficient image both domestically and internationally." [24] There is no doubt that income-tax revenue has risen (by as much as 70 percent in 1968 alone), but indirect taxation has risen roughly twice as fast again. The "squeezing" of the rich must be placed in context: the urban working class, the main target of indirect taxation, has been squeezed even harder.

Nevertheless, the point remains that in the area of taxation the military regime has demonstrated its ability to make several classes of Brazilians pay for development. Although the burden has fallen disproportionately on the working class (and regressive indirect taxes are particularly difficult to bear when real income is stagnant or falling), even the middle and upper classes, the principal beneficiaries of post-1964 development policies, have been forced to contribute significant sums. A dramatic increase in the effectiveness of taxation is extremely difficult under populist, democratic regimes in the underdeveloped world. Such a program seems to require the repressive and disciplinary powers of a military government that can afford to alienate politically mobilized segments of the population.

The foreign sector is another example of a policy area where programs adopted after 1964 would have been difficult to administer under an elected government. On the eve of the coup Brazil faced a crushing short-term international debt, a product of the cumulative balance-of-payments pressures described in chapter 3. It could be renegotiated only if the new government could convince the country's creditors, especially the IMF, that domestic stabilization plans were both serious and likely to be successful. The Castello Branco government fell over itself to do a convincing job on this front. The first task it set itself was to repudiate the strident economic nationalism, of the Goulart period. The profit remittance law passed in Congress in 1962 was repealed, and there was a rapprochement with foreign private investors. This was important as the government hoped for a rapid increase in private foreign investment to strengthen the balance of payments and to take up the slack resulting from the deflationary squeeze on Brazilian business. Such a rapprochement could also be offered as proof to the international agencies and the United States government that Brazil was firmly committed to capitalist development.

These policies achieved their purpose. As described earlier in this chapter, between 1964 and 1968 United States economic assistance to Brazil increased dramatically; after this date Brazil's economic recovery rendered aid less urgent, and the United States cut back its support. The World Bank and IADB, however, have maintained a high level of lending throughout the recent period.

The incentives given to firms engaged in the export trade also tended to favor foreign capital. As we saw in chapter 3, before 1964 Brazil had conspicuously failed to expand nontraditional exports, and this neglect had contributed to both balance-of-payments and inflationary pressures. The post-1964 government was determined to pursue a vigorous export promotion program. This featured export incentives for manufactured goods and, in practice, often meant yet another subsidy for multinational corporations, since foreign firms were better equipped to export than domestic manufacturing concerns. Because it relied so heavily on multinationals, it is at least debatable whether a successful export promotion program could have been carried out by an elected government.

In summary, it seems that a repressive state was an absolute necessary condition for successful stabilization, and that, in its turn, successful stabilization was an essential prerequisite for a new cycle of capitalist growth within the Brazilian domestic economy. Other parts of the post-1964 policy package (the rapprochement with foreign capital and the export promotion program) were also aided by authoritarian rule and would have been difficult to follow under a more responsive populist government.

The first government of the military regime, that of Castello Branco, was increasingly forced to adopt hard-line policies despite the liberal preferences of this president. Harsher measures were prompted by the unpopularity of the stabilization program, which by late 1964 was producing falling real wage levels and industrial recession, particularly in small-scale and traditional Brazilian industry. Two actions were symptomatic of the move toward authoritarianism. First, the Second Institutional Act of the Castello Branco government abolished all existing parties and made the 1966 elections indirect. The president and the vice-president were to be chosen by Congress, and congressmen themselves were made subject to immediate dismissal by the president. The president was also empowered to suspend the political rights of any person for a period of ten years. Second, this first military government decided to rewrite the constitution so as to bequeath to succeeding administrations a new institutional structure that would ensure their policies and priorities into the future. The new rules controlled elections through "official" parties and gave the federal executive greatly expanded powers to control the policy-making apparatus, the judicial system, and the law enforcement agencies.

The Costa e Silva government, which came to power in 1967, was able both to build on the stabilization efforts of the previous administration and to trigger the economic "miracle" (see the description in chapter 3). However, economic success was accompanied by increased repression.

At the beginning of his administration Costa e Silva flirted briefly with giving the military a more humane image. This aroused hopes in the militant opposition, particularly amongst students and labor unions. Wildcat strikes broke out in São Paulo and Minas Gerais, and Congress defied a presidential ultimatum, and this despite the fact that it was now controlled by the official government party, ARENA (Aliança Renovadora Nacional).

The ensuing crisis provoked major changes. Congress was closed indefinitely; yet another institutional act was issued (the fifth and the harshest to date) giving the president virtually unlimited powers to protect national security. Habeas corpus was suspended for people charged with a variety of crimes against the state; hundreds had their political rights taken away. Federal universities were hit with a new wave of dismissals, and scores of political dissidents and intellectuals fled into exile. An important victim of this period was the Supreme Court which had remained the last line of defense against authoritarian rule. Three judges were purged, another was forcibly retired, and the president of the court resigned in protest. A short while later the court's jurisdiction was further reduced by the Sixth Institutional Act.

During 1968 and 1969 violence and repression reached new heights. The radical opposition became much more active and much more daring. Carlos Marighela launched his pro-Cuban Action for National Liberation (ALN) which staged a series of armed uprisings in the cities of Brazil and was responsible for the kidnaping of the American ambassador, Charles Burke Elbrick.[25] By 1969 revolutionary bandits had taken over a million dollars from the banks of Rio and São Paulo in order to finance their activities. The authorities, alarmed and threatened by this new level of armed insurrection, began a systematic drive to eliminate the terrorist underground. Police and military authorities did not hesitate to torture and kill their suspects, and the pattern became one of kidnapings, bank robberies, and terrorist attacks on military installations being answered by the regime with widespread and increasingly systematic brutality. During this period violent repression became institutionalized and acquired a momentum of its own. Police and military security organizations proliferated, and their interrogation centers routinely tortured, maimed, and killed suspects in the attempt to root out subversion. SNI (the National Intelligence Service) came to control a veritable labyrinth of sixty-eight regional and municipal agencies. The web included separate security services for each of the regional commands of the three military services. The federal police had its own security agency, as did each of the state police forces. All the ministries —except the Foreign Office—had a division of security and information. In 1972 when Amnesty International published its famous report documenting 1,081 cases of torture in Brazil, the most notorious interrogation centers were run by DOPS (Department of Political and Social Order), OBAN (Bandeirantes Operation), CENIMAR (Information Center for the Navy), CODI (Operations Center for Internal Defense), and CIE (Information Center for the Army).[26] They all had a grim and proven record of torture, which included the regular use of electric shocks, near drowning, simulated execution, *Pau de Arara* (hanging from a parrot's perch or rack), sexual abuse, and detention in refrigerated concrete cells, in their interrogation procedures.

This vast security crackdown had the desired effect. By 1973 most radical student and labor leaders and the great majority of the urban guerrillas had been killed or imprisoned or had fled the country, while their sympathizers had been effectively cowed by the brutality and the efficiency of official reaction.

The big question remains, What caused this escalation in violent repression in the 1968–73 period? Very simply, the Brazilian military was determined to wipe out the Left, because it feared a socialist revolution similar to the one in Cuba. Analysts have disputed the scale and the significance of the militant opposition during this period, but there clearly was a disgruntled and disappointed labor movement, an alienated student body, and a small but violent urban guerrilla group. In short, the opposition was conspicuous and threatening enough to provoke a new and nervous military regime into a determined and brutal attack on dissident groups. We should also remember that the sheer weight and inertia of the vast security infrastructure built up in the 1968–69 period bred a momentum of its own, which carried the more extreme measures through the early 1970s. In early 1974, for example, SNI censored one of the first policy speeches of the president-elect Ernesto Geisel; it was too liberal for the liking of the security chiefs! [27]

However, by the time Geisel came to power in March of 1974, the threat from the Left had been destroyed, and the new government was able to begin cautious opening up of the political system. Geisel appointed as his civilian chief of staff, General Golbery, a well-known advocate of social and political reform; and together they fashioned a program of *distensão* (decompression) which was meant to be a gradual liberalization of the more objectionable features of authoritarian rule. The new policies were encouraged by the fact that Brazil was at the crest of the "miracle": growth rates were exuberant, and the government felt that it could afford to be generous.

The post-1974 period has seen some steps in the direction of greater political freedom. The more violent forms of repression have died down (for example, there has been a significant decrease in the incidence of reported torture); arbitrary arrest and detention seem on the wane; Institutional Act No. 5, which greatly increased the autocratic powers of Brazilian presidents, has been allowed to lapse (in January of 1979); and there has been an amnesty for many types of political offender (in August of 1979).[28] There have also been some positive changes in the spheres of electoral politics and freedom of the press.

In November of 1974, Geisel began his gradual liberalization of political life by permitting relatively free elections for Congress and for the state legislatures. For the first time the official Brazilian opposition party, MDB (Movimento Democrático Brasileiro) was able to utilize the same broadcasting time as the government party, ARENA (Aliança Renovadora Nacional). However, a slowdown in economic growth and renewed inflation led voters to support the opposition in large numbers. The MDB tripled its seats in the Senate, almost doubled its support in the Chamber of Deputies, and captured many of the state legislatures, thus confirming the suspicions of the hard-line generals that "if you give the people the chance they vote for the wrong people." [29] Geisel was forced on the defensive. He personally supervised the selection of all governors in consultation with the majority party's leaders in each state, so that the MDB's governors had to be acceptable to him and to his military colleagues. As further assurance against the emergence of an effective opposition, and to placate the hard-liners, he invoked Institutional Act No. 5 and annulled the mandates of a number of politicians who appeared too critical of the regime.

The November 1978 elections saw a similar pattern of intervention and control by the military. The original hope was that the November 1978 elections would be free. This hope was crushed in the *Pacote de Abril* (April package) when Geisel, alarmed that the official opposition

party was going to obtain a majority in both houses, suspended Congress, expelled by decree some of the more radical members of the
MDB party, and put into effect some "electoral reforms." [30] These stip-
ulated that one-third of all senators would be chosen by the president,
and effectively ensured that a majority in the Senate would be held by
the ruling party, ARENA. However, despite this gerrymandering, the
MDB did well in Congress (particularly in urban constituencies), and
a move is now afoot to set up four or five parties that could be a more
genuine expression of real political forces than the highly artificial
two-party system that has existed for the last twelve years. One proposal is that there should be a party for the extreme Right, for con-
servatives, and for a centrist group (which would contain elements from
the National Democratic Union and the Social Democratic party—
political groupings that flourished before the coup). On the Left there
would be a labor party and a socialist party.[31] All this is of course
highly speculative; and, whatever the eventual shape of the party system, the likelihood is that it will be structured so that the military
retains effective control over government. The experiences of 1974 and
1978, when gerrymandering kept the opposition in its place, together
with the personal preferences of the new president (Figueiredo op-
poses "excessive liberalism") delimit fairly narrow boundaries for electoral reform. (Indeed, in the fall of 1979 Figueiredo began to back off
the idea of a free multiparty system proposing, in its stead, one official
party that would represent the government's viewpoint and several
parties in opposition. In his words, it is "essential to remain unified so
that it does not become necessary for the army to intervene in the political life of the country as a result of the liberalization policy." [32])

The "opening up" of the Brazilian political system has been most pronounced in the sphere of freedom of the press. Most newspapers are no
longer subject to prepublication censorship, and this lessening of control has permitted increased criticism of the regime, including more open
reporting of human rights violations. In 1977, for example, the prominent *Jornal do Brasil* published a letter by fifteen political prisoners
describing how they had been systematically tortured by the military
police.[33]

However, although less controlled than it was at the beginning of the
decade, the press still experiences limits to its freedom. Official dis-
pleasure may result in the withdrawal of government advertising or in
the arrest of individual journalists. In March 1978, Milton Soares, an

investigative reporter for *Agências Folhas,* was beaten up in a police station in São Paulo after he had published a report about the torture of common prisoners by the Guarulhos police.[34] During the same month Antônio Carlos Fon, author of a book documenting torture in Brazil, was arrested and charged under the national security law for bringing the armed forces into disrepute.[35]

In numerous other ways freedom of expression remains curtailed in Brazil. Books too critical of the government or ideologically offensive have been suppressed; and in the case of Renato Tapajós (who wrote *Em Câmara Lenta,* an exposé of political torture), the author was arrested.[36] Films and television are closely monitored, and the opposition has been virtually excluded from the use of the media. In 1977, for example, MDB was limited to two one-hour programs of political commentary per year. However, after using its first hour (in June of that year) to criticize economic policy and demand greater protection of human rights, even this access to the media was eliminated.[37]

The liberalization drive of the post-1974 period has made little progress in the sphere of social welfare. The original aim of the Geisel government was to allow the minimum wage to rise faster than prices, thus ensuring that some of the fruits of the "miracle" would trickle down to the working class. For a while it looked as though this policy might work. In 1975 wages did rise faster than the official rate of inflation. However, after this date a combination of a world energy crisis with domestic stagflation (described in chapter 3) made it increasingly difficult for Geisel to raise real wages for workers. In May 1976, for example, Geisel promised a 64 percent hike in the minimum wage but granted a mere 44 percent (which barely kept pace with inflation). When it came to light that the previous government had juggled the 1973 official figures in order to seriously underestimate the real rate of inflation (by 12 percent), the Geisel government refused to compensate workers. As João Paulo dos Reis Velloso, planning minister, said, "The government has no intention whatsoever of making up the loss in workers' purchasing power." [38] This squeezing of wages in the renewed fight against inflation was not distributed across the board. In February 1976, Geisel granted pay increases to all public servants on the federal payroll, ranging from 300 percent at the top of the scale to 30 percent at the bottom.[39] The armed forces were among the principal beneficiaries. This was clearly a move to strengthen his political support among elite groups, which had flagged in the wake of the 1974–75 economic recession. By this time, expediency seems to have replaced the earlier commitment to improved living standards for the Brazilian lower classes.

The first few months of the Figueiredo government demonstrate a similar pattern of initial concessions being followed by harsher policies. Union militancy in late 1978 and early 1979 forced first the Geisel and then the Figueiredo administrations to grant generous wage settlements to engineers, teachers, nurses, and other relatively privileged groups within the work force (see discussion in chapter 9). However, the new round of OPEC price increases, initiated in May 1979, intensified the inflationary and balance-of-payments pressures within the Brazilian economy and prompted Figueiredo to adopt tougher measures toward labor. For example, the minimum wage adjustment in May of 1979 was 45.4 percent, less than the rate of inflation for the previous twelve months,[40] and in August 1979 a strike by construction workers in Belo Horizonte was put down with armed force.[41]

A few groups of workers have managed to gain some material concessions as a result of the political opening of recent years, but one should not exaggerate the significance of these cases and forget that gains have been confined to privileged groups within the population. Most Brazilians have not significantly improved their standard of living in the years since 1974.

Remember the harsh logic spelt out in chapter 3 that makes massive poverty and increasing inequality a necessary consequence of economic growth in this late-developing nation. The basic framework of modern industrialization strategies has been incompatible with greatly enhanced social welfare for the mass of the people; and during the 1960s and 1970s the imperatives of inflation control and balance-of-payments constraints have periodically served to worsen the plight of the working classes. It is true that Geisel did repeatedly attempt to raise wages, but these well-meaning initiatives were often squashed by economic considerations. In the few instances where groups of workers have won pay awards, they have been part of a labor aristocracy. In short, the wretchedness and the misery of the mass of the Brazilian people cannot be affected by the marginal adjustments of some enlightened leader.

When we turn to political freedoms and civil liberties, we find that the scope for marginal improvements is greater. It should be obvious from earlier sections of this chapter that for several decades in the history of Brazil it has proved possible to award the normal menu of political and civil rights to mobilized segments of the urban population. This was particularly true in the 1946–64 period, before economic chaos and the threat from a militant Left made democratic structures untenable. Stabilization means the prolonged application of extremely unpopular policies which in Brazil could be enforced only in an authoritarian and repressive political setting.

Economic constraints do explain many of the harsh policies of post-1964 governments. For example, sustained and significant wage suppression did mean the tightening of controls over trade unions and the imprisonment (without trial) of the more militant labor leaders. In the same vein, increasing the price of basic foodstuffs and public transportation and increasing the rate of personal taxation were incompatible with electoral politics.

However, the more violent types of political repression in the late 1960s and early 1970s should not be directly connected to economic circumstances. The systematic and widespread use of torture, the violent crackdowns on urban guerrillas and on radical students and labor leaders, the increased incidence of arbitrary arrest and detention, can best be understood in geopolitical terms. During the administrations of Costa e Silva and Medici, the Brazilian military regime was new and unestablished, and the generals in charge had every reason to be nervous of what could be interpreted in those years as armed insurrection with at least some explicit ties with Communist Cuba (remember Marighela's ALN movement!). The more violent kinds of repression in the 1968–73 period should therefore be seen as the product of a ruling class that was deeply frightened at the possibility of socialist revolution.

By the mid-1970s conditions had changed. Despite the economic problems thrown off by the 1974–75 recession, the Geisel government did manage to institute a program of political liberalization. Reforms have proceeded "at an uncertain and uneven pace," [42] with heavy-handed intervention by the military periodically undercutting the growth of an effective political opposition. However, despite these qualifications, Brazil has more civil and political freedoms than it had a decade ago; and such progress has much to do with the presence of a more restrained and more secure ruling class. Memories of the chaos of the 1961–64 period have faded, radical groups have been wiped out, and communism does not seem to be spreading through Latin America. As a result there is much less overreaction to either economic or political problems.

NOTES

1. The term "ideology" is used throughout this book in a relatively loose manner that does not correspond to the more rigid interpretations, for example, as in the written ideologies of political parties and codified religious doctrines. The use in this book is consistent with Karl Mannheim's definition of "ideology" as "an integral set of ideas for systematically ordering and evaluating social reality" (*Ideology and Utopia*, translated by Louis Wirth and Edward Shils [New York: Harcourt, Brace & Co., 1936], p. 71). It should be remembered that dominant ideologies reflect the interests and concerns of dominant groups. "Ideologies do not tend to challenge common knowledge; rather they place different weights on its different truths. By stressing and elaborating some and neglecting others, they offer an image of society comfortable to the needs of economic and political elites" (Mannheim, *Ideology and Utopia*, p. 97).

2. Celso Furtado, *The Economic Growth of Brazil: A Survey from Colonial to Modern Times* (Berkeley: University of California Press, 1963), p. 204.

3. Despite instruments such as the *Caixa de Conversão* which did favor the import of machinery and raw materials between 1910 and 1914, the overwhelming direction of domestic policy was against industrialization. For an interesting study of the school of thought favoring industrialization in Brazil, see Nicia Vilela Luz, *A Luta Pela Industrialização do Brasil* (São Paulo: Corpo e Alma do Brasil, Difusão Européia do Livro, 1961).

4. Robert M. Levine, *The Vargas Regime* (New York: Columbia University Press, 1970), p. 175.

5. Thomas E. Skidmore, *Politics in Brazil, 1930–1964* (New York: Oxford University Press, 1964), pp. 7–8.

6. Guillermo A. O'Donnell, *Modernization and Bureaucratic Authoritarianism: Studies in South American Politics* (University of California at Berkeley: Institute of International Studies, 1973), p. 57.

7. This process of accumulation of elite groups in the power arena has been noted by several theorists; see Octavio Ianni, *Crisis in Brazil* (New York: Columbia University Press, 1970), pp. 47–67; and Luciano Martins, *Pouvoir et Développement Économique: Formation et Evolution des Structures Politiques au Brésil* (Paris: Éditions Anthropos, 1976), pp. 79–106. The main point made by these theorists is that modern Brazilian development has incorporated rather than overthrown the previously existing landed elite.

8. James M. Malloy, ed., *Authoritarianism and Corporatism in Latin America* (Pittsburgh: University of Pittsburgh Press, 1977), p. 8.

9. Malloy, *Authoritarianism*, p. 12.

10. Frank Ackerman, "Industry and Imperialism in Brazil," *Review of Radical Political Economics* 3 (Spring 1971) : 26.

11. The level of registered voters in the population hovered around 20 percent between 1946 and 1950, or less than half of the adult population. Kenneth Paul Erickson, *The Brazilian Corporative State and Working Class Politics* (Berkeley: University of California Press, 1977), p. 22.

12. Fernando Henrique Cardoso, "Associated-Dependent Development. Theoretical and Practical Implications," in Alfred Stepan, ed., *Authoritarian Brazil* (New Haven, Conn.: Yale University Press, 1973), p. 142.

13. Golbery do Couto e Silva, *Geopolítica do Brasil* (Rio de Janeiro: José Olympio, 1967), p. 198.

14. Golbery, *Geopolítica*, p. 199.

15. Alfred Stepan, *The Military in Politics: Changing Patterns in Brazil* (Princeton, N.J.: Princeton University Press, 1971), p. 178.

16. Stepan, *The Military*, p. 176.

17. Barrington Moore, Jr., *Social Origins of Dictatorship and Democracy: Lord and Peasant in the Making of the Modern World* (Boston: Beacon, 1966), p. 437.

18. José Nun, *Latin America: The Hegemonic Crisis and the Military Coup* (Berkeley: University of California Press, Institute of International Studies, 1969), p. 37.

19. Philip Siekman, "When Executives Turned Revolutionaries," *Fortune*, September 1964, pp. 147–49.

20. Philip Agee, *Inside the Company: CIA Diary* (Harmondsworth, England: Penguin Books, 1975), p. 321.

21. Jan Knippers Black, *United States Penetration in Brazil* (Philadelphia: University of Pennsylvania Press, 1977), p. xi.

22. Black, *United States Penetration*, p. 49.

23. Black, *United States Penetration* (note 20), p. 50.

24. Philippe C. Schmitter, *Interest Conflict and Political Change* (Stanford, Calif.: Stanford University Press, 1971), p. 378.

25. Carlos Marighela, *For the Liberation of Brazil* (Harmondsworth, England: Penguin Books, 1971), pp. 7–15.

26. Amnesty International, *International Report on Allegations of Torture in Brazil* (London, 1972); see also Amnesty International, *International Report on Allegations of Torture in Brazil* (London, 1975), pp. 15–33.

27. *Jornal do Brasil*, 17 February 1974.

28. See discussion of these new freedoms in the *New York Times*, 18 March 1979; and *Latin American Political Report*, 31 August 1979, p. 270.

29. *Latin American Political Report*, 9 December 1974, p. 174.

30. *Latin American Political Report*, 8 April 1977, p. 105.

31. *Latin America Political Report*, 6 July 1979, p. 206.

32. *Latin America Political Report*, 5 October 1979, p. 311.

33. *Jornal do Brasil*, 27 October 1977.

34. *Latin America Political Report*, 24 March 1978, p. 93.

35. *Latin America Political Report*, 21 September 1979, p. 292. Fon's book is entitled *Tortura: A Historia da Repressao Politica do Brazil* (São Paulo: Global Editora e Distribuidora Ltda, 1979). P.E.N. (International Association of Writers) has identified twenty-four writers and journalists who were arrested in Brazil between 1972 and 1975 and who are still imprisoned or have disappeared. See P.E.N., *Freedom to Write: Global Report* (New York, 28 October 1977), pp. 11–12.

36. *Latinamerican Press*, 24 February 1977; and *Amnesty International News Release*, 16 August 1977.

37. Committee on International Relations, *Human Rights Conditions in Selected Countries and the U.S. Response* (Washington, D.C.: Government Printing Office, 25 July 1978), p. 42.

38. *Latin America Political Report*, 26 August 1977, p. 263.

39. *Latin America Economic Report*, 27 February 1976, p. 68.

40. *Latin America Political Report*, 4 May 1979, p. 134.

41. *Latin America Economic Report*, 3 August 1979, p. 233.

42. *Human Rights Conditions in Selected Countries* (note 36), p. 40.

PART II

Dominant Issues

CHAPTER

5

Inflation

Since 1945 not a single major Latin American nation has been able to preserve a competitive political system and at the same time achieve sustained control of the inflation once the latter has exceeded 10 percent per year. Indeed, the social tensions exacerbated by inflation have contributed significantly to authoritarian coups in Brazil (1964), Argentina (1966), and Chile (1973).

Thomas E. Skidmore

OVER the last three decades inflation has emerged as a crucial issue linking contemporary growth processes to both poverty and repression. In the Brazilian case inflationary distortions grew out of the structural conditions of late industrialization and have served to deepen the social and political costs of development. As we have seen in previous chapters, inflation was the major economic catalyst of the 1964 military coup, and in the recent period stabilization policies have been directly responsible for increased inequality and heightened repression.

Theoretical Frameworks

There have been two main theoretical approaches to inflation in the Third World, structuralist and monetarist. Followers of each school of thought have been fervently disagreeing over the causes of and the cure for inflation since the 1950s.[1]

Structuralist theories of inflation are strongly associated with Latin America and with ECLA (the United Nations Economic Commission for Latin America). The central idea of this school of thought is that inflation is a product of the structural rigidities encountered by late-industrializing countries, and that these constraints are deeply embedded in the economic, the social, and the political frameworks of these nations.[2]

Many of the critical inflation-producing rigidities can be traced to the colonial age.

1.   Traditional land tenure systems were extremely inegalitarian and did not provide incentives to cultivators to exploit the potential of the land for food production.

2.   The infrastructure, insofar as it existed, was geared to primary exporting activities and was inappropriate to the needs of domestic industry.

3.   Foreign exchange earnings were inadequate and fluctuated unpredictably with world prices for primary products.

4.   Since government revenue had typically come from export taxes or foreign borrowing, there were no developed internal financial institutions or habits of saving among domestic elites.

5.   An inadequate educational system made unavoidable shortages of skilled labor.

Given these structural rigidities, widespread inflationary pressures became the inevitable concomitant of modern industrialization. The inflationary attributes of import substitution can be traced to the fact that this industrialization strategy was attempted within the context of an unplanned laissez faire economy and yet required far-reaching changes in structure that were beyond the power of the price mechanism to achieve. For the market to work well, factors of production must be able to respond to profit opportunities. In Latin America (and in the Third World more generally) this assumption has often been conspicuously invalid, because the institutional structure has prevented supply from being responsive to price. Take the agricultural sector. The peasant tied by debt and ignorance to the landlord is often incapable of increasing production and of responding to a profit opportunity in the shape of a burgeoning urban population hungry for food. Given such a market imperfection, shortages appear in the sphere of food production, and prices rise. This inelasticity of supply constitutes a "structural" inflationary pressure, which the market cannot rectify since it is rooted in an institutional and political reality—namely, a powerful landlord class. And we must remember that the modernizing governments of the 1930s and 1940s often co-opted rather than destroyed the landed elite of the primary exporting era.

These supply constraints emphasized by the structuralist school of thought lead to policy prescriptions that advocate long-run reform of institutional frameworks, and these theorists discount the efficacy of short-term stabilization policies. Structuralists have generally been convinced that short-run monetary and fiscal policies (the usual ingredients of stabilization) trigger severe recession before the rate of price increase slows down, and when restrictions on demand are finally relaxed, inflationary pressures on the price level remain unaltered because the institutional reality has not changed.

The monetarist school of thought sees inflation as stemming from expansionary monetary and fiscal policies—that is to say, government deficit spending, expansionary credit policies, and the exchange rate operations of central banks.[3] In Latin America the first factor is often the most significant and results from an inflated bureaucracy, huge investments in infrastructure, and an unwillingness on the part of populist governments to charge the public what the services cost. Credit expansion is also at fault because it has frequently been extended by governments convinced that to lend for directly productive activity is not inflationary—a notion that, of course, ignores time lags and the possibility that monopolistic structures may prevent the expansion of supply. Finally, multiple exchange rates (resorted to by governments anxious to increase the availability of foreign exchange earnings) have invariably led to a need for subsidization by the Central Bank. In essence, the bank ends up paying more to exporters for their foreign exchange than it receives from importers; this ultimately leads to a further expansion of the money supply.

The supply constraints that dominate the structuralist analysis are generally not denied by the monetarists; however, the causal chain is reversed. Freely operating market incentives are seen to be the best method of eliminating the bottlenecks that accompany inflation. For example, a monetarist would argue that a deficient agricultural sector is to be blamed not on any inherent structural condition such as land tenurial arrangements, but on government policy, which through price controls has undermined profit opportunities in agriculture and thus induced low levels of investment.

The monetarist analysis thus blames structural problems on inflation itself and then attributes that inflation to excess demand arising primarily from government spending. This leads to the following series of policy prescriptions. First and foremost the budget deficit must be ended by cutting public expenditure and increasing tax revenue. Second, credit to the private sector must be restricted. Third, all distortions in market prices must be eliminated, and the exchange rate left to find its own level. The cuts in credit and in government spending will obviously have a depressing effect on the economy in the short run, but it is the conviction of the monetarist school that, once prices are right, supply will respond accordingly, and one can then enter a new era of inflation-free growth.

With these theoretical constructs in mind, it is time to turn to the detail of the Brazilian situation.

Brazilian Inflation

Previous chapters of this book have made us abundantly aware of the chronic tendency toward inflation which has afflicted Brazil during the modern period.

A brief glance at table 7 shows that the rate of price increase has averaged 23 percent per year since the late 1940s, reaching a peak of 90.8 percent in 1964. These extremely high rates of inflation have constituted a recurrent problem in Brazilian economic policy making since the Second World War. As we saw in chapter 4, there have been numerous abortive attempts to control inflation. Until the 1960s these failures did not prevent a resumption of growth, but the inflationary distortions increased; and by 1964 it was doubtful whether any elected regime could carry out the extended and ruthless stabilization program that was needed before the economy could move into a new cycle of growth. What were the roots of these inflationary pressures?

The Structural Component

Many of the critical inflation-producing conditions in Brazil are a legacy of that long period based on the production of primary commodities for export which I described in some detail in chapter 3. As Furtado puts it, during this era:

The development model in question was one that did not require much structural flexibility, or rather that it was compatible with structures having little capacity for change. Import substitution, on the other hand, is a form of development requiring rapid changes in economic structures.[4]

Let us first look at supply constraints in the food sector. Despite the fact that this has been emphasized by the structuralist school as an immediate and powerful inflationary pressure, it was not significant in Brazil during the import-substitution period. Price controls over food, instituted by populist governments in the 1946–64 period, did serve to weaken incentives for expanding food production; but, generally speaking, the existence of an agricultural frontier allowed supply to respond to increased demand without major institutional change. However, in the 1970s government policies favoring agricultural exports have contributed to severe inflationary pressure in the food producing sector. Massive public subsidies for cash crop exports, designed to alleviate the trade deficit, have artificially increased the relative profitability of export over domestic crops and produced a decline in the acreage devoted to food production. By the late 1970s Brazil was importing beans, corn, rice, and other staples at uncomfortably high levels, and foodstuff was rising more rapidly than any other item in the domestic cost of living index.[5]

An inadequate and inappropriate infrastructure has been a second source of inflationary pressure. At the onset of modern industrialization the Brazilian infrastructure was geared to primary exporting activities. As it had been developed for trading activities, it was totally unsuited to domestic industrialization and the needs of the local market. Consequently, shortfalls in transportation, communications, and energy served to aggravate inefficiency and increase costs in the Brazilian industrial sector throughout the import-substitution period.

The telephone system, for example, was originally built and operated by foreign firms. During the 1946–64 period, successive Brazilian governments satisfied important elements in their urban constituency by not allowing rates to keep pace with rising price levels. The telephone companies reacted predictably by not making any investments (in fact, there seems to have been net disinvestment). The result was a deterioration in telephone services. By the early 1960s the wait for a dial tone in the city of Rio de Janeiro could take as long as forty-five minutes, and some residents had been on the telephone waiting list for twenty years! All this added up to a gigantic loss of time and greatly increased the costs associated with doing business. In the wake of the 1964 coup, most of the firms were nationalized, rates were raised, and considerable progress was made on improving the telephone service.

Electric power has been another chronic problem area. Despite large public and private investment in this sector (and installed capacity did grow at 9 percent per year in the late forties and fifties), Brazilian industry did not enjoy a reliable supply of electric power at reasonable cost during the import-substituting period. As Judith Tendler has put it:

The power supply to metropolitan Rio and São Paulo was almost always on the brink of crisis during the postwar period. . . . After 1946 the two subsidiaries never ended a year without a backlog of unattended requests for power connections. . . . The continuous existence from 1946 through 1954 of substandard voltage and frequency during the peak hours [was] one method of limiting load to fit within the bounds of installed capacity.

In 1954 the Joint Brazil–United States Economic Development Commission described graphically what it was like to be engaged in industrial production in a region with chronic power shortages: "At times of serious system overload the power company has no option but to disconnect certain circuits . . . without warning to the power users concerned. . . . Tiremakers lose a day's production when such stoppage occurs, and another day is required to clean out the machinery. Stoppage of power to glass furnaces cuts off the air circulation used to cool the walls of furnaces, endangering the strength and life of these walls.

[Another] difficulty arises from low voltage and low frequency during periods of overload. Motors burn out, much equipment operates improperly with very widespread losses. . . . [Textile] looms operate improperly because shuttles slow down at such times, resulting in cloth whose quality is substandard." [6]

Such is the reality of a supply bottleneck in the production of electricity. However, I should like to stress that it is not just a case of pronounced structural rigidity; government policies in the 1946–64 period also contributed to the problem. As in the case of telephones, rates in the electricity sector were held below cost for years, thus impeding the industry in financing its own expansion. After 1964 this situation was rectified.

A third bottleneck emphasized by the structuralist school is the foreign exchange or balance-of-payments constraint. One of the prime legacies of that long period associated with primary exporting which preceded the Great Depression was a reliance on the fluctuating fortunes of primary exports for foreign exchange earnings. This dependence continued into the postwar period, Brazilian planners being under the impression that import substitution would decrease the country's reliance on export earnings. This notion had a superficial validity, since sub-stituting for imports meant acquiring the domestic capability to satisfy demand for manufactured goods. However, as we learned in chapter 3, import substitution in its initial phases merely transforms a demand for imported final consumer goods into a demand for a variety of imported industrial inputs, which actually makes the economy more vulnerable to a foreign exchange constraint.

Exchange rate policies of the import-substituting period demonstrates the interrelationship between inflation and balance-of-payments prob-lems. In the immediate postwar period, the exchange rate of Cr$18.50 per dollar which had been in force throughout the war remained un-changed until 1953 despite the fact that the domestic price level rose 285 percent between 1945 and 1953. The result was a seriously over-valued *cruzeiro* which triggered a steady decline in both the quantum and the value of exports from 1946 to the Korean War. After the war (which saw a short-lived boom in exports), the general picture was one of continually rising domestic prices and occasional (and insufficient) readjustments of the exchange rate. Bergsman estimates that in the period 1954–64 there was an implicit export tax of 31 percent on Bra-zilian goods.[7] This may not have been too serious with regard to the export of primary commodities (where demand was price-inelastic), but it constituted "a significant discouragement to a number of industrial firms." [8]

Brazil's actual export performance during the 1946–64 period was as follows: The volume of primary commodity exports remained essen-tially stagnant. The price of coffee rose overall, while the price of other agricultural and raw-material exports fell. Exports of manufac-tures, while never significant, were also stagnant or declining. All of this boiled down to a net increase of 4 percent in Brazilian export earnings,[9] a figure dramatically short of that which was needed for import-substituting industrialization. The foreign exchange gap which was created was gradually bridged by the inflow of foreign capital (see discussion in chapter 7).

A fourth supply constraint emphasized by structuralist theorists is the lack of adequate internal sources of finance. As Furtado puts it: "The financing of homogeneous products of a standard type and with assured demand in the great international centers is a relatively simple opera-tion compared with the financing of a highly diversified industrial production." [10]

In other words, in the era of primary exporting, government revenues had typically come from foreign bonds and from export taxes, and there were no developed internal financial institutions or habits of saving among domestic elites. In populist political settings these structural legacies were greatly exaggerated by the inability of government to increase personal taxation drastically.

In Brazil, government expenditure increased rapidly during the import-substitution phase of growth. There was a dramatic rise in investment by the federal government (which increased from 3 percent of GDP in 1947 to 7 percent in 1964) and a significant increase in the amounts spent on transfers and on the public bureaucracy. Tax revenues were increasing rapidly, but not rapidly enough to counteract these inflationary forces. Total tax revenues rose steadily throughout the postwar period, reaching a peak of 23 percent of GNP in 1960; and there was a distinct shift toward indirect taxation (from 10 to 15 percent of GNP). By the early 1960s the federal budget was running a pronounced deficit.

A final inflationary supply constraint emphasized by the structuralist school of thought is to be found in the inadequacies of the labor force. Most Latin American countries have an abundant supply of labor, but a large proportion of this labor pool lacks the education and the skills needed by workers engaged in modern industrial activity.

During the modern period Brazil has run into a pronounced bottleneck in the supply of skilled labor largely as a result of an extremely inadequate educational system. In Harbison and Myer's correlation of their "composite index of human resources development" with GNP per capita, Brazil had one of the largest negative deviations.[11] That is to say, Brazil's level of human resource development in the 1960s was more deficient—given its income level—than all countries in the sample of seventy-two except nine (which in Latin America includes Haiti, Guatemala, and the Dominican Republic).

Some of these problems were a result of the colonial era. For example, higher education was explicitly forbidden when Brazil was ruled by the Portuguese, and it was not until the 1920s that the first university was organized by combining the existing faculties of medicine, law, and engineering. Thus, industrialization occurred in a context where higher education was extremely elitist (for every one thousand students entering primary school in the early 1960s only seventy-six were likely to go on to university), and its function seemed mainly to "enable sons of high status families to maintain their status." [12] Thus, it was difficult to find that cadre of skilled technicians and highly trained managers needed by the emerging industrial sector. This is at least one of the reasons that high-level manpower has been both scarce and expensive in Brazil.

At the lower levels the inadequacies of the educational system were even more pronounced. In the 1960s, 50 percent of the population was officially classified as illiterate; and, given an enormous rate of attrition during primary school (60 percent of those students who entered first grade did not make it into second grade), the rate of functional illiteracy must have been even higher.

Some progress has been made in the post-1964 era. Between 1964 and 1975 the number of people who went to primary school increased from 9 million to 16 million, while the official illiteracy rate fell to 21 percent of the adult population. However, this was in the face of an acute shortage of teachers, and standards seem to have slipped badly. Today, one-third of the Brazilian population is still thought to be functionally illiterate. [13]

The Specific Component

While the five structural rigidities I have described all contribute to inflationary pressures in Brazil, we need to go beyond these supply constraints. The specifics of the industrialization strategy and the particular policies of modernizing regimes have served to aggravate the structural components and have provided additional inflationary pressures. [14]

As we saw in chapter 3, import substitution produced a highly protected domestic market for the production of manufactured goods. Throughout most of the 1950s there was a five-category exchange auction system in operation. In 1956, for example, inputs to agriculture had a 4 percent rate of protection (over and above the free-trade rate); raw materials for favored intermediate goods had a 14 percent rate of protection; other raw materials, 45 percent; spare parts and equipment, 62 percent; and finished consumer goods, 210 percent. [15] This structure of protection made the importation of manufactured goods prohibitive, and firms producing in Brazil, with no external competition and little internal competition (the domestic market structure was oligopolistic), could make abnormally high profits.

At the same time, costs of production were high. Operation at less than full capacity, and the inability of firms to take advantage of the economies of scale associated with modern technology, exaggerated the structural inflationary pressures described earlier, and made average costs within Brazilian manufacturing much higher than world prices. And as import substitution widened, it produced cumulative inflationary pressures as supply shifted progressively from imports to higher-priced domestic production.

Both of these inflationary conditions—high profits and high costs— are illustrated in the development of the automobile industry, which was one of the most conspicuous "success" stories of the import-substituting era. In 1957 Brazil produced no passenger cars and only 30,000 other vehicles (and these contained over 50 percent of imported components). By 1964 the Brazilian automobile industry ranked tenth in the world in terms of annual production, and by that time over 95 percent of its vehicles were produced by local industry. These impressive accomplishments went along with high prices for Brazilian-made vehicles. In the mid-1960s the retail price of cars in Brazil was roughly twice the price in developed countries (for example, the average retail price of a standard VW sedan during 1966–67 cost from US$2,500 to US$2,800); ex-factory prices were 50 percent higher than ex-factory prices in Europe and the United States.

A part of the cost differential was due to the sales tax levied on all manufactured goods by the Brazilian government. But for many firms the diseconomies of small-scale production seem to have been responsible for a large proportion of excessive costs. Research in developed countries indicates that in passenger car production, economies of scale become significant when an assembly plant is producing at the rate of 100,000 units per year. Since the Brazilian market was split among eight firms, none of them was large enough to capture these kinds of scale economies.

I would like to stress that some of the cost pressures in the Brazilian automobile industry could have been avoided:

If Brazilian policy had limited itself to promoting production of only high volume models (say, one low-priced and one intermediate-priced car such as the Volkswagen or Citroen 2CV, and the Opel or Ford Falcon), with only 80 or 85 percent domestic procurement then real costs of these cars to Brazil need not have exceeded the C.I.F. cost of imports.[16]

However, given the consumption preferences of the Brazilian elite (for numerous models of cars), the oligopolistic behavior of multinational firms (which entailed competition through product differentiation), and the expedient nature of much economic planning, it is hardly surprising that a high-cost automobile industry emerged in Brazil.

Costs were of course but part of the picture. Ex-factory prices were 50 percent higher, but retail prices were 100 percent higher than world prices, so it does seem that multinational firms operating in the highly protected Brazilian automobile market were able to make substantially larger profits than in their home operations. (This theme is taken up again in chapter 7.)

So far I have been describing those specific inflationary pressures that were rooted in the costs and the profits of Brazilian industrialization. I would now like to turn to the political dimensions of the import-substituting era.

As we already know from chapter 4, the modernizing regimes of the 1930–64 period were populist in spirit, and governments relied on the support of the mobilized urban classes to maintain their place in office. This political reality produced a variety of inflationary pressures.

In the first place, governments could not radically increase the incidence (or the efficiency in collection) of personal income taxes, and thus generated a growing dependence on indirect taxes (which pushed prices up) and caused the soaring expenditures of an interventionist state to exceed governmental revenues. The vastly increased public investments of the Kubitschek era were part of the reason the federal budget was in deficit by the late 1950s; and deficit financing is a classic route to inflation.

But government expenditures were not limited to investment in infrastructure and basic industry. The populist years also saw high levels of expenditure on the public bureaucracy. "Clientelist" politics meant that political supporters of an incumbent president felt that they had a right to at least a part-time job in government, a state of affairs that further inflated the federal budget.

A second and less direct inflationary pressure resulted from the price controls of the populist period. As I noted earlier, basic foodstuffs, rents, public transportation, electricity, and telephones were all subject to artificially low price ceilings by populist governments attempting to please their urban constituencies. This discouraged investment in these sectors, led to shortages and bottlenecks, and, in the long run, increased the costs of production for industrial firms.

A third and extremely crucial inflationary pressure in the populist period came from wages. The real minimum wage almost doubled between 1940 and the early 1960s.[17] Given the political support base of populist governments, it proved impossible to contain working-class demands for higher wages for any sustained period of time.

The 1946–64 scene is littered with attempts to control inflation, and wage restraint was a sphere in which little headway was made. In 1958, for example, the Kubitschek government announced an elaborate stabilization program designed to "allow the development of the country to proceed under conditions of economic equilibrium and social stability by means of the pursuit of monetary stabilization." [18] An essential ingredient of this program was the slowing down of the rate of expansion of wages, a policy that provoked virulent opposition. "Every class and sector wanted the burden to be borne by some other group first." [19] In January 1959 a massive upward adjustment of the minimum wage spelled the beginnings of the end of this particular inflation-control program. By June of that year stabilization was a dead letter; Kubitschek had decided to concentrate on growth and "leave the problems of inflation and foreign indebtedness for his successor." [20]

My analysis of the structural and specific components of inflation in Brazil during the import-substitution period of development illustrates the complexity of the issue at hand. In particular, it highlights the impossibility of neatly applying either of the conceptual frameworks outlined at the beginning of this chapter.

Take the problem of high and rising prices for industrial goods. During the initial industrialization drive, Brazilian industry was faced with an inadequate infrastructure, a foreign exchange constraint, and a shortage of skilled manpower (all were structural problems inherited from an earlier era of primary commodity production). However, these rigidities in supply were exaggerated by the specifics of the import-substituting strategy and the realities of political power. For example, the extremely high level of protection permitted firms to earn excessive profits, while populist politics actively discouraged the construction of a more efficient communications system.

The intertwining of the structural and specific components of Brazilian inflation is also apparent in the sphere of government spending. Given the long era of primary exporting and the lateness of Brazil's industrialization, the state had to assume a major responsibility for infrastructural investment (this is elaborated in chapter 6). However, the relatively competitive arena of populist politics meant that it was extremely difficult for Brazilian planners in the import-substituting period to balance their budgets and keep government revenues expanding at the same rate as government expenditures.

The inflationary distortions of the 1950s and the 1960s were therefore the result of a colonial and primary exporting past interacting with the economic policies of a modernizing regime attempting to industrialize in an expedient and cost-free way. But the costs of growth were not avoided. They were merely postponed. In 1964 the "chickens came home to roost," and the draconian measures of an authoritarian regime were needed to correct the accumulated inflationary distortions of the import-substituting period.

It should also be clear that my specific components, while bearing some relationship to the monetarist view of inflation, have important distinguishing characteristics. Monetarists in Latin America have laid great stress on government deficit spending and distorted price structures (both of which are elements in my own analysis); but by and large, this school of thought has focused on the symptoms of the inflationary disease and has devoted little attention to the causes. Expedient import-substituting strategies of growth and populist politics did not grow out of thin air but were part of industrial takeoff in this late-developing nation. The same factors that facilitated development produced inflation. For example, modernizing regimes in the 1930s, the 1940s, the 1950s were faced with the necessity of putting together a broad coalition of class groupings in order to move Brazil through the massive structural changes of the industrialization process. This meant buying off the planter-exporter class with price supports for primary exports, co-opting the industrial work force with paternalistic policies and material rewards, and attracting multinational corporations with permissive terms of entry and operation. In short, in the absence of radical political change, Brazil could ease its way into the modern era only through finding something for everyone who mattered.

We are left with the conclusion that inflation in Brazil during the 1946–64 period was a creature of late development, built upon the structural rigidities of a primary exporting past and directly connected with the strategies and power plays of mid-twentieth century industrial take-off. This leads to policy prescriptions (and consequences) that are very different from those advocated by monetarists.

Correcting for inflation is not merely a question of ending the budget deficit by cutting public expenditure and increasing tax revenues. Nor is it primarily a matter of "getting prices right." Both these policy items are contingent upon major changes in the political sphere. The fact of the matter is that populist governments (in Brazil and elsewhere in the Third World) have found it impossible to increase tax revenues drastically or to eliminate price controls for basic goods and services. These essential elements of stabilization packages seem to be the prerogative of repressive authoritarian regimes. In my view, monetarists have successfully defined some of the "trees" (the economic policies) without recognizing the "forest" (the political context). An additional short-coming of this school of thought is its neglect of the issue of wage levels. Monetarist thinking has been dominated by demand-pull rather than by cost-push versions of inflation. However, most stabilization programs have recognized that wage control is often the quickest way to dampen inflation, since it acts in both the sphere of supply (wages are an important ingredient in the costs of production) and in the sphere of demand (industrial workers are an effective part of the elite market). Wage restraint has therefore been given priority in the fight against inflation. A deliberate lowering of real wages was certainly an important part of the Brazilian stabilization drive in the 1964–67 period. Inflation can therefore be seen as a direct trigger of the repressive and inequitable "solutions" of the post-1964 period.

In summary, the phase of "easy" import substitution in Brazil bred industrial growth and cumulative inflationary distortions: a contradiction that was eventually resolved by an authoritarian and repressive military regime willing to deal with inflation in a harsh, systematic way. Since 1964 industry has been streamlined, made more efficient, and made more export-oriented; price controls for basic living expenses have been curtailed, personal taxation has been radically increased, and real wage gains have been restrained. Structural rigidities inherited from the primary exporting past still lurk in the background (for example, the supply of highly skilled manpower is still inadequate), and economic policy making is at times both inconsistent and ineffective; but by and large, the structural causes of inflation have been eased, and

the specific components of inflation have been eliminated. Political repression and increased inequality have been extremely unsavory by-
products of this process, but the contemporary Brazilian leadership (if
not the people) seems to have both recognized and accepted these
trade-offs.

NOTES

1. An excellent summary of structuralist and monetarist views of inflation can be
found in Rosemary Thorp, "Inflation and the Financing of Economic Development," in
Keith Griffin, ed., *Financing Developments in Latin America* (London: Macmillan, 1971),
pp. 182–225.
2. These bottlenecks have been clearly described by numerous writers. See David
Felix, "An Alternative View of the 'Monetarist-Structuralist' Controversy," in A. O.
Hirschman, ed., *Latin American Issues* (New York: Twentieth Century Fund, 1961),
pp. 81–95; and Dudley Seers, "A Theory of Inflation and Growth in Underdeveloped
Countries Based on the Experience of Latin America," in *Oxford Economic Papers*,
vol. 14 (June 1962): 174–97.
3. See G. A. Costanzo, *Programas de Estabilización Económica en América Latina*
(Mexico, 1961); and Roberto de Oliveira Campos, "Two Views on Inflation in Latin
America," in Hirschman, *Latin American Issues*. pp. 66–81, for expositions of the
monetarist view.
4. Celso Furtado, *Economic Development of Latin America: A Survey from Colonial
Times to the Cuban Revolution* (Cambridge, England: Cambridge University Press, 1970),
p. 95.
5. See discussion in José Roberto Mendonça de Barros and Douglas H. Graham
"A Agricultura Brasileira e o Problema da Produção de Alimentos," *Pesquisa e Planejamento Economico*, 8, no. 3 (1978): 695–726.
6. Judith Tendler, *Electric Power in Brazil* (Cambridge, Mass.: Harvard University
Press, 1968), pp. 9–15.
7. Joel Bergsman, *Brazil: Industrialization and Trade Policies* (London: Oxford
University Press, 1970), p. 98.
8. Bergsman, *Brazil*, p. 36.
9. Bergsman, *Brazil* (note 7), pp. 99–101.
10. Furtado, *Economic Development of Latin America* (note 4), p. 97.
11. Frederick Harbison and Charles A. Myers, *Education, Manpower and Economic
Growth* (New York: McGraw-Hill, 1964), pp. 33–42.
12. R. J. Havighurst and A. J. Gouveia, *Brazilian Secondary Education and Socio-
Economic Development* (New York: Praeger, 1969), p. 199.
13. *The Economist*, "A Survey of Brazil," 31 July 1976.
14. Some of my specific elements in Brazilian inflation are treated by the structuralist
school. See Furtado who stresses circumstantial factors and propagation mechanisms
(*Economic Development*, pp. 99–100); and Osvaldo Sunkel, "La Inflación Chilena: Un
Enfoque Heterodoxo," in *Trimestre Económico*, vol. 25 (October–December 1958). How-

ever, these analyses lack my distinction between those inflationary pressures due to industrial strategy and those due to political regime.

15. Bergsman, *Brazil* (note 7), p. 31.

16. Bergsman, *Brazil* (note 7), p. 130.

17. Werner Baer and Isaac Kerstenetzky, "Some Observations on the Brazilian Inflation," in Werner Baer and Isaac Kerstenetzky, eds., *Inflation and Growth in Latin America* (Homewood, Ill.: Richard D. Irwin, 1964), p. 369.

18. Thomas E. Skidmore, *Politics in Brazil, 1930–1964* (New York: Oxford University Press, 1967), p. 175.

19. Skidmore, *Politics in Brazil*, p. 177.

20. Skidmore, *Politics in Brazil* (note 18), p. 181.

CHAPTER

6

The State

Why not admit that we are confronting one of the gravest threats Brazilian society has ever faced? During these last ten years we have witnessed a real escalation of statism without precedent in the history of the country and comparable only to socialist states.

Estado de São Paulo

A GREAT DEAL of confusion and dismay has been triggered by the increasingly conspicuous role of the state in Brazil's development. In this chapter I shall argue that this situation is neither accidental nor ephemeral but is embedded in those economic structures and political frameworks described in earlier chapters of this book. The role of the contemporary Brazilian state is deeply rooted in the structural conditions of late development and reflects the priorities of successive political regimes.

Industrial takeoff in the mid-twentieth century necessitates considerable state intervention. The protection of "infant" manufactures against foreign competition and the provision of the elaborate infrastructural requirements of modern industry are just two of the areas where state action is crucial. However, if state intervention is a necessary part of late industrialization, the goals and the scope of such initiative are a function of the priorities of ruling classes. In modern Brazil the state has been part and parcel of the drive to *grandeza,* and it is more accurately seen as an efficient and powerful agent of accumulation rather than as a source of redistributive policies. In short, state action has generally served to bolster the inequitable patterns of Brazilian development.

My analysis of the role of the Brazilian state underlines two fundamental points. First, it demonstrates how the distinctive structural characteristics of late development can have implications for social justice. Second, it underscores the complexity of the development process. The causes and the consequences of state action can be understood only if due attention is paid to the interaction between the past and the present and between economic structures and political power.

I begin by putting the controversy over the role of the state into some theoretical perspective. I then take a rigorous look at the modern Brazilian state. I mainly focus on the state as producer and as financier, as these roles highlight the ways in which state activity has become an integral part of the modern development experience.

The Liberal-Pluralist Perspective

An extremely influential thread running through postwar "Western" social science has been a static model of the political process called liberal pluralism. This theoretical construct has tended to downplay the state as an autonomous force.

According to the liberal-pluralist perspective, society should be allowed to regulate itseif with as little interference as possible from the state:

The general rule is nothing ought to be done or attempted by the government. The motto or watchword of government, on these occasions ought to be—*Be Quiet.* . . . With few exceptions, and these not very considerable ones, the attainment of the maximum of enjoyment will be most effectually secured by leaving each individual to pursue his own maximum enjoyment.[1] [Italics in the original]

This harmony of interests is arrived at by men and women freely pursuing their own selfish ends. In the economic universe we have the doctrine of the invisible hand.[2] This describes a free enterprise system unconsciously coordinating producers and consumers through a system of prices and markets in order to achieve the best good for all:

any interference with free competition by the government is almost certain to be detrimental to the general good.

The political universe is dominated by the same atomistic, equilibrating mechanisms. Individuals pursue their own selfish ends; but because people have various interests, they tend to associate with numerous and different pressure groups whose interests crisscross. Multiple, overlapping group membership is a crucial element in pluralistic theory, for it denies the existence of a dominant group or class; it assumes that through bargaining and compromises all interests are weighed in the political arena.

The liberal-pluralist perspective rules out the possibility that the state needs to intervene on behalf of the weak or the underprivileged. Since it takes for granted that all interest groups are in on the political balancing act, it denies that some groups are powerless or illegitimate. This would seem to contradict reality, for in most societies, throughout most of history, interest groups have not been at liberty to combine freely but have been strictly chartered by the state. Doctrines of the invisible hand and the harmony of interests are cold comfort if one happens to be a worker in a country where an authoritarian regime has outlawed trade unions in the name of economic progress.

In short, liberal-pluralist theory has minimized the role of the state as an independent actor. It has also reduced the need for political and economic theorists to come to grips with the intensely moral question of what the state ought to be doing. In the nineteenth century Hegel wrote: "The State is the Divine Idea as it exists on Earth." [3] Modern social scientists are distinctly uncomfortable with such notions, and the intellectual bias of both economists and political scientists has been to solve societal problems with mechanistic, scientific, and supposedly objective tools. The self-regulating market mechanisms of Adam Smith and the atomistic, egoistic assumptions of utilitarian philosophers have been easier to deal with, if less illuminating, than those that are more explicitly bound up with value-laden judgments.

If the dominant theoretical construct of postwar social science seems unhelpful in our search for a conceptual framework that will illuminate the nature of the interaction between the state and contemporary growth processes in the Third World, where else can one go? There remain two rather neglected schools of thought that provide some relevant theoretical insights. They are classical Marxism and corporatism.

Classical Marxism

Marx's views on the state are neatly summed up in that famous statement from the *Communist Manifesto:* "The executive of the modern state is but a committee for managing the common affairs of the entire bourgeoisie." [4] In classical Marxian analysis, the institutional framework of nations has its roots in the material conditions of life, and it is the economic structures of society that provide the real foundation on which rises a legal and political superstructure. Economic progress is seen as a zero sum game where "every advance in production is at the same time a retrogression in the condition of the oppressed class, that is, of the great majority. . . . What is a boon for the one is necessarily a bane for the other." [5] In the face of this inevitable economic conflict between the classes, the state emerges as a "machine for keeping down the oppressed, exploited classes." [6]

We are left with an image of the state as having a minimal autonomous role; it is relegated to the position of being a coercive instrument of the dominant economic class. While this perspective helps us understand the underlying economic forces of society, it does little to explain "the question of the state in the light of the concrete socio-economic *and* political *and* cultural reality of actual capitalist societies [italics in original]." [7]

The Corporatist Tradition

Until recently Western scholars had thought of corporatism as a brief and closed era in the history of political institutions. This conclusion was easy to come to given the distasteful memories of Hitler's Germany and Mussolini's Italy. However, far from being an outmoded political form, it seems that partial versions of corporatism are alive and kicking, especially in Latin America.

Corporatism is based on a body of ideas that can be traced through Aristotle, Roman law, medieval social and legal structures, and into contemporary Catholic social philosophy. These ideas are based on the premise that man's nature can only be fulfilled within a political community:

The man who is isolated—who is unable to share in the benefits of political association, or has no need to share because he is already self-sufficient—is no part of the polis, and must therefore be either a beast or a god.[8]

If the happiness of man requires a well-ordered political community, the state becomes a legitimate and central guiding force. However, the theorists of corporatism go much further and ascribe to the state a *telos* or moral end. It becomes not merely:

. . . an association for residence on a common site, for the sake of preventing mutual injustices and easing exchange. . . . But it is the cardinal issue of goodness or badness in the life of the polis which always engages the attention of any state that concerns itself to secure a system of good law well obeyed.[9]

The centrol core of the corporatist vision is thus not the individual but the political community whose perfection allows the individual members to fulfill themselves and find happiness.

I would like to stress that this view of the political universe lends itself to antidemocratic formulas and is contrary to the spirit of liberal pluralism. In essence, the state has a privileged vision of the common good, and it is unnecessary for individuals or interest groups to express their opinions and preferences. It is also intensely antagonistic to Marxist formulations. An insistence on the inevitability of class conflict violates the corporatist view of a harmonious community that is to be constructed by a caring and paternalistic state.

The great mistake [is] . . . the notion that class is naturally hostile to class, and that the wealthy and the working men are intended by nature to live in mutual conflict. So irrational and so false is this view, that the direct contrary is the truth. . . . In a State it is ordained by nature that these two classes should dwell in harmony and agreement, and should, as it were, groove into one another.[10]

The state in the corporatist tradition is thus clearly interventionist and powerful. From Aristotle to twentieth-century popes there is a strong tradition in which the state is conceived of as playing an architectural role in the political life of nations and as capable of imposing major changes in the established order so as to create a more just society.

Corporatist theory with its emphasis on the interventionist state seems of immediate relevance in the Third World where the modernization process has been so intertwined with governmental action. However, given the conspicuous injustices of modern development strategies, one is perhaps less comfortable with the benevolent formulations of this strong state. Before pushing these theories any further, I should like to turn to our case study.

The State as Producer

As can be seen from table 8, the contemporary state is an extremely important producer of goods within the Brazilian economy. In 1978 a survey of the 500 largest firms showed that over 29 percent of sales was controlled by public enterprises, 35 percent by multinational corporations, and 36 percent by private Brazilian firms.[11] In 1976 there were 571 state firms operating in Brazil; the largest, Petrobrás, had reached the dimensions of a giant multinational, refining oil in Italy and selling shoes in the Soviet Union.

A second characteristic obvious from table 9 is that the state investment is highly concentrated in certain basic industries. In mining, state firms are dominant, controlling 58 percent of sales, and they tend to be particularly important in the export sector (for example, Companhia Vale do Rio Doce accounts for 80 percent of Brazilian iron ore exports). The state is also strongly represented in the metal-products sector and in chemicals. In the steel industry, state firms like Companhia Siderúrgica Nacional, Usiminas, Cosipa, and a few others are responsible for about two-thirds of sales. Within the chemical sector, Petrobrás has dominated petroleum explorations and refining and has steadily increased its share of gasoline distribution. Through subsidiaries like Petroquisa, it has enhanced its share of petrochemical production, in part by forming joint ventures with multinationals.

The dynamism of such state firms as Companhia Vale do Rio Doce (CVRD) and Petrobrás has been a function of expansion within their respective fields, of growth in areas that are complementary to their initial specialization; and, in some instances, of extension into fields that are unrelated to the original activity. For example, both firms have expanded their activities into the production of fertilizer and into shipping; while Petrobrás has gone into various fields of petrochemicals, and CVRD has gone into pelletizing plants, bauxite mining and aluminum production, pulp manufacturing, and steel plants. Such diversification has been accompanied by the growing use of joint ventures between the state and multinationals, and between the state, multinationals, and domestic firms (the so-called tripod arrangements). As we shall see in a later section of this chapter, joint ventures serve to combine the specific economic and political advantages of the alternative producing units within the Brazilian economy.

If state enterprises are important in absolute terms, especially in basic industry, they also emerge as the fastest-growing sector of the Brazilian economy. As can be seen from table 8, between 1973 and 1978 the state increased its share of the sales of the 500 largest corporations from 16 percent to 29 percent; this was mainly at the expense of private domestic firms, but multinational corporations also suffered a relative decline. Public enterprises in manufacturing are on average ten times larger than private firms.[12] Petrobrás, CVRD, and the state steel companies are immense economic units, dwarfing their private counterparts. This large scale can largely be explained by the technological imperatives of these basic industries.

Evans demonstrates that five key state firms are making significantly lower profits than a sample of ten large multinationals—11 percent as opposed to 16 percent.[13] This difference accords with a more broadly based study undertaken by Bacha.[14] Using the *Visão* listing of the largest 5,000 corporations, between 1968 and 1974 Bacha finds that multinational corporations enjoy an average rate of return of 15.8 percent per year, while state enterprises average only 9 percent per year.

What does this description of the state as producer mean in terms of its role in the Brazilian development strategy? It is my contention that the expansion of state enterprises in Brazil has not been the result of an explicitly statist ideology; rather, it has been the logical response to the imperatives of economic growth in this late-industrializing nation. In subsequent paragraphs I will take pains to demonstrate that in certain sectors the state is the natural and the efficient producer. Many Brazilians are both surprised and dismayed to find that they have created "the most successful and pervasive system of state capitalism in South America." [15] But while the growth of the state may have been unpremeditated and out of line with the free enterprise bias of many segments of the domestic elite, one may rest assured that it is not accidental. An aggressive and active state has been a necessary condition for vigorous growth in Brazil.

Second, expansion of the state has been in certain specific directions. The state is still absent from most areas of final goods manufacturing, while it dominates in the production of infrastructural items, basic industrial goods, and raw materials. The nearest the state approaches involvement with manufacturing is in the production of intermediate goods, such as steel products and basic petrochemicals. As is the case with much of the output of state enterprises, these intermediate products are inputs into the manufacturing sector, which is heavily dominated by multinational firms.

What does this clear-cut division of labor between the state and the multinational corporation imply? One influential school of thought sees it is evidence of an *entreguista* (collaborator) state, serving as a "handmaiden" to the multinational corporations. Tavares and Serra, for example, are proponents of this view and describe the state as shouldering the "responsibility of supplying the domestic market at low cost with basic inputs and external economies which were used by multinational corporations for their own expansion both domestically and in export markets." [16] Several arguments have been marshaled to bolster this hypothesis. For example, it has been pointed out that the state has invested in sectors of the economy that are characterized by either low returns, high risk, or long gestation periods; in many cases, foreign firms could not be induced to invest in these areas—they were too unattractive. Support for this theory has also been drawn from the discrepancies in profit levels mentioned earlier. The lower profit levels typical of state enterprises are seen as part of a plan to underwrite foreign capital. The products of state firms (the inputs of the multinational-dominated final goods sector) are priced artificially low and thus serve as a subsidy to foreign capital; this partially accounts for the much higher average rate of return for multinational investment in Brazil. Interestingly enough, the CVRD is the only state firm whose output is primarily exported rather than serving as an input to local industry, and it constitutes the only state enterprise that has average rates of return greater than those achieved by the multinationals.

This pattern of discrepancy in profit levels between the state and multinational firms could be modified by policy initiatives. The governmental planning apparatus—particularly the price-setting ability of the CIP (Conselho Interministerial de Preços)—has the power to boost the profit rates of state-owned firms and lower those of multinational corporations. For example, higher prices for steel or electric power would simultaneously raise profits within the state sector and, by raising the cost of inputs, would squeeze profits in the multinational-dominated final goods sector.

Despite the fact that this second scenario is theoretically feasible, it represents a highly unlikely turn of events. Utilizing this capacity to depress profit margins in the multinational sector would be tantamount to lowering industrial growth rates. If multinational corporations were unable to earn high rates of return in Brazil, they might begin to contract their activities in that country. Thus, suppressing their profits would impede growth and ultimately imperil the goals of the contemporary Brazilian regime, which, as we saw in chapter 4, are focused on the rapid attainment of world power status.

For this reason, I find it more convincing to view the division of labor between the multinational corporation and the state as a partnership rather than as a relationship of exploitation with an *entregulsta* state serving as a "handmaiden" to the multinationals. It is a partnership that has been built up over the last forty years, is centered around complementary economic roles, and is grounded in common interest in rapid growth. Let me probe this statement in greater depth.

State enterprises have distinctive traits as producing units. In the first instance, they can exert control over national economic resources, such as mineral deposits and hydroelectric power potential. Second, through access to government revenues they are able to mobilize huge sums of capital. Third, due to the nature of public as opposed to private accountability, they do not have to recoup investments within a few years and are able to contemplate much longer time horizons than are private firms. Finally, since their objective is to maximize the national product rather than merely the product of a firm or a sector, they can afford to ignore the indivisibilities and the externalities characteristic of much infrastructural investment.

The distinctive traits of multinational firms as producing units are more familiar, since they are more nearly in accord with the textbook model of a profit-maximizing firm. As we shall see in chapter 7, their economic strengths are vested in various types of technology and in easy access to finance (particularly to foreign exchange and to cheaper investment funds). These factors give them a competitive edge both over domestic private firms and over state firms in the production of sophisticated consumer goods. In most late-developing nations, not just Brazil, the multinational corporation is the most effective and efficient vehicle for the production of consumer durables, which often constitute the dynamic sector of final goods production.

However functional this division of labor between state enterprises and the multinational firm, it is wrong to view it in too static a way. The spheres of influence of the two principal economic actors have shifted through time, and the relationship between them has grown closer. Nothing shows this more aptly than the increasing use of joint ventures.

The recent history of the petrochemical industry in Brazil is an excellent example of the building of joint ventures based on a complementarity of roles between state, foreign capital, and national capital.

Prior to the early 1960s oil refining was in the hands of Petrobrás and various other, much smaller, state companies, while the production of final petrochemical products, such as plastics and synthetic rubber, was to dominate petrochemical production in the São Paulo area for Rhone Poulenc. In other words, the petrochemical industry was distinguished by a clear differentiation of roles between state and foreign capital and by pronounced gaps in domestic production capability; that is to say, both basic and intermediate petrochemical products had to be imported.

Since 1964 serious efforts have been made to fill these empty spaces (*espaços vazios*) of the productive structure.[17] The first cycle of development was marked by: an abortive attempt by Union Carbide to produce ethylene on a large scale; a more successful attempt by the Capuava group of domestic capitalists, to do the same thing; and the eventual creation of the UNIPAR group (União da Indústria e Petroquímica)—a mixture of local, state, and foreign capital in a venture that was to dominate petrochemical production in the São Paulo area for several years in the late 1960s.

A second cycle began in the early 1970s with the growth of Petro-

quisa, a wholly owned subsidiary of Petrobrás. One of the most successful ventures of this new firm is COPENE (Petroquímica do Nordeste),
set up in 1972 and located in the northeast of Brazil. COPENE itself
produces ethylene, propylene, benzene, and other basic petrochemicals;
but it has also put together a set of eighteen user firms which are owners of 50 percent of the stock in COPENE itself. Eleven of these firms
are tripartite alliances between state, local, and foreign capital; five
others involve two types of capital (local and multinational, or state
and multinational); one is controlled by local capital; and one is wholly
state-owned. Additional diversity is provided by the fact that a dozen
multinationals from six advanced countries are involved in the ownership
of this new petrochemical complex.

COPENE is typical of recent trends in the petrochemical industry in
Brazil and is a particularly vivid illustration of the complementarity of
roles between state, foreign, and national capital. First, from the point of
view of the multinational firm, a major petrochemical venture in the
northeast of Brazil has many "risky" dimensions. Foreign capital was
persuaded to join the scheme because the state, in the guise of Petroquisa, was prepared to underwrite much of the uncertainty. Perhaps
most important was the fact that Petroquisa assumed many of the direct
risks. For example, it took responsibility for those parts of the project
that were likely to sustain losses in the early stages of production.
And, it underwrote the construction of such infrastructural facilities as
electrical generators and water supply systems. These were peculiarly
absent given the location of the petrochemical complex in the underdeveloped northeast, and they are precisely the type of investment that
private entrepreneurs dislike. In this particular case infrastructural facilities were bound to lose money until all the plants were operating
at full capacity.

Petroquisa was also able to negate some of the more indirect risks
associated with this venture. It guaranteed that the move to Bahia would
be collective and therefore would carry with it many of the external
economies normally associated with location in a more developed area.
Particularly important was the fact that the new complex would be
large enough to attract a skilled work force and would be capable of generating a market for intermediate and final goods. Another indirect
benefit of having Petroquisa as a partner was that it minimized the
problems inherent in access to inputs. The availability and the price of
raw-material inputs to the petrochemical industry obviously depend on

Petrobrás and on government policy. A favorable resolution of both problem areas was and is greatly facilitated by partnership with a wholly owned subsidiary of this state firm.

Such are the advantages gained by the multinational in going into partnership with the state. What does the state get in return? The main contribution of the multinational firm is technological. Given the sophisticated and advanced nature of production techniques within the petrochemical industry, foreign capital was and is essential. Theoretically it is always possible to purchase technology, but this is rarely an efficient solution. As Evans put it, "Getting technology from a partner whose local profits depend on its efficient operation is the best way to ensure that it will work." [18] And this is particularly true when that technology is highly complex and constantly evolving.

The participation of multinationals has also had a significant financial impact on the viability of the petrochemical complex in the northeast—the total costs of which are estimated to be three-quarters of a billion dollars. Not only did multinationals contribute directly as partners in the project, but they also added international credence to the venture and facilitated the raising of funds on the private international capital market. Through Petrobrás, Petroquisa has access to an enormous financial capability; but for much of the recent past the Brazilian government has preferred to expend its own resources on oil exploration. For this reason financial help from the multinationals has not been redundant.

The advantages to private national capital in joint ventures are very clear-cut. Fundamentally, participation in a petrochemical project with foreign and state capital enables domestic firms to appropriate part of the action in a sphere where, left to themselves, they would be squeezed out. It should be obvious from previous sections that both state and multinational firms have a multifaceted, competitive edge over domestic firms. Specifically important in the sphere of petrochemicals are the scale, the time horizons, and the resources of state enterprises, and the superior command over technology enjoyed by multinationals.

The contribution of private national capital is more difficult to gauge. Some local groups (for example, the construction firm Camargo Corrêa) seem to have been brought into the petrochemical industry with no obvious raison d'être. Others have a more convincing function—for example, the Grupo Ultra which managed to gain an important niche in the industry through political influence (it is headed by Beltrão, minister of planning under Costa e Silva), good management, and some initial experience in the bottled-gas business.

In the main it seems that private domestic capital contributes to joint ventures in a loosely defined "political" sphere of action. Some offer relevant industrial experience; many supply expertise with the local bureaucracy and help interpret the numerous regulations and incentives of Brazilian governments; and all help legitimize these projects in the eyes of that segment of Brazilian public opinion that still supports the national bourgeoisie.

A final point on this topic: very few private national concerns can take advantage of joint ventures. Generally the larger and/or politically advantaged firms are incorporated in the tripartite arrangements, and the result is often increased polarization within the private national sector—the successful few drawing away from their locally owned competitors.

The subsidiaries of the Companhia Vale do Rio Doce provide a second example of joint ventures—this time linking the state and multinational firms. CVRD is an impressive concern:

With 21,500 employees the company is a giant even by standards of concerns in industrialized countries. It is the world's largest exporter of iron ore. . . . For the next five years, the company has budgeted investments of $10 billion. This represents about 10% of the total investments in the Brazilian economy.[19]

Over the last few years CVRD has established various joint ventures with European, American, and Japanese companies in such spheres as metal pelletizing plants, bauxite, aluminum production, pulp manufacturing, and iron ore excavation. This latter project is typical: it is designed to exploit the vast ore reserves of the Amazon basin and has as its partners both European and Japanese firms.[20] In all of these ventures CVRD has retained 51 percent of the equity.

How has CVRD managed to construct this empire? In this sector the principal economic advantages of the state are vested in its control over national resources—specifically the vast Brazilian reserves of iron ore. The multinational corporations need the raw materials CVRD can provide for their operations within Brazil and for their industrial activities elsewhere in the world. For them, involvement in exploiting this significant source of iron ore is an integral part of a global strategy of profit maximization.

The strength of the contribution of the multinationals once again lies in access to advanced technology and privileged sources of finance. However, it should be pointed out that the technological superiority enjoyed by multinational firms is not so pronounced as it was in the petrochemical industry. Techniques employed in mineral extraction and processing are less volatile and complex, and thus they are more accessible to domestic firms than those typical of the petrochemical sector. Because of this, CVRD is in a much more clearly dominant position than is Petroquisa, and it can exercise greater control over the rules of the game.

Why have joint ventures in the iron ore sphere tended to exclude private national capital? First, CVRD's important local customers are state-owned and foreign-owned steel companies; the private national share of the Brazilian steel industry is small and shrinking. Second, national capital appears to play a much less important political role in the iron ore sector than it does in the petrochemical industry. CVRD's position vis-à-vis the multinationals is strong, and the legitimacy question is not so urgent. Thus the state does not need a domestic ally. Iron ore simply does not have that load of nationalist sentiment that has pursued the oil industry in Brazil during the modern period. It is at least conceivable that there is no need artificially to incorporate private national capital in this particular joint venture precisely because the pressures to legitimize foreign participation are not acute.

As a final example of the role of state as producer in Brazil, I would like to take the case of CEME (Centro de Medicamentos).[21] Unlike the ventures already described, CEME was not a success story, and it serves to illustrate both the contradictions and limitations of state enterprises.

CEME was created in 1971 by the Brazilian state in an effort to fill a major gap in social welfare—providing basic drugs to the mass of the Brazilian people.[22] The INPS (Instituto Nacional da Previdência Social) guaranteed minimal hospital care and also enabled poor patients to consult with physicians. But patients, more often than not, lacked the money to buy the drugs the doctors prescribed. CEME was designed to make medication available to poor people.

Thus, from the outset, the justification for CEME was its role in promoting social welfare. This flew in the face of the mainstream of state policy and created huge problems. For example, given the "life or death" connotations of drug sales, it was extremely awkward for the state to make profits by selling medications. CEME therefore defined its purpose as the distribution of medications without charge to those whose family income did not exceed the minimum wage. Pregnant women, nursing mothers, and children under five were also included; but, generally speaking, it was low-income families that took advantage of CEME.

The venture was dogged by the fact that the state lacked the sources of leverage or competitive strength we have described in previous case studies. For example, the Brazilian state controls no significant natural resource relevant to pharmaceuticals. Indeed, the inputs of the industry tend to be produced in advanced countries by multinational firms. The overall technological edge enjoyed by multinationals in this sector is enormous. The volatility and sophistication of the production technology, the emphasis on product differentiation, and the importance of marketing techniques made the gap between CEME and the leading foreign firms (in terms of production capability) truly impressive. CEME did manage to bring together twenty publicly owned pharmaceutical laboratories, but they were able to produce only eighty types of medications as compared with the thousands of products produced by the subsidiaries of multinational firms. Indeed, CEME's laboratories were unable to produce the advanced antibiotics, steroids, and hormones needed in modern medical practice.

Some of these limitations did not matter. After all, the aim of CEME was to distribute essential medicines that would help cure the illnesses common to the masses. Many of the more sophisticated products of multinational firms were redundant to this goal. However, CEME's weaknesses in the sphere of production undoubtedly undermined its raison d'être in the eyes of Brazilian critics and made it vulnerable to displacement by the much more powerful multinationals.

CEME failed because it was seen as a threat by multinational corporations operating in Brazil, and because the state was not a sufficiently strong supporter of its role and function. In essence, foreign firms wanted CEME to go away, and the Brazilian government was not entirely convinced that it wanted or needed CEME to stay around.

Objectively speaking, there was no real competition between CEME and the multinationals. Their markets and their products were quite different. Multinationals sold expensive, highly differentiated, sophisticated drugs to the middle and upper classes of the prosperous southeast of Brazil. CEME distributed free of charge a small range of basic medications to the poor, many of whom lived in the underdeveloped northeast. Indeed, CEME even helped the multinational firms. For example, in 1973 one-third of the drugs CEME distributed could not be produced in their own laboratories and had to be purchased from the private sector. Thus, CEME actually increased the profitability of multinationals operating in the pharmaceutical sector. However, "buying their products was not enough to turn the multinational corporation into CEME's ally. CEME defined the purposes of the pharmaceutical industry in a threatening way and was looked upon as a potential competitor in the long run." [23]

By mid-1975, CEME had been dismembered. The job of distributing drugs was placed under the Welfare Ministry, and CEME's research activities were transferred to the Ministry of Industry and Commerce.

The history of CEME shows that the growth of state enterprises is far from being automatic. Built around welfare goals, CEME was a long way from reflecting the mainstream of state policy or priorities. Its sole, unequivocal support came from needy members of the lower classes, a group that has little political leverage in contemporary Brazil. CEME also lacked the wherewithal to sustain itself as an independent production unit. Its existence hinged upon a distributive rather than upon a profit-maximizing function; and unlike other "profitable" state enterprises, it could not generate its own investment funds; it therefore could not become an autonomous, self-sustaining entity.

The role of CEME was further compromised by the fact that it was attempting to enter an industry where the competitive strength lay firmly with multinational corporations. CEME might have been forgiven its welfare function if it had successfully combated foreign penetration of the pharmaceutical industry. Indeed, President Scardua went so far as to define the agency goal as "not statism but nationalism, a gradual nationalism." [24] But for technological reasons, the pharmaceutical industry was firmly in the hands of foreign capital, and CEME made little headway on this front.

Before leaving this analysis of the state as producer, we should consider the management and the goals of state firms. A recent survey of the senior personnel in Brazilian public enterprises found that they see themselves as business executives rather than as high government officials.[25] With educational backgrounds and salary levels that compare well with relevant peer groups in private industry, the managerial echelon of state firms have attitudes and behavior patterns more characteristic of aggressive entrepreneurs than of government bureaucrats; and they are as capable of being hostile to "government regulation" as management is in the private sector. This accords well with the notion that the state as producer is primarily concerned with growth, profitability, and efficiency—that is to say, it is propelled by the same logic of accumulation as the private sector.

The financial structure of state firms illustrates this point. From 1966 to 1975 the key public enterprises in Brazil were able to finance from 40 percent to 60 percent of gross investment from retained profits and depreciation funds.[26] This compares favorably with the figure of 50 percent for Brazilian private firms during these years. The bulk of the remaining investment funds were obtained from the foreign-capital market on strictly commercial terms. Estimates vary, but it seems that under 20 percent of total investment was obtained as transfer payments from the government.[27]

State firms in Brazil do not fit the conventional image of government enterprises as inefficient, unprofitable, and overstaffed drags on national growth goals. This view is widespread in the literature. Witness a recent IMF publication: "Government-owned enterprises, rather than serving as a focal point for collecting financial resources for their own investment, or for other purposes, have generally placed a financial burden on parent governments." [28] This statement is certainly not upheld by the Brazilian experience. Indeed, the hardest questions Brazilian public enterprises have to face are not in the sphere of efficiency but in the sphere of equity. On a general level of analysis, it is obvious that state firms have been critical components of a development strategy that has produced a worsening distribution of income and has failed to relieve poverty. But there are more specific ways in which state firms have exacerbated unequal and uneven development.

In the first place, state enterprises have been low absorbers of labor. In the years between 1966 and 1975, value added in the major state firms increased 3.7 times, while employment increased only 1.2 times.[29] In certain enterprises low rates of labor absorption have been particularly pronounced; for example, over the last ten years there has been virtually no growth in employment in the public steel sector despite impressive rates of growth. The fact that Petrobrás generates seven times as much profit and employs one-half as many people as Pemex (the Mexican state oil monopoly) is an eloquent comment on the priorities of Brazilian state enterprises.

Second, the provision of low-cost basic inputs to the manufacturing sector of the economy tends to have inequitable effects. One of the main functions of the state steel industry is to provide adequate supplies of low-cost steel to the auto industry. But the auto industry is dominated by multinational firms and the auto market is confined to an affluent minority group within the population. The end result is that the benefits of public investment are carried off by large foreign-owned firms and the upper-income groups of Brazil.

In summary, it would seem that the expansion of state firms in Brazil has had a private cost-benefit rationale. The overall function of public investment in the production sphere has been to aid and abet the growth process, and scant attention has been paid to ways in which state enterprises might enhance employment or the standard of living for the majority of the Brazilian people.

The State as Financier

The financial roles of the Brazilian state in the modern period serve to illustrate the tremendous scope of state intervention in this late-developing nation.

The use of taxation and expenditure powers is the classic way in which governments have attained their allocative, stabilizing, and distributive goals. In Brazil, government expenditure as a proportion of GDP has risen steadily in the postwar period, from 17 percent in the late 1940s to 37 percent in the mid-1970s.[30] However, such growth in government spending should not be interpreted as the rise of a "welfare state." Data on the allocation of the federal budget show the extremely low priority that has been attached to health and education, areas of social concern that have been allocated a small and shrinking proportion of governmental funds.[31] In 1973, for example, a mere 1.1 percent of the federal budget went to health care, while 21.7 percent was spent on defense.[32] In the same year Brazil spent twice as much on roads and public works as it did on education and health! In view of this it is not surprising that Brazil has the second highest rate of illiteracy in South America and one of the worst infant mortality records in the region.[33] In short, the priorities displayed in the federal budget are in keeping with the military's developmental philosophy described in chapter 4.

Especially since 1964, "order and progress" rather than social welfare for the masses, has been the keynote of government policy making.

In recent years the Brazilian state has moved beyond these traditional financial roles to more innovative areas where it has directly served the needs of the contemporary development strategy. The pre-1964 financial system was clearly inadequate to deal with a rapidly growing and increasingly internationalized economy, and state initiatives and state institutions have been bent to the task of enhancing the capability and efficiency of Brazilian capital markets.[34]

Housing finance is perhaps the area in which financial reforms have been the most thorough and the most far-reaching. This sector constitutes an excellent example of how and why the state has intervened in the capital accumulation process.

There was an early period of "institution building" marked by the creation of an indexing system;[35] by the establishment of the National Housing Bank (BNH); and by the setting up of social security funds under the aegis of the state—for example, the public trust funds, PIS (Programa de Integração Social) and PASEP (Programa de Formação do Patrimônio do Servidor Público), and the National Unemployment and Seniority Fund, or FGTS (Fundo de Garantia do Tempo de Serviço). A second phase saw the creation of private savings and loan institutions that came to contribute significantly to the total finance available for housing through the sale of BNH-guaranteed *Letras Imobiliárias*. This latter development was a function of new public confidence in government and of a tremendous increase in small private savings accounts, guaranteed by the BNH.[36] In other words, it is possible to detect a distinct evolutionary sequence in the housing sector: an early period when state initiatives and state resources set the groundwork for a greatly expanded housing financial network, was followed by a period when the private sector began to contribute to the development effort. A final feature of this process is that the very success of these strategies created savings in excess of what could be absorbed in the housing sector. Consequently the housing bank has broadened its definition of real estate financing to include loans to industries producing building materials and to municipal authorities for sewage systems. While all this activity has helped the civil construction sector, it has done little to increase the provision of low-income housing. In general, unskilled working-class families have been excluded from this program because of the relatively high cost of the individual housing units. (All buyers of BNH housing are subject to indexation and pay a positive rate of interest on their loans.) [37]

However, despite this important qualifier on the equity front (which is after all in line with the mainstream of state policy), the state housing system does represent a significant effort in both the construction and the employment spheres. Most of the initiative has come from the government; indeed, it could hardly have been otherwise, given inflation and the long-run mortgage loans typical of this market. In recent years the private sector has begun to play a more important part in rechanneling savings in this sector, but this happened only after the basic financial institutions had been established by the state.

In the general area of mobilizing "forced" savings, the innovative role of the Brazilian state can be seen most clearly in the creation of PIS and PASEP. These were public trust funds established in the early 1970s to provide retirement benefits for private (PIS) and public (PASEP) employees, through employer contributions in the former case and through an earmarked portion (1 percent) of value-added tax revenue in the latter case. The impact of these programs on income distribution tends to be regressive because the annual distribution of yields (3 percent) is based on each worker's share in the trusts which is determined by wage level and seniority.[38] However, despite this qualifier (which is again in the equity sphere), the PIS and PASEP funds have acquired a massive role in the financial sector. In 1975, for example, they generated a volume of financial resources equal to 45 percent of all the bills of exchange issued by the *Finançeiras* [39] and 80 percent of the resources captured through investment banking institutions. Thus, this particular public-sector initiative in mobilizing funds has reached a stage where it produces a resource base that exceeds that of the major private savings institutions. These funds have now stabilized as a constant proportion of GDP and are *the* major source of savings in the Brazilian economy.

It would be wrong to imagine that state incentives have always been well conceived or successful, as is illustrated by the effort to stimulate the stock market to mobilize equity investment. From early 1968 until June of 1971, stock prices rose twelve times, and the volume of stock transactions rose thirty-five times in real terms. After mid-1971 the market suffered a sharp and prolonged decline; from 1971 to the end of 1974, stock prices fell by a multiple of four, while the general price level rose 1.75 times. Transactions in real terms fell 75 percent. This erratic and disappointing behavior of the Brazilian stock market has been the subject of much debate.

In the first instance, the rapid expansion of the demand for stocks in the late 1960s was due, in part, to the stimulus of general fiscal incentives; and this policy entailed large social costs. Tax exemptions on the distribution of dividends of up to 12 percent of tax liabilities, and tax credit to individuals who purchased mutual funds, were just two of an impressive list of fiscal incentives set up after 1968 by the Brazilian state. Such large-scale use of tax incentives implies substantial forgone government revenue and reduces the ability of the state to intervene more directly, and perhaps more effectively, in capital markets.

A second problem involved the fact that a small number of state enterprises, not private firms, were the major beneficiaries of the expansion of the stock market. In 1974, for example, five state enterprises accounted for 41 percent of total transactions. This constitutes a natural preference on the part of investors, since large state enterprises (such as Petrobrás and Electrobrás) are the only Brazilian companies that guarantee a reasonable dividend and protect the interests of minority stockholders. Thus, in the financial sphere as in the industrial sphere, private national firms suffer from pronounced structural weakness.

A final criticism focuses on the lack of careful planning. The absence of a state regulatory agency similar to the SEC in the United States (compounded by such problems as an inflationary environment, the absence of substantial institutional investors, and thin markets in most stocks) opened the way to considerable manipulation by the large stockholders. It is therefore not surprising that small and medium-sized investors generally abandoned the stock market after 1971 and placed their money in savings accounts.

In summary, the stock market in Brazil, except for the brief period 1971–72, did not turn out to be an important vehicle for capturing private savings. This failure was at least partially the result of ill-considered government action. The stock market proved both expensive and risky and has been abandoned as a major policy instrument.

A distinct division of labor has thus emerged between the public and the private sector over the recent period. The public sector has become much more important in the higher-risk and longer-term credit markets (such as agriculture, housing, and long-term industrial expansion); while the private sector continues to confine its activities to the lower-risk and shorter-term areas of consumer credit (via the *Finançeiras*), and to the rechanneling of government and foreign loans to private borrowers for working capital purposes (via the commercial and investment banks). It is obvious that, because of the pivotal role of the state in mobilizing savings through forced as well as voluntary means (PIS, PASEP, FGTS, and the Caixas Econômicas), Brazil's financial markets differ dramatically from those of developed countries. Given the weakness of the stock market, the private sector's capacity to mobilize savings is limited to *Letras de Câmbio* and the recent growth of private savings accounts. These efforts are still insignificant in comparison with funds generated by the state.

I would like to stress the ways in which a large proportion of the resources for the new financial institutions has been provided, in large part, by a system of forced savings whose burden has been borne by the working classes. Since the late 1960s a number of social security and retirement funds has provided an increasing proportion of national savings, and they comprise the bulk of the funds borrowed by the national treasury, the housing bank (BNH), the national development bank (BNDE), and the official savings banks (Caixas Ecônomicas). In chapter 9 I will explore in some detail the social welfare implications of these new financial structures.

Finally, a word on state financing in the agricultural sector, as this issue also has important welfare repercussions. Throughout the last thirteen years the Brazilian government has made a serious effort to increase agricultural output and productivity. Pro-agriculture policies have included price support programs for crops, subsidies for the purchase of agricultural inputs (such as fertilizer and tractors), and the provision of rural credit at subsidized or even negative interest rates. The programs have been managed by the National Monetary Council (CMN) and channeled through the branches of the Bank of Brazil.

State support of agriculture is an extremely apt demonstration of both the achievements and the limitations of the current development strategy. In sheer growth terms the programs have been a great success. As we saw in chapter 3, commercial cash crop agriculture has prospered and become the nation's "trump card" in the wake of the oil crisis. Agricultural exports reached US$9 billion in 1977, giving Brazil its first trade surplus in four years and making this nation the second largest exporter of agrarian products in the world. But the agricultural success story has incurred large social costs.

The rapid expansion has taken place almost exclusively on lands recently brought under cultivation by rich farmers, and there has been a concentration on cash crops for export. These farmers receive the tax incentives, the soft loans, and the price supports from the state. The older and more traditional agrarian areas, cultivated by small farmers who produce staples for domestic consumption, have been neglected. As a result, domestic food prices have risen at a rate higher than the rate of inflation, with deleterious effects on standards of living among lower-class Brazilians.

Domestic food prices have been so high . . . and have aggravated the widespread malnutrition among the poorest Brazilians. According to the Ministry of Social Assistance, of 800,000 urban residents hospitalized in the first half of 1975, at least 120,000 were children suffering from malnutrition.[40]

There is an interesting distinction between the ways in which the state has structured the money markets in the urban and rural sectors of the economy. In urban financial markets, recent governments have moved toward indexation of loans, positive interest rates, and encouragement for the entry of the private sector; the agricultural sector, on the other hand, constitutes the most deliberately subsidized area of the Brazilian economy.

Self-conscious state underwriting of agriculture is caused by several factors. In the first instance, it is felt that many other policies discriminate against agriculture (for example, overvalued exchange rates and price controls on food products), and it is necessary to redress the balance. Second, it clearly accords with the imperatives of the Brazilian growth strategy, especially the current need to ease the balance-of-payments position by increasing the amount and range of primary commodity exports.

The Theoretical Issues

How does the state as producer and as financier illuminate the theoretical preoccupations of this book? In the first place, the role of the state is bound up with the economic structures of late development described in chapter 3. In the early primary producer economy, laissez faire was the order of the day, and the state kept a generally low profile. The most conspicuous interference with the market by government was in price supports for the coffee sector, a function that the Brazilian state serves to this day. With the onset of industrialization, the state began to play a major role in the structuring of economic reality. Throughout the 1930–64 period governmental initiatives fostered industry in a variety of ways: directly, through investments in basic industry and infrastructure, and indirectly through the creation of a protected internal market, and by devising incentive schemes for industrial investment; the state became the central actor in the import-substituting process. During the recent period of export-led growth, the influence of the state has been even more pervasive. Indeed, as Barros and Graham have put it "the momentum of state activity with its economic and financial power grew substantially more during this period than the [government] either anticipated or desired." [41] As we have seen in previous sections of this chapter, the state as producer of basic goods and services has become the fastest growing segment of the Brazilian industrial economy, while the state as financier has become the prime source of savings.

Second, the role of the state revolves around the political and ideological factors discussed in chapter 4. The modernizing urban-based regime which came to power in the 1930s was strongly committed to industrialization and internal growth. Later on, in the 1960s when the dynamic phase of import-substituting industrialization had come to an end, an authoritarian military regime led the nation into a new cycle of export-led growth. Throughout the modern period the national goals of Brazil have been premised on rapid rates of economic growth. The military tends to couch its goals in terms of a great and secure nation, but *grandeza* (greatness) invariably depends on a rapid expansion of national output.

The timing of industrialization combines with the goals of the modernizing regimes to explain both the causes and the consequences of massive state intervention in Brazilian development processes.

Brazil is a late developer: it did not begin large-scale industrialization until the 1930s. By this stage in the evolution of international economic structures, state intervention was an absolutely necessary condition for industrial takeoff. Government action was required to protect domestic "infant" industries from the goods of advanced nations, and public investment was needed for basic goods and services. The early industrializers in Western Europe and North America were obviously not faced with the problem of having to compete with producers who had more than a century's "head start," and their infrastructural needs were less sophisticated than those faced by twentieth-century developers. Modern industry has a multitude of needs which range from electricity grids to elaborate communication systems. The long gestation periods, the indivisibilities, and the externalities inherent in many of these items make them candidates for public rather than for private investment.

But late development is only part of the explanation. The role of the state is also a function of the goals of Brazilian regimes. Since 1930 national aspirations have been focused on rapid internal growth and *grandeza,* and the state has been part and parcel of this vision of the future. Which is to say, it has become an efficient and powerful agent of accumulation rather than the source of redistributive actions or policies. If the national project had been defined differently, or if, for example, the goals of government had been dominated by such issues as employment creation or the raising of the standard of living of the rural population, the scenario would have been different. In this case the role of state firms may have been to create jobs rather than to produce profits, and the purpose of state agricultural credits would have been to subsidize food production rather than cash crops for export.

Thus, both the timing and the goals of development need to be considered before one can adequately account for the role of the state in the Brazilian growth experience. The pursuit of rapid economic growth in the mid-twentieth century has led to a massive state presence in the modern Brazilian economy, and this fact has confirmed rather than countered the inequitable properties of contemporary growth strategies.

It is important to note that state intervention in the Brazilian economy has not been a deliberate goal of policy. Indeed, many members of the Brazilian elite (particularly private capitalists) are intensely antagonistic to state control or *estatização* (statization). Reasons range from an ideological preference for free enterprise and market mechanisms to a bitter awareness of the fact that state firms have become more powerful than private Brazilian firms and are eating up public resources that might have been used to bolster the private sector. Vocal opposition has resulted in some recent attempts to sell off subsidiaries of state firms to the private sector.[42] However, it is not clear that Brazilian private firms have the wherewithal to buy or manage such companies, and to sell state firms to multinational corporations would offend nationalist feelings within Brazil. The consensus seems to be that state ownership and control of the economy, however much disliked by the Brazilian elite, is here to stay. The contemporary growth strategy is tremendously dependent upon state intervention, and it is difficult to imagine circumstances that would "significantly reverse the increased state involvement in the economy." [43] In short, it is more accurate to see state intervention as an inevitable concomitant of late development than as a self-conscious aim of recent Brazilian governments.

It should be clear by now that liberal-pluralist perspectives are of little help in understanding the Brazilian reality. A minimal state presence and free markets do not describe the optimal path for a nation if that nation is trying to promote industrial growth in the mid-twentieth century. Underdeveloped nations have needed strong interventionist states to compensate for being latecomers to industrial processes and techniques.

More important, the liberal-pluralist school of thought does not begin to address the question of the goals and the priorities of a strong interventionist state. Interest-group theory carefully avoids this issue, as it assumes that all groups within a nation participate in a competitive political arena where rival claims and programs are adjudicated. This is clearly not true in post-1964 Brazil where power resides firmly in the hands of an authoritarian military regime. Precisely because of this lack of representation in a competitive political arena, the Brazilian state has been able to pursue a ruthless, progrowth strategy which has redounded to the benefit of elite groups. In chapter 8 I shall explore the degree to which the rich have got richer in the modern period. The fact that in 1970 the top 1 percent of the population appropriated the same proportion of national income as the bottom 50 percent gives some idea of the contemporary distributional picture.

Marxian analysis is useful in that it underscores the importance of economic imperatives. State firms have become the fastest growing entity in the Brazilian economy *not* through some self-conscious policy of state control but because of the growth requirements of this late-developing nation. Similarly, the state and the multinational corporations have assumed complementary roles *not* because they are natural political partners but because of their common interests in the accumulation process.

However, one can take the economic determinism of much Marxian theory too far. As we found out in chapter 4, the intensity of the drive to *grandeza* in the modern period, the role of a military caste in promoting this objective, and the articulation of both factors with the class structure are extremely complex processes in contemporary Brazil. For example, if the state is merely a committee for managing the affairs of the bourgeoisie, which bourgeoisie are we talking about? In nineteenth-century Britain it might have been clear that we were talking about the national bourgeoisie, but in a late-developing nation such as Brazil this assumption cannot be made. Most policies have promoted the interests of the multinational corporation and the state productive sector (the dominant economic actors of modern growth strategies), and these policies are often contrary to the self-interest of national capitalists. I would agree with Ralph Miliband that understanding the underlying economic forces of society is crucial, but one also has to address the complex interrelationship between economic structures and the social and political reality of actual nations if one is to comprehend the role of the modern state. In this task classical Marxism does not help us.

Corporatist theory sheds light on the contemporary Brazilian reality in at least two ways. It is unambiguous in its acceptance of a strong, interventionist state charting the course of nations; and it is centered on the conviction that the state has a privileged vision of the common good that it can legitimately impose on the populace without the trappings of liberal democracy. However, in some fundamental respects the modern Brazilian state diverges from the corporatist ideal. We must remember that embedded in the corporatist image of the political universe is a state with a moral end, a state that rules in such a way so as to create a good and a just society:

It must forcefully change parts of the actual order which have grown unjust. . . . It must use force against the selfish resistance of the privileged interests that range themselves against the new and juster order.[44]

From the preceding analysis it should be clear that the Brazilian state has played a massive role in forging a highly inequitable development strategy that cannot be the basis for a good and a just society. The morality of such a role is a complex issue and involved around some of the themes of chapter I. For example, how necessary are these costs of growth, and how long will they last, and are there alternative routes to the modern world that involve less human suffering? These questions will be taken up again in the final chapter of this book.

NOTES

1. Jeremy Bentham, "A Manual of Political Economy," in Alan Bullock and Maurice Shock, eds., *The Liberal Tradition* (Oxford: Oxford University Press, 1967), pp. xxiii–xxiv, 28–29; quoted in Alfred Stepan, *The State and Society: Peru in Comparative Perspective* (Princeton, N.J.: Princeton University Press, 1978), p. 8. Part I of this book contains an extremely valuable analysis of concepts of the state.

2. This doctrine was, of course, originally elaborated by Adam Smith in *The Wealth of Nations*, vol. 1, Everyman's Library Edition (London: J. M. Dent, 1954), p. 398.

3. Quoted in Harold J. Laski, *The State in Theory and Practice* (New York: Viking, 1935), p. 3.

4. Karl Marx and Frederick Engels, *Selected Works*, vol. 1 (Moscow: Foreign Languages Publishing House, 1958), p. 36.

5. Frederick Engels, "The Origin of the Family, Private Property and the State," in Marx and Engels, *Selected Works*, vol. 2, p. 295.

6. Engels, "The Origin of the Family," p. 294.

7. Ralph Miliband, *The State in Capitalist Society* (New York: Basic Books, 1969), p. 6; quoted in Stepan, *The State and Society* (note 1), p. 29.

8. Aristotle, *Politics*, Book 1, chap. 2, secs. 14, 15; quoted in Stepan, *The State and Society* (note 1), p. 30.

9. Aristotle, *Politics*, Book 1, chap. 9, secs. 8, 12; quoted in Stepan, *The State and Society* (note 1), p. 30.

10. Leo XIII, *Rerum Novarum* (1881), in Anne Freemantle, ed., *The Papal Encyclicals in Their Historical Context* (New York: New American Library, 1963), p. 174.

11. These data are compiled from the Brazilian magazine *Exame*. See "Melhores e Maiores," *Exame* (Edição especial, September 1979), pp. 125–28. For a discussion of the problems involved in interpreting the data on Brazilian firms, see Werner Baer, Richard Newfarmer, and Thomas Trebat, "On State Capitalism in Brazil: Some New Issues and Questions," *Inter-American Economic Affairs*, 30, no. 3 (Winter 1976): 63–93.

12. Carlos Von Doellinger and Leonardo C. Cavalcanti, *Empresas Multinacionais na Indústria Brasileira*, Coleção Relatórios de Pesquisa no. 29 (Rio de Janeiro: IPEA, 1975), pp. 42–47.

13. Peter Evans, "Entrepreneurship and Alliances: State Enterprise and the Process of Industrialization at the Periphery," mimeographed (Department of Sociology, Brown University, Providence, R.I., 1977), p. 22.

14. Edmar Bacha, "Issues and Evidence on Recent Brazilian Economic Growth," mimeographed (Harvard Institute for International Development, Cambridge, Mass., 1976), p. 32.

15. *New York Times*, 11 April 1976.

16. Maria da Conceição Tavares and Jose Serra, "Beyond Stagnation: A Discussion of Recent Developments in Brazil," in J. Petras, ed., *Latin America: From Dependency to Revolution* (New York: John Wiley, 1973), p. 78.

17. For a comprehensive account of these developments, Peter Evans *Dependent Development: The Alliance of Multinational, State and Local Capital in Brazil* (Princeton, N.J.: Princeton University Press, 1979).

18. Evans, "Entrepreneurship and Alliances," p. 38.

19. *New York Times*, 11 April 1976.

20. The major partner of CVRD in this project was United States Steel. In mid-1977 this corporation was replaced by European and Japanese multinationals.

21. For a detailed analysis, see Evans, "Entrepreneurship and Alliances" (note 13), pp. 49–55.

22. CEME took as its inspiration a statement by President Medici: "I will not allow anyone to become sick because of lack of prevention, or to die from lack of assistance" (quoted in Evans, "Entrepreneurship and Alliances [note 13]," p. 57). This statement is particularly ironic given the fact that Medici presided over Brazil at a time when nutritional standards were falling among poor people and infant mortality rates were skyrocketing. See, for example, Candido Procopio Ferreira de Camargo et al., *São Paulo 1975: Cresimento e Pobreza* (São Paulo: Edições Loyola, 1976).

23. Evans, "Entrepreneurship and Alliances (note 13)," p. 60.

24. João Felicio Scardua, *Opinião.* 20 October 1974, pp. 15–16.

25. Luciano Martins, "A Expansão Recente do Estado no Brasil: Seus Problemas e Seus Atores" (paper presented at the Social Science Research Council, New York, 10 April 1976).

26. Thomas J. Trebat, "The Role of Public Enterprises in the Brazilian Economy: An Evaluation" (paper presented at the Seventh Annual Meeting of the Latin American Studies Association, Houston, November 1977), p. 13. This study analyzes the larger, more established firms in six sectors, including utilities, rails, steel, petrochemicals, and mining.

27. Trebat estimates that, for the larger state firms, public subsidy accounts for one-tenth of total investment needs (see "The Role of Public Enterprises," p. 13). Martins (note 25), on the other hand, for his wider sample, estimates the public-subsidy element to be larger—approximately one-fifth of total investment.

28. Andrew H. Gantt and Guiseppe Dutto, "Financial Performance of Government-Owned Corporations in Less Developed Countries," *IMF Staff Papers.* (Washington, D.C., March 1968), p. 126.

29. Trebat, "The Role of Public Enterprises" (note 26), p. 11.

30. "Quem e quem na economia Brasileira," *Visão,* 31 August 1975, pp. 573–6.

31. A recent report by the World Bank records the fact that between 1965 and 1976 the Brazilian Ministry of Health actually saw its budgetary allocation decline in real terms. The vacuum has been progressively filled by the social security institutes which provide high-cost individual health care for 80 percent of the urban and 40 percent of the rural population. The institutes do not cater to the poorest and the neediest segments of the population. (IBRD *Brazil: Human Resources Special Report* [Washington, D.C., 27 November 1978], pp. 39–41.)

32. United Nations Statistical Yearbook 1976, issue 28, (New York: United Nations), p. 759.

33. Inter-American Development Bank, *Economic and Social Progress in Latin America,* Annual Report of 1974, Washington, D.C. This report finds that Brazil has the third lowest rate of government expenditures on public education per capita in South America.

34. For a comprehensive analysis of these developments, see José Roberto Mendonça de Barros and Douglas H. Graham, "The Brazilian Economic Miracle Revisited: Private and Public Sector Initiative in a Market Economy," *Latin America Research Review* 13 (1978) : 16–29. See also Werner Baer, I. Kerstentsky, and A. Villela, "The Changing Role of the State in the Brazilian Economy," *World Development.* 1, no. 11 (1973) : 23–34; and Maria da Conceição Tavares, *Da Substituição de Importações ao Capitalismo Financeiro* (Rio de Janeiro: Zahar Editora, 1972).

35. I should like to stress the importance of the move toward indexation. The inflationary distortions of the pre-1964 economy had produced a chaotic financial market and low rates of savings within Brazil. Thus, one of the first steps of the new regime was to index all financial instruments. That is to say, a system was set up whereby the principal and the interest on debt instruments were adjusted in accordance with the rate of inflation. It was initially applied to government bonds allowing a noninflationary basis for financing the budget deficit. Indexing was then gradually extended to other financial instruments—the national housing bank (BNH), to savings deposits, savings and loan

associations, and corporate debts. See discussion in Werner Baer and Paul Beckerman, "Indexing in Brazil," *World Development* 2, nos. 11, 12 (October–December 1974): 35–49.

36. It should be remembered that indexed returns for private savings accounts are, in effect, guaranteed by the government through the BNH. Thus, private savings institutions have their risks significantly reduced by state intervention.

37. The relatively high rents charged for BNH housing (which had been billed by the government as housing for the poor) became the subject of the satirical play by Chico Buarque and Pavlo Pontes, *Gota D'Aqua* (Rio de Janeiro: Editora Civilização Brasileira, 1976).

38. See Alfonso C. Pastore and José Roberto Mendonça de Barros, "O Programa de Integração Social e Mobilização de Recursos para o Desenvolvimento," *Estudos Economicos*, 2, no. 4 (1972): 2–17.

39. Consumer credit, operated by the *Financeiras*, is the oldest segment of the private financial market in Brazil. They appeared at the end of the fifties accompanying the growth in consumer durables manufacturing. *Financeiras* acquired funds by issuing bills of exchange (*letras de câmbio*) which could be sold with a discount, thereby permitting a real rate of return for buyers of this paper. The typical installment plan could range from three months to three years.

40. *New York Times*, 14 April 1977.

41. Barros and Graham, "The Brazilian Economic Miracle Revisited (note 34)," p. 6.

42. In February 1979 key economic figures in Figueiredo's new government announced their intention of selling state companies to the private sector. For example, there was a proposal to sell all the Petrobrás subsidiaries. However, "it is obvious that no-one in the private sector possesses sufficient funds to make a serious bid for companies of such magnitude" (*Latin America Economic Report*, 9 February 1979, p. 175).

43. *Latin America Economic Report*, 19 August 1977, p. 253.

44. Heinrich A. Rommen, *The State in Catholic Social Thought: A Treatise in Political Philosophy* (St. Louis and London: B. Herder, 1945), p. 292.

CHAPTER

7

The Multinational

Corporation

Working through great corporations that straddle the earth,
men are able for the first time to utilize world resources with
an efficiency dictated by the objective logic of profit.
George W. Ball

MULTINATIONAL CORPORATIONS dominate the most important
and most dynamic sectors of Brazilian manufacturing industry. In the late
1970s, 50 percent of total assets in manufacturing were owned by multinational firms, and 41 percent of the largest firms in Brazil were subsidiaries of multinational corporations. Sectors such as automobiles, pharmaceuticals, and electrical equipment were almost totally controlled by
the multinationals. This massive presence of foreign capital in Brazilian
industry has been the subject of much debate. The multinationals have
been accused of undermining the sovereignty of the nation, of worsening
the plight of the poor, and of creating a development model for the rich
molded in the image of Madison Avenue.

Many of these accusations contain at least a grain of truth. Multinational firms have monopolized some of the key sectors of industry
and weakened the role of private national capital. They have also been
the vehicle through which rich country goods and capital-intensive
technologies have been transferred into Brazil from the advanced world.
However, despite these facts, it is wrong to place too heavy a burden
of guilt on the shoulders of the multinationals. Multinational firms, in
and of themselves, do not destroy national independence or cause poverty; they are merely part of that chain of causality spelled out in other

sections of this book. The main purpose of this chapter is to demonstrate how the pursuit of rapid growth in the mid- and late-twentieth century has led to a large and increasing role for foreign capital within the domestic economy, and how this has exacerbated the uneven and unequal attributes of Brazilian development.

Some Background Characteristics

Multinational corporations are large and enormously powerful components of the world's economic system.[1] Taking the usual criterion and comparing the gross annual sales of multinationals with the gross national product of countries, one comes to the rather startling conclusion that General Motors is slightly bigger than Switzerland and a good deal bigger than Venezuela; Ford is bigger than Iran, South Africa, and Colombia; and IBM is twice as big as Chile and Peru. Even when one takes the more limiting criterion of value added to production, the gross annual sales of the top ten multinationals are still bigger than the GNP of eighty nations, and the value added by all the giant corporations is equal to one-fifth of world production. All of which contributes to a formidable picture.

Second, their rate of growth is extremely rapid. Over the last two decades multinationals have grown at an average rate of 10 percent per year, or three times the rate of growth of most advanced industrial nations. Much of this dynamism is due to expansion abroad rather than in home operations, and it is in the overseas markets that profits are highest. In the early 1970s, 122 of the top United States-based multinationals had a higher rate of profit abroad than at home. To cite some examples: the pharmaceutical industry earned a rate of return of 22.4 percent on its overseas assets and 15.5 percent on its domestic operations; while in the office equipment field, the overseas profit was 25.6 percent as compared with 9.2 percent at home. Needless to say, this discrepancy in profit margins has spurred United States corporations to shift an increasing proportion of their total assets abroad. By the mid-1970s, 40 percent of the United States auto industry and 75 percent of the electronics industry were located overseas. Indeed, today the foreign operations of United States firms constitute one of the largest economies in the world, smaller only than the domestic economies of the United States and the Soviet Union.

A third and extremely important feature of multinational corporations is their oligopolistic structure. There is a high degree of concentration in geographic origin—the United States alone accounting for one-third of the total number of foreign affiliates; Britain, France, West Germany, and the United States together accounting for over three-quarters. Moreover, direct foreign investment tends to be a characteristic of a small group of large firms within each country of origin. For example, in the mid-1970s, 250 firms controlled 70 percent of the direct foreign investment emanating from the United States, while in Britain 165 firms accounted for over 80 percent of the total. In the host country, the affiliates of multinational corporations exhibit typical oligopolistic behavior. They operate in markets that are dominated by few sellers; they compete largely through product differentiation; and they rely on barriers to entry to preserve their competitive edge. This latter condition is created both by economic factors (economies of scale, threshold size), and by the protectionist policies of host governments (tariffs, import licenses). As we shall see later in this chapter, through such factors as privileged access to capital, advanced technology, and sophisticated managerial and marketing techniques, multinationals are able to sustain and reinforce their oligopolistic position.

In short, multinational corporations are huge, rapidly growing oligopolistic structures which increasingly control the productive processes of the capitalist world.[2] To understand the raison d'être of these corporations and to assess their impact on national economies in the Third World, we need to place these facts in a wider perspective.

The Theoretical Background

The theoretical literature on direct foreign investment in the underdeveloped world is vast—full of attempts to explain, justify, or cure the phenomenon in question.[3] The various schools of thought are products of radically different conceptions of what constitutes the optimal development path for nations.[4]

On the right hand of the theoretical spectrum lies the business school approach.[5] The essential ingredients of this school of thought are: (1) an acceptance of the existing distribution of income both between and among nations; (2) an implicit belief in the moral and practical virtues of the free enterprise system; (3) a disregard for the overall social and political effects of an extension of this system to other countries; and (4) recommendations for government policy that center on the well-being of business enterprises and call for an environment of stability and noninterference. In other words, policies that are conducive to good business.

A related but more academic line of analysis can be found in neo-classical economic theory. While this orthodox brand of economics is only marginally concerned with the inner workings of multinational firms, it is, nonetheless, based on assumptions that lead to similar prescriptions of laissez faire and maximization of capital flows.

Neoclassical theory is grounded in the notion that since foreign investment constitutes a flow from capital-rich to capital-poor countries, it comprises a net addition to the investible resources of the host country and, as such, contributes positively to the growth process. The underlying assumption is that the resultant style of development is desirable. In particular it implies that the market constitutes the best determinant of economic and social welfare, and that the distribution of income produced by market forces is both appropriate and beneficial to the populace. In the case of foreign investment in underdeveloped countries, this assumption is fairly strong. It takes as a given that the products introduced by the multinational firm, the technologies used to produce these products, and the tastes induced in the indigenous population all enhance social welfare in the host country.

In summary, the business school and the neoclassical approaches to foreign capital are based on the premise that the free enterprise system is the most efficient means of promoting growth, and growth is assumed to enhance social welfare. The policy implications of these schools of thought are clear: nations are advised to minimize controls on capital, to restrict government interference in the market, and generally to cooperate with foreign investors.

A shift in emphasis from the virtues of international capital to a more critical stance leads to the dependency and Marxist schools of thought. These theories question in a fundamental way the role of foreign capital in the Third World; and the viewpoint is the interest of the host country rather than of the investing firm or the capital exporting country.[6]

The dependency school, which originated in Latin America, stresses the following factors.[7] Foreign investment has various external effects that are capable of damaging underdeveloped countries. These include the suppression of domestic entrepreneurship; the adoption of unsuitable technology and inappropriate products; and the extension of oligopolistic practices, such as product differentiation and heavy advertising, into the Third World.

An important distinguishing characteristic of the dependency approach is the way in which it stresses the broad ramifications of the capitalist development process, of which foreign investment is but one element. This school of thought analyzes the social, political, and economic consequences of the penetration of capitalist institutions and methods into underdeveloped countries and concludes that the dependent status of these countries can never permit genuine development. The remedies are seen as sweeping changes in both external relations and internal power structures.

The Marxist approach to foreign investment is distinguished by its emphasis on class conflict.[8] While the dependency school is concerned with promoting a national development strategy in which the eventual class structure is left ambiguous, the Marxist School is quite explicitly concerned with socialist development. The final class structure is thus clearly defined and is neither attainable within the existing political framework of most underdeveloped countries, nor compatible with integration into the international capitalist system. The remedy therefore is seen as internal revolution and complete rejection of foreign capital. Modern Marxists have generally employed the concept of an economic surplus being extracted from, or pumped out of, underdeveloped countries by foreign investors. Where the dependency school talks of the dangers of dependence, the Marxist approach speaks of neo-imperialism and exploitation. The analysis therefore lies even further outside the scope of orthodox economics, and all the values of the capitalist system are under attack.

Before assessing the relevance of these conceptual frameworks to the themes of this book, we need to turn to a detailed examination of the Brazilian case. My main preoccupation will be with the interaction between foreign capital and social welfare issues. Specifically, I explore the degree to which industrialization via the multinational corporation has affected—or failed to affect—the standard of living of the mass of the Brazilian people.

Foreign Capital and the Industrialization of Brazil

Foreign capital had been present in Brazil before 1930 and the advent of modern industrialization. During the last half of the nineteenth century both Britain and the United States invested large amounts of money in Brazil, mostly in portfolio holdings. Bonds and other capital notes were important factors in the expansion of railroads, telegraphs, and utilities. By 1880 the stock of foreign capital was estimated at US$190 million; this was to grow to US$2.6 billion by 1930.[9] About one-half of foreign capital in Brazil during this period was British and one-quarter was American. However, one should not overemphasize the importance of foreign investment in the early development of Brazil, since little foreign capital was involved in producing the country's major export commodities of sugar, minerals, and coffee.

As we have seen in previous chapters of this book, in the 1930s and the 1940s a complex series of factors led to the self-conscious industrialization of Brazil; and, as a result, the role of foreign capital changed dramatically. World events (the Great Depression, World War II), the organization of industrial activity in the advanced nations (the emergence of the giant oligopolies and their spread overseas), and changes in domestic policies (the setting up of barriers to trade and the strategy of import-substituting industrialization) all led to a significant shift in the pace and the format of industrial development. Over the last fifty years, Brazil has evolved from being a stagnant agricultural country into the most important industrial nation in Latin America. This transformation has been intimately linked to the multinational corporation.

By the 1930s the Brazilian market was beginning to look immensely attractive to United States corporations; and in order to avoid the new tariff barriers, direct investment in manufacturing plants within Brazil came to replace exports from home operations. This change in emphasis can be followed in the pages of *Brazilian Business*, a magazine published by the American Chamber of Commerce.[10] Throughout the 1920s it concerned itself with Brazilian imports from the United States. Numerous articles analyzed potential markets for United States business, and it was obvious that investment was seen primarily as a way of stimulating trade. In the 1930s, with the new international climate and the protectionist policies of the Vargas government, direct foreign investment became a major theme in this business journal. The April 1932 issue contained an editorial on the difficulty of importing with the lowered exchange rate, and it suggested that United States corporations invest in manufacturing in Brazil in order to avoid losing these markets to local competition. By 1935 the editorials were describing at great length, and with considerable enthusiasm, the advantages of foreign capital and foreign skilled labor for Brazilian development. The editors' hopes were not disappointed, for during this period an increasing number of United States firms opened subsidiaries in Brazil.[11]

Foreign direct investment in manufacturing rose rapidly in the postwar period of accelerated import substitution. Total United States investments tripled between 1946 and 1961, and the percentage going to manufacturing increased from 39 percent to 54 percent (see table 10). By the end of the Kubitschek era, roughly one-third of Brazilian manufacturing was controlled by foreign capital.

This dramatic expansion of the multinational corporation into Brazil was a direct result of the import-substituting policies of successive Brazilian governments.

As we saw in chapter 3, a program of protecting the domestic market inaugurated, somewhat inadvertently, in the depression and war years was greatly strengthened in the post-1946 period of self-conscious and accelerated industrialization. Key policy instruments included prohibitive tariffs for light consumer goods and consumer durables, and the subsidization of capital goods imports. Because of recurrent foreign exchange shortages and the lack of a domestic technological capability, Brazilian governments increasingly favored foreign investors who would agree to import industrial equipment for the production of those goods given high priority by the government. These tended to be sophisticated consumer durables, products urgently desired by Brazilian elite groups. An example of governmental encouragement in this period is SUMOC Instruction 113 issued in 1955. This measure allowed foreign enterprises to import equipment at 45 percent below the tariff level and exempted them from providing foreign exchange cover for imported machinery. This latter privilege was not enjoyed by Brazilian-owned firms and provoked the following rather bitter comment from the president of the Brazilian Federation of Industry: "In this way, there was created veritable discrimination against national industry. We do not plead for preferential treatment but for equal opportunities." [12]

This increasingly favorable official attitude toward foreign investment was also reflected in the profit remittance regulations. Between 1946 and 1953 a complex set of controls on foreign exchange and remissions was in operation, and these controls had the effect of curtailing outflows. In 1953 a system of free currency exchange was adopted; and for the rest of the decade, controls on profit remittances were virtually eliminated.

In short, the era of easy import-substituting industrialization (1930–64) saw rapid industrial growth, particularly in the consumer-durables sector, and a heavy reliance on foreign direct investment. Industrial production grew at 9.6 percent per year during this period, and one-third of this growth was due to the activities of multinational corporations.[13] This phase of growth reached a climax in the vigorous "developmentalism" of the Kubitschek era. His government offered foreign enterprises easy credit, protection from imports, favorable profit remission conditions, and a vastly improved infrastructure.

As we know from previous chapters, economic growth rates began to fall precipitately in the early 1960s. Goulart, faced with soaring inflation and balance-of-payments difficulties, responded with a leftist stabilization program that included a severe limit on profit repatriation. Private foreign investment slowed to a trickle. In 1962 only US$9 million entered the country—down from an average of US$110 million in the four previous years.

In 1964 the Goulart government fell in a military coup, and the new authoritarian regime quickly moved to contend with the severe problems of the Brazilian economy. To deal with the critical state of the balance of payments, the military regime aggressively sought out foreign investment. The *cruziero* was devalued, capital markets were reorganized, and the laws that placed a ceiling on profit remittances from the affiliates of multinational corporations were rescinded. As a result of these policies, foreign capital once again began to flow into Brazil in large amounts.

Multinational corporations have played an extremely important role in the post-1964 development strategy. Multinationals have remained dominant in the manufacturing economy but have become increasingly concentrated in the larger-scale and more profitable sectors. Table 8 illustrates that 35 percent of the largest five hundred enterprises in Brazil were foreign-controlled in 1978; the foreign presence was especially significant among the largest firms (41 percent of the top twenty-five were foreign-controlled). These large multinational firms tend to be in the fastest growing and the most profitable segments of manufacturing.[14] For example, in the late 1970s the multinationals controlled 99 percent of the automobile industry, 84 percent of the pharmaceutical industry, 76 percent of the plastics industry, and 66 percent of the electronics industry (see table 9). Over the last decade these sectors have been the fastest growing areas of the Brazilian industrial economy (see table 3). Generally speaking, the slower growing and less technologically sophisticated areas of industry (such as clothing, shoes, and food processing) have remained the preserve of Brazilian private capital.

As a response to the elaborate export promotion programs of recent Brazilian governments (see discussion in chapter 3), multinational corporations have become successful exporters. By 1976, Brazilian multinationals were exporting manufactured goods worth close to US$5 million—45 percent of the total exported that year. Some 63 percent of this trade was interaffiliate, meaning that multinationals are increasingly choosing Brazil as a base from which to serve other markets.[15] This decision is eminently rational. The Brazilian government offers exporters an elaborate series of subsidies and provides a stable, pro-business political climate in which to operate. It is also true that, given the products of multinational firms and the highly unequal income distribution in Brazil, it makes better sense for firms to expand horizontally and tap elite markets in other Third World nations than to rely on the emergence of a mass market within Brazil.

In summary, multinational corporations have been critical actors in the modern industrialization of Brazil. In the period of import substitution they were largely responsible for creating the domestic capability to manufacture sophisticated consumer goods. And in the succeeding cycle of export-led growth they have been crucial in making Brazil a successful exporter of manufactured goods. In both eras they have been a prime stimulus to extremely rapid rates of growth within the Brazilian manufacturing economy, and they constitute an important reason for the fact that Brazil is now the most important industrial nation in Latin America.

Why have multinational corporations played such an important role in the industrialization of this late developing nation? And how have they managed to oust national firms from the "commanding heights" of the Brazilian manufacturing economy?

The Economic Power of Multinational Firms

Despite the conventional wisdom of orthodox theory, direct foreign investment rarely constitutes a simple flow of monies from capital-rich to capital-poor countries. An analysis of time-series data demonstrates that the net flow is often the other way around and that the sums involved can be dramatic. A recent inquiry by the Brazilian Congress (reported in table 11) found that the eleven most active multinationals have brought US$238 million into the country throughout the history of their operations (some going back half a century); and that over the last ten years they have taken out US$774.5 million.[16]

It is rather surprising that direct foreign investment has ever been thought of as a straightforward addition to capital formation in the host country. After all, a rational capitalist will invest only if the asset is likely to yield a return above and beyond the original investment.

Therefore, the economic power of multinational corporations is not primarily vested in their role as suppliers of capital. As Shane Hunt puts it,

Capital presents the fewest problems. It can be borrowed overseas from banks, bond markets, or international official agencies, and it can be mobilized domestically. For all the emphasis given foreign investment in Latin American development, it should not be forgotten that the bulk of savings funneled into investment in Latin American countries comes from domestic sources.[17]

Recent research by both orthodox and dependency theorists has emphasized the competitive edge of multinational corporations that is vested in production, managerial, and marketing technologies and in privileged access to finance, particularly foreign exchange.

Let us first examine the question of technology. It is obvious that important segments of Brazilian industry are technologically dependent on multinational corporations. This has been true throughout the period of modern industrialization and is a predictable consequence of the strategy of development followed by successive Brazilian regimes (described in chapter 3 and summarized in earlier sections of this chapter). Put simply, given that the original import-substitution drive was geared to demand emanating from the middle and upper classes in Brazilian society, domestic manufacturing was increasingly engaged in producing sophisticated goods. This led to a reliance on the technological and organizational skills monopolized by the giant corporations of the advanced capitalist countries. Even with ample capital and foreign exchange, Brazilian industrialists could not compete in the dynamic sector of their own home market without taking foreign firms as partners. Witness the Matarazzo empire.

When *Fortune* described it in 1960, it was the largest Latin American firm, with sales of over 1% of Brazilian GNP. It had been completely internally financed until 1959. Yet it was quite backward technologically. Over half its production was in textiles, and a large part in food products. To begin to produce more advanced products, it had to enter into partnership with B. F. Goodrich, Dow Chemical, and Union Carbide, among others.[18]

The technological superiority of multinational firms over local producers is a multifaceted phenomenon; but whether one is talking about techniques of production or marketing know-how, it is the economics inherent in using tried processes over and over again that makes it so difficult for private domestic firms to compete with multinational operations. As the Brazilian elite group reproduces the demand profile of advanced capitalist countries, multinationals are able to capitalize on the production and administrative know-how that they have developed in their home operations. While this technical capacity is available to the foreign firm at zero marginal cost, Brazilian companies, beginning manufacture of these products, have to acquire it through licensing agreements and production experience. This situation is the basis for technological dependency. Multinational corporations are profit-maximizers; they have a huge vested interest in the extant technology. As 98 percent of research and development expenditure has taken place in the advanced world, this technology is capital-intensive and labor-saving and produces goods appropriate for the mass markets of rich countries.[19]

I find this argument fundamental in explaining the raison d'être of technological transfer from the advanced to the underdeveloped world.

Once these basic premises are accepted, it becomes inevitable that multi-national corporations should attempt to translate their products and their technologies into the new environment. If they find a certain lack of congruence between advanced world techniques and Third World markets, it is more profitable to change the market to fit the product than vice versa.

Many economists seem surprised when they turn up such findings as "there has been very little in the way of technical adjustments in product designs or production techniques," [20] as multinational firms move into developing countries, and a burgeoning literature attempts to define more suitable technologies for the Third World. Amartya Sen, for example, views the current "menu" as inappropriate and seeks technological solutions that better fit the factor endowment of the country concerned.[21] While E. F. Schumacher in his search for more relevant techniques has suggested three types of labor-intensive manufacturing (which he calls home industry, village industry, and small industry), ranging from US$30 per work position to US$750 per work position.[22] These schemes are extremely attractive in that they can create jobs at a fraction of the current cost of work positions in technologically advanced industry.

However, despite the theoretical appeal of these more appropriate technologies, they have had little practical impact in poor capitalist nations. The reason should be obvious from my previous discussion. National industrialization strategies have often been built around elite demand for sophisticated consumer goods. This had led to a heavy reliance on the multinational corporation whose self-interest lies in the transfer of well-tried, capital-intensive techniques from the advanced world. Thus the technology utilized in an underdeveloped country such as Brazil has little to do with the indigenous-factor endowment or with the needs of the mass of the population. Of course, in theory there exists a wide range of techniques for making most products, and the number of possible product-mixes is virtually limitless. But actual industrialization strategies are minimally concerned with theoretical plausibility: the choice of both product and technology is a function of political power and economic constraints.[23] In Brazil political power has been wielded by an elite group that has promoted an industrialization strategy geared to its own consumption needs. While the constraints of late development have given multinational firms a critical competitive advantage in producing the goods desired by this elite group.

What is the precise nature of the technological edge exercised by multinational firms? First, I would define technology as the skills, the knowledge, and the procedures needed for making and selling products. This broad definition includes administrative systems and sales apparatus as well as machinery, and it helps one get away from the notion that technology should be equated with hardware. We must remember that many of the products manufactured by multinational firms in under-developed countries have standard and relatively well-known engineering and production techniques. Obviously there are exceptions. As mentioned in chapter 6, the petrochemical and pharmaceutical industries are characterized by complex and highly volatile production technologies that in themselves give multinationals a competitive edge. But in the late 1970s it is not difficult to find out how to make an automobile or a refrigerator; and in these sectors the competitive strength of multinational firms is increasingly vested in management and marketing know-how rather than in the hardware of production.

Management technology (the administrative superstructure of modern firms) has become increasingly important to multinational corporations. The huge size and the far-flung nature of contemporary operations involve, among other things, elaborate corporate hierarchies, finely tuned incentive structures, sophisticated financial systems, advanced planning techniques, and a vast weight of specific skills embodied in senior personnel. It should be obvious that local firms in underdeveloped countries find it inordinately hard to compete in this sphere. Ever since Joseph Schumpeter's famous work on the subject, economists have recognized the huge, comparative disadvantage that poor nations labor under while acquiring the managerial skills of modern industry. Moreover, because of the long gestation period inherent in the educational process, it is impossible to rectify the situation overnight. Brazil did not have a university until the 1920s, and until very recently only a tiny proportion of the adult population received a college education. As a result, the country has experienced a chronic shortage of high-level manpower.

In the sphere of marketing technology, multinational corporations undoubtedly wield a great deal of economic power through their use of sophisticated sales and communications techniques. Barnet and Muller have called it "that extraordinary competitive edge they acquire by using the techniques of market manipulation to shape tastes, goals and values." [24]

The main avenue for market conditioning is advertising. It is an extremely powerful tool in shaping tastes and promoting desires for the products of advanced consumer societies.[25] The advertising industry in Brazil has been heavily dominated by such international giants as McCann-Erickson, J. Walter Thompson, and Ogilvy and Mather, who represent European and Japanese firms as well as the principal American multinational corporations. It seems that advertising agencies have followed multinational firms into the markets of the Third World. In 1954 the top United States advertising agencies derived a mere 5 percent of total billings from overseas campaigns; in the early 1970s, one-third of the US$7 billion business came from outside the United States, and a significant proportion of this came from less-developed countries.[26]

Advertising has played a critical role in promoting the Brazilian style of development. To give an idea of the level and rate of growth of advertising expenditure: in 1974, US$911 million, or 1.3 percent of the Brazilian GNP was spent on advertising; this represented an increase of 33 percent over the previous year, and it was more than the federal government spent on health care during that year.[27] Television, magazines, and newspapers are the most effective weapons for tapping the elite market, while radio, billboards, comic strips, and again television seem to be the favorite media for disseminating the advertising message to lower-income groups. In essence, the Brazilian elite has been induced into American-style living, and the working class has been persuaded to buy powdered milk, Marlboro cigarettes, and Ritz crackers instead of rice and beans. As we shall explore in chapter 8, this sacrifice of essentials (those goods necessary for physical survival) in order to buy luxury items has had a deleterious effect on the standard of living of the poor.

Marketing technology is an extremely potent source of power for the multinational firm and yet it has been neglected in the literature. This is because economists, preoccupied as they are by the myth of consumer sovereignty, have ignored the phenomenon of induced demand. As Tibor Scitovsky has put it, "The economist's approach to his subject tacitly assumes that consumers know what they are doing and are doing the best they can, so that the economist's only task is to see to it that the economy delivers what consumers want." [28]

But most goods produced in affluent capitalist economies are unnecessary in the physiological sense of that word, and the sale of these goods is dependent upon the creation and conditioning of tastes. We are not born needing, or even wanting padded bras, pegged jeans, or deodorants: demand for such items is created by the elaborate battery of advertising techniques devised by Western consumer society. In other words, "production only fills a void that it has created itself!" [29]

One is led to the conclusion that multinational corporations are not engaged in a vicious attempt to subvert and impoverish the peoples of the Third World; instead, they are merely transmitting to underdeveloped countries techniques of demand manipulation that are typical of their home countries. At least part of the explanation of why capital-intensive luxury products are marketed through glossy magazines and color television in poor countries lies in the rational profit-maximizing behavior of the giant corporations. Multinationals extend tried techniques of production and marketing to the underdeveloped world because it is the least-cost solution for themselves. They know how to make, manage, and sell their current bundle of goods, so why trade in a perfected product and successful marketing technique for some costly alternative? It makes much better sense to shape consumer tastes to fit the product, rather than to embark on the costly business of changing the product to fit the needs of a poor country. The social welfare repercussions of this behavior within the host country are often extremely negative, but from the viewpoint of the firm it is eminently rational behavior.

Special Privileges

A second source of power for the multinational firm revolves around privileged access to finance—namely, easier access to foreign exchange, availability of intra-firm capital, access to cheaper credits, and superior ability to take advantage of government subsidies. I should like to stress that in all these areas the multinational corporation has an advantage over private national firms, not in the availability of money in any simple sense, but in the form of finance (whether in the local currency or in foreign exchange) and in its terms (the rate of interest and the length of the loan).

The foreign-exchange constraint on Brazilian industrial growth has often become apparent with a fall in the price of coffee on the world market. For example, in the mid-1950s coffee prices fell severely, and the Brazilian government immediately redoubled its efforts to increase the inflow of foreign capital to replace export earnings. Two government policies, Instruction 113 (described earlier in this chapter) and a series of decrees encouraging foreign automobile companies to start manufacturing vehicles in Brazil were particularly instrumental in encouraging direct foreign investment into Brazil. The automobile industry is worth emphasizing as it represents one of the more spectacular success stories of the modern period. Growth rates in this sector have been extremely rapid, and by the mid-1970s Brazil was the eighth largest producer of cars in the world. Operating under oligopolistic market conditions and behind tariff barriers, foreign car manufacturers in Brazil have been able to make large profits. As *Business Week* has put it:

Though the risks are high as the auto makers move out into the "third" world markets, the potential for big rewards is also high. Nothing shows this more graphically than the sudden surge in auto production in Brazil. . . . Josef Rust, Chairman of VW's supervisory board says that "the company chose Brazil as the country for our greatest investment outside Germany." And he chortles, "the returns to the parent company are frightening." Indeed, many in the industry maintain that it was only because of the high returns from its South American operations that VW remained in the black during its disasterous years in the Northern Hemisphere markets in 1970 and 1971.[30]

The foreign exchange constraint was not the only reason for a foreign-dominated auto industry in Brazil—there were also severe technological problems; but in the mid-1950s local firms would have found it extremely difficult to import the capital equipment necessary for such a venture given the balance-of-payments situation of the Brazilian economy.

The greater intra-firm capital resources available to multinational corporations are a result of the wide profit margins of these firms and their consequent ability to reinvest. Table 11 demonstrates that multinationals have typically reinvested more than their initial capital, despite significant profit remittances to the parent company.

A third factor is cheaper credit. Multinational corporations are generally seen (by both the national and the international lending communities) to be better credit risks than local firms. As a consequence, they often receive longer-term loans with lower interest rates than domestic enterprises. Multinationals are also more flexible in their source of finance. When domestic sources dry up or become expensive, they are able to turn to alternative credit sources (international or home country) in a way that is impossible for local firms. This differential in the cost of credit becomes particularly important in times of recession. In the 1964–67 "stabilization" period and during the 1974–75 slowdown, domestic firms had a rough time. In the more recent period *Latin America Economic Report* predicted that "The tightening of credit will hit the smaller Brazilian businesses more than the transnational subsidiaries which have much greater ease in obtaining overseas loans. It is thus feared that the numbers of mergers and bankruptcies may well increase recalling the bad old days of 1966–67."[31]

A final consideration is their ability to take advantage of government subsidies. Over the last decade, the military government in Brazil has set up an elaborate panoply of incentives, at least some of which are directed at multinationals. They include tax holidays, export subsidies, and the underwriting of capital goods imports. The result has often been discrimination in favor of foreign enterprises. This has provoked bitter comment from members of the Brazilian Congress.

Apparently, Brazil is to grant General Motors tax exemptions and other advantages worth over $1 billion in the next ten years to enable the company to hike sales by 5% and export local GM goods more aggressively. . . . Or, there is the case of Volkswagen, whose budget is bigger than the budgets of several of Brazil's northeastern states; in 1973, its operations came to $1.76 billion. Last year, because of tax exemptions offered by the government, the company was allowed to buy 1,400 square miles of land in Para state—an area only slightly smaller than Luxembourg—for a cattle ranch! This kind of investment incentive reportedly cost the Brazilian government $707 million or almost what it has had to pay for all its chemical imports during an entire year.[32]

No wonder Brazilian capitalists complain of unfair competition!

The Impact of the Multinational Corporations

Thus, through their control of production, managerial, and marketing technology, and through their privileged financial status (both nationally and internationally), multinational corporations have increasingly dominated the leading sectors of the Brazilian manufacturing economy. What impact has this had on the course of Brazilian development? There have been immediate and dramatic consequences in the spheres of growth, national sovereignty, and social welfare.

In the realm of economic growth, foreign direct investment has played an extremely positive role. The modern history of Brazil demonstrates that multinational corporations have stimulated impressively high rates of industrial growth within the domestic economy. By providing foreign exchange, cheaper investment funds, and a multifaceted technological capability, multinational firms have helped Brazil to radically and permanently expand her productive capacity. Whether one likes the political and social results of this style of development is a much more complicated issue and revolves around those value judgments discussed at the beginning of this chapter.

Business school and neoclassical theorists have, in the main, been content to demonstrate the growth-producing properties of foreign investment. The effect of this growth in host economies is simply assumed to be positive. The more critical dependency and Marxist schools of thought have been intensely concerned with the impact of direct foreign investment on national control of the productive apparatus and with the social welfare repercussions of this pattern of development.

The fact that half of Brazil's manufacturing economy is controlled by foreign firms produces two types of vulnerability. In the first place, decisions as to what products are going to be produced and which technologies are going to be used are made to further the global profit-maximizing goals of multinational firms, rather than to promote the objectives of national governments. Second, decisions as to levels of investment are intimately bound up with how parent companies view the business climate in the host country, and they may have little to do with targets set by domestic planners. If a regime becomes stridently nationalist and sets limits on the activities of foreign firms, or if labor becomes restive and disruptive, multinational corporations may just "clear off" and set up subsidiaries in another "friendlier" host country.

Brazil has dealt with these problems of national control fairly successfully. The priorities of modern regimes (particularly in the post-1964 period) have not diverged fundamentally from the private profit calculations of multinational corporations, and, in the main, foreign firms have advanced the growth goals of successive Brazilian governments. In addition, over recent years, Brazil has been able to limit the activities of multinational corporations in certain politically sensitive areas of the economy.

Since the late 1960s both Western Europe and Japan have dramatically increased their investments in this country, and today at least three advanced nations (the United States, Japan, and West Germany) are heavily invested in Brazil (see table 10). This allows the national government to play firms off against each other and dictate tougher terms to multinationals operating within the domestic economy. As we saw in chapter 6, in some sectors of the economy, joint ventures between the state and multinational corporations have become the norm, and over the course of the last two years, state companies have managed to exert control over the important minicomputer market (despite strong pressure from IBM and Burroughs).[33] In addition, Brazil has moved toward tighter controls on payments for foreign technology.[34] However, such "renegotiation of the terms of dependence" has been within strict limits. Brazil has gained a little more state control over her productive apparatus, but multinationals still operate in what they rightly view as an environment extremely favorable to their activities.

In the sphere of social welfare, the repercussions of multinational firms have been quite negative. One of the most direct ways of tracing the interaction between multinational corporations and poverty in Brazil is to examine the impact of these firms on employment.

In chapter 9 I describe the broad demographic and employment trends in contemporary Brazil. Briefly, fast rates of population growth (particularly in urban settings) have combined with relatively slow rates of employment creation in the industrial sector to produce a situation where only one-sixth of the total working population has industrial jobs. And "the service sector has become a refuge for an overgrown urban labor force, mopping up those who would otherwise be unemployed."[35]

What responsibility do the multinationals bear for this situation? The concensus seems to be that despite their dominant position in the manufacturing economies of countries such as Brazil "the size of the workforce directly created by and within the activities of the TNE's [Transnational Enterprises, another term for multinational corporations] appears to be quite marginal as compared to the requirements for employment in the Third World."[36] Indeed, the total labor force of the multinational subsidiaries in the manufacturing, mineral, and commodities sectors of all developing countries "is smaller than four million people, and more likely it should be around the two and a half million mark." [37] This approximates the employable population of the city of São Paulo!

This pronounced tendency of multinational firms to generate little employment despite their rapid expansion in the Third World hinges on three factors.

First, there is their scale of operation. The large-scale production techniques typical of multinational firms greatly facilitate capital-intensive activities.[38] Second, the products and the processes introduced by the multinationals create an industrial structure in underdeveloped countries that is geared to the factor endowment of rich countries (where labor is less plentiful and much more expensive). This seriously limits employment possibilities in the Third World.[39] According to the United States Tariff Commission, multinational affiliates accounted for only 8 percent of total employment in the Brazilian manufacturing sector in 1970, despite the fact that they controlled almost half of this sector.[40] In chemicals, multinational majority-owned affiliates accounted for 18 percent of total employment, in electrical machinery 34 percent, and in transport equipment 28 percent of total employment. In all of these individual sectors multinational firms were dominant (see table 9).

A final factor is that foreign companies tend to displace a large number of labor-intensive, small-scale national enterprises, thus significantly decreasing the number of jobs available in the private national sector. In Brazil, for example, the percentage of new manufacturing affiliates established through the acquisition of local firms was 60 percent of the total in the early 1970s.[41] And as national firms are progressively displaced in the domestic market, the remaining ones are driven to adopt production and marketing practices similar to those of multinational corporations if they wish to compete effectively with foreign subsidiaries. In the process of adopting modern, sophisticated technology, local firms become less labor and more capital intensive.[42]

Theoretical Implications

Left-wing theorists from both the dependency and the Marxist schools of thought have highlighted the ways that multinational corporations have distorted development strategies in the Third World so as to create extremes of wealth and poverty. These interpretations are often too simplistic and linear and tend to seriously underestimate the interactions between domestic power structures and foreign capital. As we have seen, the products and the technologies of multinational firms tend to exaggerate inequality in poor countries (primarily through their failure to create enough employment), but in no straightforward sense do multinationals cause poverty.

We are in that world of multiple and cumulative causation I first described in chapter 1. Multinational corporations entered Brazil, not in a self-conscious effort to "distort" national development, but in response to the industrialization policies of post-1930 modernizing regimes. In the years of easy import substitution, successive governments threw up barriers to trade (import licenses and tariffs) which gave the greatest degree of protection to goods that had previously been imported (sophisticated goods for an elite group). As the financial capability (in particular, access to foreign exchange) and the technological expertise required to manufacture these identical products were effectively monopolized by the giant international firms, the dynamic sectors of Brazilian manufacturing came to be dominated by foreign capital and by the multinational firm. In the post-1964 period this pattern was reinforced as multinational corporations benefited from the new policies of export promotion. In short, foreign capital has obviously exacerbated the uneven and unequal properties of modern industrial growth in Brazil, but it seems that the fault lies at least as much with the programs and priorities of successive Brazilian regimes as with the multinationals.

The interaction between the domestic power structure and foreign capital takes on various guises. For example, some of the policies of Brazilian governments have affected multinational corporations in an extremely direct and tangible way. The 1964 change in the profit remittance regulations, and the subsequent series of tax incentives designed to attract direct foreign investment, had an obvious and fairly immediate impact on multinational firms operating in Brazil. Other government policies have had a less direct effect. Export incentives, for example, are available to most segments of Brazilian industry, and yet the multinationals have been in the best position to take advantage of such subsidies. Similarly, the infrastructural and basic industrial investments of Brazilian governments have indirectly promoted the profitability of multinational firms by subsidizing the inputs to their manufacturing processes.

Conversely, the multinational corporation has affected the domestic power structure in a variety of ways. As we learned in chapter 4, foreign capital was extremely supportive of the 1964 coup and had at least some responsibility for the coming to power of a "pro-business" authoritarian regime in Brazil. Multinational corporations have also played a role in bolstering the contemporary Brazilian power structure. Multinational firms are both capital- and skill-intensive; that is to say, they employ a small and well-educated segment of the urban population. This privileged group of Brazilians have realized large material gains over the last two decades. (As we shall see in chapter 8, managerial salaries in the manufacturing sector rose at the rate of 8 percent per year in the late 1960s and early 1970s.) Naturally there is a realization that much of this new affluence is linked to the pro-foreign capital policies of recent military governments. In other words, the multinational corporations have contributed to a highly concentrated form of prosperity and have enhanced domestic support for an elitist and authoritarian power structure. As Bruton has put it:

Multinational corporations are there because of national strategies yet we must always remember that the presence of powerful multinational corporations in the local economy will itself tend to affect the political forces in a way so as to reinforce the *status quo*. Firms do not simply react to market signals but also contribute towards shaping them.[43]

By now it should be obvious that the multinational corporation is not the evil genius of the conspiratorial literature, capable at one fell swoop of installing military dictatorships and producing grinding poverty within Third World nations. In Brazil, at least, there is a much more interactive and symbiotic relationship between foreign capital and successive domestic power structures.

An important consequence of this complex intertwining of factors is that it makes poverty and inequality singularly intractable. As inequitable development is at least partially rooted in the policies and priorities of domestic power structures, "getting rid of the multinationals" will not guarantee a better deal for the poor. Simply turning over the productive structure to "national firms, producing the same goods and services as those of the TNE's and exercising similar business practices" [44] will not create more employment or generate a more positive social welfare result than leaving things in the hands of multinationals. Indeed, the net effect of such reformist policies might actually be detrimental to the well-being of the populace. Multinational corporations have, after all, promoted rapid growth and created prosperity for a minority. Kicking them out usually entails large economic costs. These themes will be taken up again in my final chapter.

NOTES

1. For some of the best-known critical accounts of the activities of multinational firms, see J. J. Servan-Schreiber, *Le Défi Américain* (Paris: Editions de Noël, 1967); Raymond Vernon, *Sovereignty at Bay: The Multinational Spread of U.S. Enterprises* (New York: Basic Books, 1971); John H. Dunning, ed., *The Multinational Enterprise* (London: George Allen and Unwin, 1971); John H. Dunning, ed., *International Investment* (London: Penguin, 1972); C. Tugendhat, *The Multinationale* (London: Penguin, 1972); Richard J. Barnet and Ronald E. Muller, *Global Reach: The Power of the Multinational Corporations* (New York: Simon & Schuster, 1974); United Nations, Department of Economic and Social Affairs, *Multinational Corporations in World Development* (New York: Praeger, 1974); Constantine Vaitsos, *Intercountry Income Distribution and Transnational Enterprises* (Oxford, England: Clarendon Press, 1974); T. H. Moran, *Multinational Corporations and the Politics of Dependence* (Princeton, N.J.: Princeton University Press, 1974); Robert Gilpin, *U.S. Power and the Multinational Corporation: The Political Economy of Foreign Direct Investment* (New York: Basic Books, 1975); United Nations, Centre on Transnational Corporations "Transnational Corporations in World Development: A Re-Examination" (New York: United Nations, 1978).

2. Figures relating to size, rate of growth, and oligopolistic structure of corporations were obtained from Vernon, *Sovereignty at Bay*, pp. 3–26; Barnet and Muller, *Global Reach*, pp. 13–26; UN, *Multinational Corporations*, pp. 1–29.

3. For an excellent survey of the literature relating foreign investment to the development process in the Third World, see Sanjaya Lall, "Less-developed Countries and Private Foreign Direct Investment: A Review," *World Development* 2 (April–May 1974):43–48.

4. The relevance of value judgments in development economics has been treated by Gunnar Myrdal in *Asian Drama: An Inquiry into the Poverty of Nations* (New York: Vintage Books, 1972), pp. 30–55.

5. A good illustration of this kind of work is S. M. Robbins and R. B. Stobaugh, *Money in the Multinational Enterprise* (New York: Basic Books, 1973). Robbins and Stobaugh build a sophisticated model of how multinational corporations can greatly raise

their profits by a better use of transfer prices and other financial channels. The fact that the cost of such policies is often borne by the host country is not considered relevant to the "optimum" strategy proposed.

6. See discussion in P. P. Streeten, "The Multinational Enterprise and the Theory of Development Policy," *World Development* 1, no. 10 (October 1973):1–14.

7. See, for example, Theotonio dos Santos, "The Structure of Dependence," *American Economic Review: Papers and Proceedings* 60, no. 2 (May 1970): 231–36; O. Sunkel, "National Development Policy and External Dependence in Latin America," *Journal of Development Studies* 5 (1969–70): 23–48; and S. Hymer, "The Multinational Corporation and the Law of Uneven Development," in J. N. Bhagwati, ed., *Economics and World Order* (New York: Macmillan, 1972), pp. 113–40.

8. See, for example, H. Magdoff, *The Age of Imperialism* (New York: Monthly Review Press, 1969); A. G. Frank, *Lumpenbourgeoisie and Lumpendevelopment* (New York: Monthly Review Press, 1972); and T. E. Weisskopf, "Capitalism, Underdevelopment and the Future of the Poor Countries," in J. N. Bhagwati, ed., *Economics and World Order*, pp. 43–77.

9. Richard S. Newfarmer and Willard F. Mueller, *Multinational Corporations in Brazil and Mexico: Structural Sources of Economic and Noneconomic Power*, Report to the Sub-Committee on Multinational Corporations, Committee on Foreign Relations, U.S. Senate, 94th Congress, 1st session, (Washington, D.C.: Government Printing Office, August 1975), p. 96.

10. See analysis of this source in Frank Ackerman, "Industry and Imperialism in Brazil," *Review of Radical Political Economics* 3 (Spring 1971):22.

11. Eric N. Baklanoff, ed., *New Perspectives on Brazil* (Nashville, Tenn.: Vanderbilt University Press, 1966), p. 112.

12. Andre Gunder Frank, *Capitalism and Underdevelopment in Latin America* (New York: Monthly Review Press, 1969), p. 182.

13. Newfarmer and Mueller, *Multinational Corporations* (note 9), p. 98.

14. Newfarmer and Mueller demonstrate that if one confines the analysis to the manufacturing sector of the Brazilian economy, multinational corporations controlled 50 percent of the net assets of the 300 largest firms in 1972 (*Multinational Corporations*, p. 113).

15. Peter Evans and Gary Gereffi, "Foreign Investment and Dependent Development: Comparing Brazil and Mexico," mimeographed (Brown University, Providence, R.I., March 1979), p. 46.

16. Brazilian–American Chamber of Commerce, Inc., *News Bulletin* 6, no. 75 (1976): 2.

17. Shane Hunt, "Evaluating Direct Foreign Investment in Latin America," Discussion Paper no. 23 (Princeton University, Princeton, N.J.), p. 14.

18. Sylvia Ann Hewlett, "The Dynamics of Economic Imperialism: The Role of Direct Foreign Investment in Brazil," *Latin American Perspectives* 11, no. 1 (Spring 1975):140.

19. Frances Stewart, "Technology and Employment in LDC's," in Edgar O. Edwards, *Employment in Developing Nations* (New York: Columbia University Press, 1974), p. 100.

20. Stewart, "Technology and Employment," p. 117.

21. See Amartya Sen, *Employment, Technology and Development* (Oxford, England: Clarendon Press, 1975), pp. 3–81.

22. E. F. Schumacher, *Small Is Beautiful* (New York: Harper & Row, 1973), pp. 163–223.

23. See discussion of this point in Frances Stewart, "Choice of Technique in Developing Countries," *Journal of Development Studies* 9, no. 1 (October 1972):114.

24. Barnet and Muller, *Global Reach* (note 1), p. 175. A more complete treatment of the same theme can be found in Stuart Ewen, *Captains of Consciousness: Advertising and the Roots of the Consumer Culture* (New York: McGraw-Hill, 1976); and Armand Mattelart *La Cultura como Empresa Multinacional* (Mexico City: Serie Popular, 1974).

25. A good example of taste transfer to poor nations can be found in Steven Langdon, "Multinational Corporations, Taste Transfer and Underdevelopment: A Case Study from Kenya," *Review of African Political Economy*, no. 2 (1975):12–35.

26. *Advertising Age*, August 1974, vol. 45.

27. *Advertising Age*, January 1977, vol. 48.

28. Tibor Scitovsky, *The Joyless Economy* (New York: Oxford University Press, 1976), p. 9. See also discussion by Joan Robinson in *Aspects of Development and Underdevelopment* (Cambridge, England: Cambridge University Press, 1979), pp. 113–14.

29. John Kenneth Galbraith, *The Affluent Society* (Boston: Houghton Mifflin, 1958), p. 153.

30. *Business Week*, 24 November 1973.

31. *Latin America Economic Report* 4, no. 12 (March 1976):47.

32. *Latin America Economic Report*, 6 January 1978, p. 7.

33. Capre, the government body that sets the rules for the electronics industry, has banned multinationals from important market sectors such as minicomputers. The idea is to reserve these markets for Brazilian firms. *Latin America Economic Report*, 6 July 1979, p. 207.

34. *Latin America Economic Report*, 3 March 1978, p. 66.

35. See discussion in Stephen H. Hellinger and Douglas A. Hellinger, *Unemployment and the Multinationals* (London: Kennikat Press, 1976), p. 22. In 1960 in Brazil one-third of the working population was in the service sector; a decade later, the percentage had grown by 5 percent, and much of the work consisted of marginal activities.

36. Constantino V. Vaitsos, "Employment Problems and Transnational Enterprises in Developing Countries: Distortions and Inequality," mimeographed (Geneva: International Labor Organization, 1976), p. 1.

37. Vaitsos, "Employment Problems," p. 2.

38. Most research undertaken in developing countries demonstrates that large-scale production is significantly less labor-intensive than small-scale firms. See discussion in *ILO Employment, Incomes and Equality: A Strategy for Increasing Productive Employment in Kenya* (Geneva, 1972).

39. For an excellent analysis of how sophisticated technologies can seriously limit employment, see Stewart, "Choice of Technique" (note 23), pp. 92–121; and G. K. Helleiner, "The Role of Multinational Corporations in the Less Developed Countries' Trade in Technology," *World Development* 3, no. 4 (April 1975):161–90.

40. *United States Tariff Commission, Implications of Multinational Firms for World Trade and Investment and for U.S. Trade and Labor*, Report to the Committee on Finance of the U.S. Senate (Washington, D.C.: Government Printing Office, January 1973), pp. 609–11. The Tariff Commission's figures are generally agreed as being an underestimation, since they represent only the sample of parent firms that were "reporters" in the Commerce Departments 1970 survey. However, even if one doubles the figures, multinationals still generate very little employment in Brazil relative to their share of manufacturing.

41. Evans and Gereffi, "Foreign Investment" (note 14), p. 40.

42. The following example illustrates this process very well.
One country imported two plastic injection-moulding machines costing $100,000 with moulds. Working three shifts and with a total labour force of forty workers they produced 1.5 million pairs of plastic sandals and shoes a year. At $2 a pair these were better value (longer life) than cheap leather footwear at the same price. Thus, 5,000 artisan shoemakers lost their livelihood; this, in turn, reduced the markets for the suppliers and makers of leather, hand tools, cotton thread, tacks, glues, wax and polish, eyelets, fabric linings, laces, wooden lasts and carton boxes, none of which was required for plastic footwear. As all the machinery and the material for the plastic footwear had to be imported, while the leather footwear was based largely on indigenous materials and industries, the net result was a decline in both employment and real income within

the country. (Edgar Owens and Robert Shaw, *Development Reconsidered* [Lexington, Mass.: D. C. Heath, 1972], p. 107).

43.   H. J. Bruton, "Economic Development and Labour Use: A Review," *World Development* 1, no. 12 (December 1973) :22.

44.   Vaitsos, "Employment Problems" (note 36), p. 18.

PART III

Social and
Political Results

CHAPTER

8

Poverty and Inequality

In human societies extremes of wealth and poverty are the
main source of evil. . . . Where a population is divided into
the two classes of the very rich and the very poor, there can
be no real state; for there can be no real friendship between
the classes and friendship is the essential principle of all
association.

Aristotle

THE PURPOSE of this chapter is to examine the nature and the depth
of poverty and inequality in Brazil, and to explore the relationship of
these phenomena to the growth process. As I explained in chapter 1, the
recent "discovery" of persistent and massive poverty in the Third World,
and the suspicion that economic growth "by itself may not solve or even
alleviate the problem within any reasonable time period"[1] has triggered an awakening of interest in the link between growth and equity.

The controversial work of Adelman and Morris in 1973 set the terms
for much of the recent debate. In a large cross-sectional sample of
underdeveloped countries, they found that the development process is
accompanied by an absolute as well as a relative decline in the average
incomes of the very poor, and that "the only hope of significantly improving the income distribution in these countries lies in a transformation of the institutional setting."[2] In concluding their book they state
that:

The frightening implication of the present work is that hundreds of millions of
desperate people throughout the world have been hurt rather than helped by
economic development. Unless their destinies become a major focus of development policy in the 1970s and 1980s, economic development may serve merely
to promote social injustice.[3]

These findings have certainly frightened orthodox economists. Papanek, Paukert, and Little have all tried hard to discount the book, pointing to methodological and statistical problems; [4] and a more sophisticated study of Ahluwalia does seem to undermine some of the more pessimistic findings of the Adelman and Morris work.[5]

When one goes from these aggregate cross-sectional studies to the experience of particular countries through time, the picture is even more confusing. The burgeoning literature in this field has uncovered evidence of increasing inequality juxtaposed with rapid growth in a sizable number of the more mature, underdeveloped countries. These include Brazil, Peru, Argentina, Mexico, and Malaysia.[6] South Korea and Taiwan, on the other hand, seem to have achieved some redistribution with growth; [7] while in India, the distribution has apparently remained invariant with nearly stagnant income levels.[8] Colombia and Puerto Rico demonstrate yet another relationship between growth and equity.[9] In these countries growth has proceeded at satisfactory rates with highly concentrated but unchanging patterns of income distribution.

This recent flurry of empirical investigations has produced little consensus as to the trends in the relationship between growth and equity in the Third World and few suggestions as to what might be the causal link between these two phenomena. This is at least partially because of long-established biases in economic theory.

Some Conceptual Problems

Modern economic theory has, for the most part, ignored questions of poverty and inequality. Neoclassical theorists have concentrated on maximizing efficiency within society and taken themselves "out of the theoretical-philosophical discussion of how income ought to be distributed." [10] This stance has generally been justified on the ground that "more is better," and as long as economic analysis concerns itself with producing more aggregate income, the equity question will take care of itself. The implicit assumption has been that growth is accompanied by improved social and political conditions, and that the main barrier to a better world order lies in the sphere of production (see discussion in chapter 1).

This bias has produced a situation where much of orthodox welfare theory is concerned with issues that carefully avoid judgments on the distribution of economic rewards in society.[11] Take the concept of Pareto optimality. There is an infinite set of Pareto optimal points open to society; each point is characterized by a distinct distribution of income. The theory properly used does not tell us how to distinguish between various Pareto optimal points; it only guarantees that each point represents a position from which no change is possible, such that someone could become better off without making someone else worse off. In other words, if the lot of the poor cannot be made any better without cutting into the affluence of the rich, the situation would be Pareto optimal despite glaring disparities between the rich and the poor. This conclusion hardly makes the air electric with expectations when discussing questions of social justice in underdeveloped nations!

Another influential thread running through conventional economics is the conviction that the appropriate measure of social welfare is the level and rate of growth of GNP. However, GNP is merely the money measure of the overall flow of goods and services in an economy. It tells you nothing about the interpersonal distribution of this sum. It therefore is possible to conceive of a situation where the mass of the people receive stagnant or falling incomes, but GNP continues to grow because of the enhanced prosperity of a rich minority. This is particularly possible in an underdeveloped context where aggregate production figures are often little affected by what happens to the incomes of the bottom 60 percent of the population. In Brazil, for example, the combined share of the top 40 percent of the population amounts to well over three-quarters of total GNP. Thus, the rate of growth of GNP measures essentially the income growth of the more prosperous urban classes.

In some of the recent literature, alternative criteria have been suggested. One idea is that equal social value be given to a 1 percent increase in income for any member of society. Thus, a 1 percent increase in income for the poorest group would have the same weight in the overall performance measure as a 1 percent increase in income for the richest group, even though the absolute increment involved is very different. Another suggestion is a "poverty-weighted" index that would strengthen the relative influence of lower-income groups.[12] However, interesting as these alternative measures are, they have yet to be used seriously as yardsticks of economic performance.

It should be stressed that economists have not ignored or assumed away distributional issues through some collective slip of the memory. Ignorance is rarely arbitrary, and this lacuna in the discipline exists for some highly rational reasons. As Myrdal has put it:

People who are better off have usually done their best to keep their minds off the equality issue. In the first place, they have tried to remain ignorant of the poverty and distress of the poor people—even of the living conditions in their own national communities. . . . In every country there have been whole systems of psychological and ideological barriers protecting the well-to-do from knowledge of social facts which would be embarrassing to them.[13]

Economists have not been eager to face the fact that economic growth does not and cannot mean prosperity for all, and, with few exceptions, they have chosen to bury their heads in the sand on this uncomfortable issue.

Poverty and Inequality in Brazil

The existence of massive poverty, the extreme concentration of income, and the increase in inequality during recent years are now accepted facts of contemporary Brazilian development.[14]

The distribution of income in Brazil is highly unequal. As can be seen from table 12, concentration of income in the hands of the top 20 percent of the Brazilian population is considerably more exaggerated than in developed countries, and somewhat more exaggerated than in several other capitalist Third World nations. Furthermore, there has been a considerable increase in inequality over recent years.

Table 13 details the nature of the distributional trends during the 1960–76 period. Despite the high growth rates that characterized much of this period, and at least some absolute gain by each decile, the majority of the Brazilian population lost out in relative terms in the years 1960–76, while the richest 10 percent increased its share of national income from 39.6 percent in 1960 to 50.4 percent in 1976. In other words, of the total gain in the Brazilian GNP during this period (and we must remember that the global product more than doubled) the richest strata of the population appropriated three-quarters, and the poorest, 50 percent less than one-tenth. This dramatic increase in inequality within the size distribution of income was matched by polarization on other fronts. Urban incomes grew much more rapidly than did rural incomes; those with university education increased their incomes four times as fast as those with little or no education; and, of the various regions of Brazil, only the richest, the state of São Paulo, registered an above-average increase in income. A striking example of the degree of concentration of income in contemporary Brazil is the fact that in 1976 the top 1 percent of the population received a larger slice of national income than the bottom 50 percent of all Brazilians!

Table 13 presents the most recent overall figures for the distribution of income in Brazil. However, various more fragmentary types of evidence help us obtain a more detailed picture.

Data published by the Ministry of Labor in Brazil demonstrate a significant widening of wage differentials within the urban labor force during the late 1960s and early 1970s. Wages in the lowest earnings bracket fell in real terms, and the ratio of the average wage in the top class relative to the bottom class rose from 28.2 percent in 1969 to 40.5 percent in 1973. To make the polarization more pronounced, there was a rise in the population for both these classes.[15]

Edmar Bacha and Eduardo Suplicy have analyzed relative wages in specific Brazilian industries. The most dramatic points to emerge from these studies are the steadily worsening position of the unskilled and the extremely rapid rise in managerial salaries. The Bacha data, for example, indicate that unskilled workers experienced a steady decline in their wage rates between 1966 and 1972.[16] Skilled workers gained a modest increase in wages over this interval, while managers, starting from an extremely high-base salary level, increased their earnings at the rapid rate of 8 percent per year (in real terms) over the 1966–72 period. The Suplicy figures dealing with a different sample and a slightly later time period, reveal a similar picture of big gains going to managerial groups; however, in this study, low-level workers do experience a small absolute increase in their incomes.[17]

In summary, it seems that a variety of sources points to a widening of the gap between the rich and the poor in Brazil and to an extremely dramatic concentration of income within the top decile of the population.

When we turn from this relative picture to absolute standards of living, the data are less clear cut.

Defining the poverty level in any national context is a tricky business because of the degree to which minimum standards of food, clothing, and shelter are culturally as well as physically determined.[18] In Brazil a rather crude measure of poverty can be obtained by using minimum wage figures, as these represent a minimum standard of living that is specifically geared to national economic and social conditions. Applying this criterion to 1970 census data, we find that slightly more than 50 percent of working individuals and 30 percent of families failed to earn the minimum wage in this year.[19] Regional disaggregation reveals an even more depressing picture, for the bulk of the population in the poorer states lived on incomes that were well below the official minimum. In Piaui (a small state in the northeast of Brazil) census figures show that in 1970, 90 percent of employed individuals earned less than the minimum wage for that state.

Other non-income indicators of living standards tend to confirm the presence of widespread and miserable poverty in Brazil.

The National Household Expenditure Study (ENDEF) conducted in 1974–75, contains the most complete and careful data to date on nutrition in Brazil.[20] This survey finds that first-degree (that is, mild) malnutrition affects 37 percent of all Brazilian children through age seventeen, while 20 percent are estimated to be suffering from second-degree (that is, severe) malnutrition. Severe malnutrition stunts growth, and this growth deficit becomes permanent if it is not made up before adolescence. Many experts suspect that brain growth is impaired by severe malnutrition, and that such mental impairment is irreversible.

In regard to health, "it appears that general health conditions in Brazil are poor compared with countries at similar per capita GNP levels." [21] Infant mortality is twice as high as this comparable sample, and estimates based on official death registration statistics show increasing infant mortality rates in certain metropolitan areas during the middle and late 1960s (see table 14). The incidence of malaria, Chagas' disease, and schistosomiasis remains high over wide geographic areas (malaria, for example, is reported over 80 percent of Brazil), and the Brazilian government has failed to produce effective mass-control measures for any of these debilitating diseases. In addition, there are large regional disparities in health standards. In the 1960s and early 1970s life expectancy in the prosperous southeast of Brazil was over sixty years, while for low-income urban households in the five northeastern states life expectancy was forty years.

While there is little dispute over the continued existence of massive poverty in Brazil, trends in absolute living standards over the last two decades have been hotly disputed.

On the optimistic side, the data contained in table 13 do seem to indicate that all deciles of the Brazilian population improved their absolute income levels in the 1960–76 period. There are additional positive signs from the years of the "miracle." In the early 1970s, when the growth rates were impressively high, there was considerable evidence of a tight labor market particularly in the industrial heartland of São Paulo. This would seem to be confirmed by the Suplicy figures, which demonstrate that both unskilled and skilled labor gained wage increases over these years.

However, this positive image has to be qualified by some negative evidence. As can be seen from table 15, the post-1964 period has witnessed a shrinking in the real value of the minimum wage. Between 1964 and 1968 the minimum wage fell dramatically, and since that date there has been some sporadic slippage (see discussion in chapters 3 and 4). This drift downward in the value of the minimum wage has been countered by some fall in the number of workers earning the minimum wage.[22]

Other negative signs come from recent trends in the labor market. The slowdown in growth since 1974–75 has produced stagnant or shrinking real wages and higher rates of unemployment in at least some sectors of the economy. IBGE (Instituto Brasileiro de Geographia e Estatística) in a recent publication demonstrated a mere "2.6% increase in employment between August 1976 and August 1978."[23] This represented half the rate of growth of the population of Brazil during these years and a quarter of the rate of population growth in the urban centers. The construction sector is an excellent example of how the recent slowdown in growth has impacted on the job opportunities and upon the standard of living of the working classes. In the early to mid-1970s, construction employed 7 percent of the Brazilian labor force, and average wages (including overtime) paid on building sites in São Paulo were two and one-half times the minimum wage. By 1978 wages in this sector were only 28 percent above the minimum wage, and the work force had been cut down considerably (by as much as 60 percent in São Paulo and Rio Grande do Sul).[24]

Finally, there is some forceful negative evidence from the city of São Paulo. Greater São Paulo is the largest (9 million people in 1972), the most dynamic, and the most prosperous region of Brazil, with only 19 percent of its workers earning less than the minimum wage (as opposed to twice this figure in the nation as a whole). Nonetheless, the fruits of economic growth have been spread around extremely unevenly, and poverty (measured in terms of income levels, infant mortality rates, and sanitary and nutritional standards) seems to be on the increase.

A study by DIESSE (Departamento Intersindical de Estatística e Estudos Sócio-Econômicos) demonstrates that the average working-class family experienced an absolute as well as a relative decline in its income level between 1958 and 1969 (see table 16). The salary of the average head of household fell by one third during these years; and in spite of the fact that other members of the household entered the work force in order to compensate for this decline, family income still fell by 9.4 percent.[25]

On the health and nutritional fronts, recent trends have been similarly depressing. Between 1960 and 1973 the rate of infant mortality in São Paulo increased 45 percent (to a high of ninety-seven deaths per thousand live births). The proportion of dwellings served by running water fell from 61 percent in 1950 to 56 percent in 1973; the percentage of the population linked to sewage fell from 35 percent in 1971 to 30 percent in 1975; and, in 1970, 52 percent of the population of greater São Paulo was officially classified as suffering from malnutrition, as opposed to 45 percent in the mid-1960s. All this adds up to an extremely grim and deteriorating social welfare picture in this, the most prosperous city of Brazil.[26]

It is precisely this juxtaposition of great and growing wealth with massive human suffering that has most offended critics of the Brazilian military regime. As the *New York Times* has put it:

the Brazilian dictatorship proclaims in the press and at international conferences the Brazilian economic miracle with a GNP growth of 11%. But it hides from the world the fact that out of every 1,000 children born in Brazil, 100 die before reaching the age of one; that in 1968, in the region of Amarizi, near the city of Recife, all the children born between the months of July and December died without the occurrence in the region of either an epidemic or a catastrophe. . . . Why did they die? They died victims of diarrhea, vitamin deficiency, lack of medical assistance or due to poor hygienic conditions.[27]

Before concluding this account of the nature and the depth of poverty in contemporary Brazil, a word is in order on the fate of the Amazonian Indians. They have been largely forgotten in the heated debate that has raged over Brazilian development, and yet the systematic destruction of the remaining Indian tribes in the Amazon basin constitutes a dramatic example of the human costs of Brazilian development. As Shelton Davis has put it:

the massive amount of disease, death and human suffering unleashed upon Brazilian Indians in the past few years is a direct result of the economic development policy of the military government of Brazil. . . . large private, state and multinational corporations, the principal ingredients in the Brazilian model of development, have systematically expropriated Indian resources.[28]

Despite a long history of disease and deculturation, as the Brazilian frontier moved westward, there remained in the mid-1950s a major concentration of indigenous tribes (numbering approximately 200,000 people) in the Amazon and central regions of Brazil. Over 120 Indian communities inhabited this immense area, living in small tribal groups that numbered between 100 and 500 individuals. Most of the tribes subsisted from hunting, fishing, and gardening activities and maintained close attachments to their ancestral territories.

This way of life became increasingly incompatible with Brazilian development goals. By the early 1960s the Amazon basin was seen as a source of vital economic resources. With "79.7% of the country's lumber resources, 81% of its fresh water, half its iron ore deposits, 93% of its aluminium and the largest deposit of rock salt in the world," [29] it became the target for active exploitation.

The 1964 coup was decisive, as the new military government was more firmly committed to rapid economic growth and less concerned with the human consequences of its economic programs than had been true of previous Brazilian regimes (see discussion in chapter 4). Three policies have been particularly important in worsening the plight of the Indian population in the post-1964 period.

First, the military regime has endorsed the rights of private companies to exploit the rich mineral and agricultural resources of the

Amazon basin. Second, the government has introduced a series of fiscal and tax incentives for promoting cattle raising and agribusiness projects in the interior. Third, a series of crash-spending programs has been launched to open up and colonize this area. For example, "Operation Amazon" was set up in 1966 with the goal of spending US$2 billion on the development of transport, power, communications, and natural resources in the region; and PIN (Plano de Integracão Nacional), inaugurated in 1971, was an immensely ambitious scheme centered around the building of a trans-Amazon highway and the colonization of land by settlers from the northeast.

The disastrous effects of these programs on the indigenous Indian population have been documented by the International Red Cross and by APS (Aborigines Protection Society) reports on Indian policy in Brazil.[30]

Take the Waimiri-Atroari tribe which lives in a large jungle area north of Manaus. In the early 1970s the Brazilian government decreed a special reserve for the Waimiri–Atroari in the state of Amazonas. At the same time plans were laid for a road that would connect the city of Manaus with Boa Vista and pass through the new Indian reserve. It provided the only military route to the Venezuelan frontier, and it terminated in the north at large molybdenum deposits. As the road threatened to destroy the territorial integrity and the economic viability of the Waimiri–Atroari, the tribesmen made it clear that they would rather die fighting than give up their lands. The last few years have seen violent confrontations between the Waimiri–Atroari and agents of FUNAI (the official Brazilian foundation in charge of Indian affairs), and the tribe is being wiped out.

A similar depressing saga can be told about the Kreen–Akarore and the Parakanan tribes which have been reduced to a handful of people as a result of highway building. A recent account describes the sickness and despair typical of the remaining tribesmen.

We found two temporary houses along the Santarém–Cuiabá highway and a population of 35 persons all suffering from colds, including Kreen Akarore Chief Iaquil, who did not know where he was. . . . The customs of the tribe have degenerated and tobacco and alcohol now form parts of their new habits.[31]

The few remaining Kreen-Akarore women were aborting their children rather than produce offspring who would have to face the new conditions of their tribal life.

In summary, the likelihood of survival of the indigenous Brazilian population has diminished considerably in the recent period. In the pre-1964 era, the major threats to the Indians were small-scale rubber collectors, hunters, and traders. Over the last fifteen years the Brazilian government has entered the picture with massive programs of highway construction, mineral exploitation, and agricultural colonization. These policies "are not to be blamed on a series of bureaucratic blunders but are an organic part of the development strategy and the 'economic miracle.' "[32] They have entailed the systematic destruction of the indigenous Indian culture of Brazil.

The facts and figures on poverty and inequality (and even mass murder) in contemporary Brazil lead to some rather dismal conclusions.

In absolute terms, approximately one-third of Brazilian families continue to exist in a state of wretched and miserable poverty unaffected by the dazzling prosperity of recent years. The census figures and the PNAD survey data tell us that every decile in the population gained some additional income in the years between 1960 and 1976; but this global picture should be qualified by three additional pieces of evidence.

In the first place, a small but not negligible number of Amazonian Indians have been killed or reduced to a state of miserable destitution as a result of the pro-growth policies of recent governments.

Second, in the mainstream of the population, at least some discrete groups of the urban working class have experienced an actual drop in income levels. Unskilled workers, earning close to the minimum wage, have seen some sporadic slippage in their standards of living; and this has been particularly true in periods of recession, when widespread unemployment has compounded the economic problems of this segment of the population. With little market-derived bargaining power in Brazil's labor surplus economy, unskilled workers have been the chief victims of government stabilization policies in the 1964–67 period and again in 1974–79 (see discussion in chapters 4 and 9).

Third, the direct evidence on high rates of malnutrition and infant mortality, on severely deficient services and appallingly bad housing, demonstrate that many aspects of family welfare in Brazil have lagged behind the growth of money incomes. The life conditions and the life chances of the Brazilian poor remain as wretched as they were before the economic miracle. These miserable circumstances have been maintained at least partially by multinational corporations and "Western Consumerism." As we learned in chapter 7, advertising has had a profound impact on the buying habits of urban Brazilians and has led to the substitution of nonessentials for essentials in the budgets of many lower-class people. In other words, if a poor family is persuaded by TV commercials to spend 25 percent of its income on cigarettes and consumer durables and only 50 percent on food, its nutritional standards are likely to fall even if its real income has risen slightly (see table 17).

The facts with regard to inequality are even more incisive. The census returns and the PNAD data demonstrate that the gap between the rich and the poor widened in the 1960–76 period; in addition, various kinds of more fragmentary evidence all point to a growing polarization of Brazilian society. But what increasing relative deprivation means in social welfare terms is less obvious. Intuitively, one feels that increasing inequality should have a distinctly negative effect on the welfare of those left behind in the race for economic improvement. To take an extreme example: if your neighbor becomes exceedingly rich and flaunts his newly acquired Rolls-Royce in front of your eyes, the "natural" reaction would appear to be envy and dissatisfaction with your own unchanged standard of living. However, most contemporary sociologists would view the matter as being a little more complicated than this. As Runciman says, "the relationship between inequality and grievance only intermittently corresponds with either the extent and degree of actual inequality, or the magnitude and frequency of relative deprivation which an appeal to social justice would vindicate." [33] In other words, the degree to which increasing inequality can be associated with a deterioration in social welfare is unpredictable and can only be determined by careful examination of the society in question.

One of the few economists to tackle the question of inequality in underdeveloped nations is Albert Hirschman. In an effort to explain the apparent ease with which many Third World countries tolerate great and increasing degrees of inequality, he puts forward the proposition: "Advances of others supply information about a more benign external environment; receipt of this information produces gratification; and this gratification overcomes, or at least suspends envy." [34] In short, in a period of fast economic growth, increasing inequality will not necessarily provoke discontent among lower-income groups; the fact that someone is moving ahead will have, at least for a while, a beneficial effect on the psyche of the poor. It is easy to see how crucially Hirschman's hypothesis hinges on a measure of social mobility. Gratification at the advance of others is based on an expectational calculus, and if the poor cannot realistically aspire to enjoy the fruits of prosperity, the basis for any present satisfaction is obviously destroyed.[35]

In Brazil the divisions of society are extremely real and rigid, embedded as they are in a long history of uneven and unequal development; and consequently, upward mobility is limited. Perhaps one of the few avenues of advance for the poverty-stricken lower classes of Brazilian society has been internal migration from the countryside to the cities. Recent studies demonstrate the existence of a two-tier migratory pattern in Brazil: an initial move from the countryside to low-paying jobs in the "informal" urban labor market is followed by an eventual move into the higher-paying "formal" sector.[36] Although some evidence suggests that men in the prime age groups (twenty-five to forty-nine) moved rather quickly into better-paying jobs during the years of the miracle, it is unclear whether these migratory patterns constitute a reliable avenue of upward mobility for the bulk of the rural poor. At the very least, prospects in this sphere would seem to depend on the rate of employment creation in the modern sector, which has been much less encouraging in the years 1974–79 than during the boom years 1968–73 (see discussion of trends in the construction sector, page 169).

To return to Hirschman's argument, the absence of independent labor organizations and the recurrent threat posed by a reserve army of the underemployed in the countryside (factors discussed in chapter 9) are dominant factors in explaining the weak bargaining position of working-class groups in Brazil. During times of great prosperity, discrete groups of new arrivals have been absorbed into the modern sector, but these trends have not been continuous (after all, no economy can grow at the rate of 11 percent per year forever!) and have conspicuously failed to reduce poverty significantly or to reverse the overall trend toward increasing inequality.

Given these difficulties in the way of the "have nots" empathizing with the "haves," it is hard to believe that the polarization typical of recent years has done anything but exacerbate the suffering of the Brazilian poor. Hirschman is right when he recognizes that the link between deepening poverty and political action is neither obvious nor automatic. But instead of turning to theories of vicarious gratification to explain the absence of seething discontent and revolutionary fervor in Brazil, I would prefer to locate the important explanatory factors in successive strategies of economic growth and in the structure of political power, as I attempt to do in the final section of this chapter. But first let me examine some of the more important theories that have emerged in Brazil to explain the meaning and function of poverty.

The Theoretical Debate within Brazil

To date, two broad groups of theories have emerged that link the rapid growth rates of modern Brazilian development with the phenomena of inequality and poverty. Both conceptual frameworks are intensely value-laden and incorporate specific sets of policy goals.

On the right end of the political spectrum, we have a group of theories that see increasing inequality as an inevitable consequence of the workings of the market during a period of rapid growth; polarization and increased deprivation become necessary accompaniments of the growth process in at least the short run. On the left end of the political spectrum, we have a constellation of theories that see increasing inequality as a direct result of the growth strategy; in particular, they see the concentration of demand within an elite group as an essential ingredient of the Brazilian economic "miracle." Right-wing theorists are of the opinion that rapid growth justifies increasing inequality because eventually there will be significant "trickle down" to the lower classes. Theoreticians on the Left tend to see as illegitimate growth strategies that depend upon deepening poverty.

The right-wing or "market forces" approach to the growth-inequality relationship is exemplified in *Distribuição da Renda*, published in 1973 by Carlos Langoni, a young, Chicago-trained government economist. In his book Langoni develops the argument that increasing inequality is an inevitable, if unfortunate, accompaniment of rapid economic growth, but that the process is self-righting. With a little infrastructural investment from the government, market forces will eventually produce both growth and equity. The reasoning goes as follows.

In the first place, due to the strong correlation between income and years of schooling in Brazil, inequality is linked to changes in the educational composition of the labor force. Second, the rapid technological transformation of the Brazilian economic structure during "the miracle" altered the demand for labor in favor of persons with high levels of skill. The supply schedule for this type of manpower is, of necessity, extremely inelastic (due to the long gestation period of the educational process); so, in spite of the expansion of higher education in the 1960s, the Brazilian labor market was unable to satisfy the huge increase in demand for skills generated by the growth rates. As a result, managerial personnel were able to command even higher levels of remuneration than were justified by productivity alone; and these high salaries obviously worsened the distribution of income. Finally, Langoni links inequality to structural change in the labor force. High growth rates that are specific to certain sectors of industry generate interregional and intersectoral employment shifts. The movement of labor from the poverty-stricken rural areas and from the lower-paying primary sector to lucrative urban occupations has the short-run effect of increasing the dispersion of incomes and, therefore, of increasing inequality.

To sum up, Langoni views the unfortunate distributional picture of the recent past as doubly transitional. As more and more people move away from the traditional sectors, and as the majority of Brazilians become city dwellers working in modern industry and commerce, the purely sectoral exacerbation of inequality will disappear. And as long as the government responds to the increased need for high-level manpower with appropriate educational investment, supply will adjust to demand and the monopoly rents earned by managers will disappear. The conclusion drawn is that, aside from providing more university education, all the Brazilian government need do is continue with the business of growing, and market forces will take care of the equality issue. In his preface to *Distribuição da Renda,* Delfim Netto (who was minister of finance in 1973 and is currently minister of planning), pours scorn on those who favor overt government action to reduce inequality, accusing them of indulging in "a veritable confidence game which would end up leaving the nation dividing up the misery more equitably." [37]

The "market forces" theory has been adopted as the official interpretation of distributional trends over the recent period for the obvious reason that it absolves the military regime from any direct guilt in the deteriorating social welfare situation. The theory is extremely convenient in that it precludes the need for any redistributional policies into the future; market forces left to themselves will eventually provide both growth and equity. It also disarms criticism from the advanced democracies. Underlying much of the analysis is an implicit comparison with nineteenth-century Europe and North America. If these nations could incur short-run costs in their development processes, why not Brazil? (See discussion of this point in chapter 2.)

Despite the attractions of the market-forces interpretation of recent events, it can be challenged on a number of accounts. On the empirical level, it has been shown that intersectoral and interregional shifts in employment account for very little of the increase in inequality. Moreover, it has been demonstrated that the major concentration of income occurred during the 1964–67 period of stabilization and slow growth rather than in the post-1967 period of economic boom. John Wells finds the critical period of increasing inequality in wages to have been between 1965 and 1966 (a year of pronounced industrial recession).[38] His gini-coefficient for industrial wages increases 20 percent between 1965 and 1966; thereafter there is a modest drift upward in the index of inequality. Thus, it is fairly difficult to maintain that concentration of income was a result of the bidding up of managerial salaries in a time of economic boom; the "iron laws of demand and supply" do not constitute an adequate explanation of growing inequality in Brazil.

On the left of the political spectrum, demand-constraint or underconsumptionist models have long been used to explain the dynamics of Brazilian development. The origins and rationale for this school of thought are as follows.

The industrialization strategy of Brazil was import substitution, a mode of development that emphasized the production of consumer durables for an elite market. Since the wealthy class was small, the market was capable of saturation. Once this happened, production would run into a demand constraint, growth rates would fall, and the whole economy would tend toward stagnation. The high growth rates of the Kubitschek years followed by the dismal economic scene of the early 1960s tended to confirm the hypotheses of the stagnationist school of thought. However, the resumption of growth in 1967 and the sustained prosperity of the Brazilian economic miracle seemed to upset both the premises and the predictions of the demand-constraint theorists; this was particularly true given that the miracle was accompanied by increasing inequality. After a period of confusion, the underconsumption thesis was reconstituted so as to incorporate the possibility of demand intensification. Increasing inequality was seen to concentrate income in the elite group, thus intensifying demand for a whole range of luxury goods and providing the impetus for a renewed spurt of economic growth.

Olivera, Furtado, and Tavares were among the theorists who contributed to this new version of the demand-constraint model.[39] They argued that by 1967 the Brazilian market was permeated with profound discontinuities. The bottom 50 percent of the population had only marginal access to manufactured goods; the next 40 percent of the population (the working classes) had access to nondurable consumer goods. The next 9 percent (the urban middle class) and the top 1 percent (the upper class) formed a highly diversified market for both durable and nondurable goods. By dint of a progressive concentration of income in this top decile, demand became sufficiently intensive so as to prevent, at least for a while, the enactment of the underconsumptionist scenario. It should be noted that the underconsumptionist theorists were convinced that a new boom based on demand concentration had to be short-lived. The elite market would eventually become saturated, and the sharp discrepancies in income and in buying power would serve as barriers to the imitation of the consumption habits of the rich by the mass of the people.

Olivera and other left-wing theorists thus saw increasing relative deprivation as directly functional to the growth strategy. The cut in living standards of the workers in the post-1964 period permitted a redistribution of personal income toward upper-income groups who were destined to be the great consumers of the Brazilian miracle. Wage cuts also resulted in an increase in profit rates. These financial surpluses were used by the corporate sector to extend credit facilities to middle-class groups, enabling them to purchase durable consumer goods. Thus, the fall in working-class incomes during the 1964–67 period becomes linked to the growth strategy in two ways—via demand creation and via credit creation.

In much of the writing in this school of thought, one can detect (with some sympathy) that "the wish is father of the theory." In their anxiety to pinpoint the essential antagonism between the Brazilian development strategy and social justice, the demand-constraint theorists overstate their case. In particular, they exaggerate the directness of the link between inequality and growth. For example, they tend to assume that the working classes are entirely excluded from the market for consumer durable goods. The data show this to be an inaccurate premise. By 1972, 48 percent of all households in Brazil owned an electric iron, 70 percent some form of radio, and 32 percent a television.[40] Via the demonstration and substitution effects discussed earlier, there seems to have been a considerable "trickle-down" of goods to the urban working class.

This kind of empirical evidence refutes some of the Left's basic premises: that demand during the miracle was restricted to an elite market; and that increasing inequality and the consequent concentration of demand was a necessary condition for the renewed economic vitality of the Brazilian economy in the recent period. In short, while the under-consumptionist school of thought has focused correctly on some important issues (the structure of effective demand, the luxury goods emphasis of the industrial strategy), it has suffered from an excess of economic determinism. These theories have tended to trace a direct and linear relationship between the concentration of income and the exact configuration of industrial growth during the years of the miracle.

My own interpretation of poverty and inequality in Brazil, while distinctly left in orientation, is more interactive and cumulative than those I have just described.[41] It rests on elements that I have dwelt upon at length in other chapters of this book: a deeply rooted and highly differentiated "colonial" social structure which has survived into the modern era; modern industrialization strategies based on the production of capital-intensive consumer durables for elite groups; demographic trends that have exacerbated the job deficit; and political frameworks that have given effective power to elite groups and have facilitated policies emphasizing growth at the expense of any egalitarian (or humanitarian) objective. It is this interaction between the past and the present, and between economic and political elements, that sets up the chain of cumulative causation responsible for the presence of massive poverty and increasing inequality in contemporary Brazil.

At a fundamental level of analysis, the highly differentiated social structure of premodern Brazil and the absence of radical political change at the onset of domestic industrialization ensured that development strategies would be designed for and by an elite. Import-substituting industrialization was therefore geared toward producing sophisticated consumer goods; and as the technological and financial capability required to manufacture these sophisticated products was effectively monopolized by the giant multinational firms, this industrialization strategy led to a situation where Brazilian manufacturing came to be dominated by multinational firms.

The cumulative effect of this process was to rigidify and exaggerate the previously existing distribution of income (which was, as we have seen, extremely unequal). The multinational firms with their capital- and skill-intensive technologies absorbed little labor; individuals who did find employment within this dynamic sector were firmly divided into workers and managers—the latter group receiving nearly all the fruits of increased productivity.

This organization of production fed through to the structure of demand. The industrial managers and other members of the Brazilian elite were able to appropriate an increasing proportion of national income; in the 1960–76 period, for example, the top 10 percent of the population increased their share of national income from 40 percent to 50 percent of GNP. This concentration of spending power in the hands of upper-income groups provided a significant and expanding market for the products of multinational firms. In essence, it enabled Brazil to adopt the consumption habits of the advanced affluent societies "prematurely." [42] Goods manufactured by multinational corporations for the mass markets of rich countries were easily absorbed by an elite market in Brazil. However, one should not overschematize this process. By the 1970s many of the sophisticated goods produced by multinational firms were being consumed by the urban working classes. At least the skilled workers were earning more, and this greater affluence combined with advertising and a greater availability of consumer credit to expand the effective market for consumer durables. In addition, the successful export drive by multinational firms further extended this market.

I should like to stress how my explanatory framework differs from that of the underconsumptionist school of thought. I see a highly unequal distribution of income as a background characteristic that has interacted with industrialization strategies and the role of multinational corporations throughout the modern period. I do not see an increase in inequality and a consequent intensification of demand as triggering the Brazilian miracle in any direct or self-conscious way. (Indeed, the increase in inequality in the 1965–66 period identified by John Wells was primarily a result of anti-inflationary policies and a dampening of demand; see discussion in chapters 3 and 4.) The roots of massive poverty and the reasons for a widening gap between the rich and the poor in Brazil lie firmly entrenched in the economic and political evolution of this late-developing nation.

At the beginning of the nineteenth century, Ricardo perceived the laws that regulate the distribution of income in society as the principal problem in political economy, not only because distributional shares are interesting per se, but because distributional factors determine the growth paths of nations.[43] This theoretical insight is critically important in understanding why a poor country, such as Brazil, can have "exuberant" growth rates in such sectors as color television sets and Mercedes-Benz cars, and yet fails to provide sufficient food and shelter for a third of its population. We must always remember that in market economies the production of goods responds to money demand, not to human needs, and that a highly unequal distribution of income will generate a healthy demand for luxury goods in the poorest of nations.

It is a pity that twentieth-century economists have concentrated their energies on maximizing output and have taken themselves out of the business of adjudicating who should get what in society. The spheres of production and distribution are intertwined in multiple and cumulative ways, and one cannot make sense of one without considering the other. In my view, more is not necessarily better, unless the increase in production satisfies conspicuous human needs.

NOTES

1.   Montek S. Ahluwalia, "Income Inequality: Some Dimensions of the Problem," in Hollis Chenery et al., *Redistribution with Growth* (London: Oxford University Press, 1974), p. 3. Much of the new concern in the mainstream of the economics discipline is pulled together in a volume edited by Charles R. Frank, Jr., and Richard C. Webb, *Income Distribution and Growth in the Less-Developed Countries* (Washington, D.C.: The Brooking Institution, 1977).

2.   Irma Adelman and Cynthia Taft Morris, *Economic Growth and Social Equity in Developing Countries* (Stanford, Calif.: Stanford University Press, 1973), p. 194.

3.   Adelman and Morris, *Economic Growth*, p. 192.

4.   See G. Papanek, "Growth, Income Distribution and Politics in Less Developed Countries," in Y. Ramati, ed., *Economic Growth in Developing Countries* (New York: Praeger, 1975); F. Paukert, "Income Distribution at Different Levels of Development: A Survey of Evidence," *International Labor Review* 108 (1973):97–125; and I. M. D. Little, Review of Adelman and Morris, *Economic Growth* (note 2), and of Chenery et al., *Redistribution with Growth* (note 1), *Journal of Development Economics* 3, no. 1 (1976): 99–116.

5.   Montek S. Ahluwalia, "Inequality, Poverty and Development." *Journal of Development Economics* 34 (1976):307–42.

6.   Albert Fishlow, "Brazilian Size Distribution of Income," *American Economic Re-

view 62, no. 2 (1972):391–402; Richard Webb, *Government Policy and the Distribution of Income in Peru, 1963–73* (Cambridge, Mass.: Harvard University Press, 1977); R. Weisskoff, "Income Distribution and Economic Growth in Puerto Rico, Argentina and Mexico," *Review of Income and Wealth* 16 (1970):303–32; David Felix, "Economic Growth and Income Distribution in Mexico," mimeographed (Washington University, St. Louis, Mo., 1976); and D. Snodgrass, "Trends and Patterns in Malaysian Income Distribution, 1957–70," mimeographed (Cambridge University, England, June 1974).

7. B. Renaud, "Economic Growth and Income Inequality in Korea." World Bank Staff Working Paper, no. 240, Washington, D.C., February 1976; and J. Fei, G. Ranis, and S. Kuo, "Equity with Growth: the Taiwan Case," mimeographed (Yale University, New Haven, Conn., 1976).

8. D. Kumar, "Changes in Income Distribution and Poverty in India: A Review of the Literature," *World Development* 2, no. 1 (1974):31–41.

9. A. Berry and M. Unrutia, *Income Distribution in Colombia* (New Haven, Conn.: Yale University Press, 1976); and Weisskoff, "Income Distribution" (note 6), pp. 303–32.

10. Alice M. Rivlin, "Income Distribution—Can Economists Help?" *American Economic Review* 65, no. 2 (May 1975):5–6.

11. A useful discussion of this point is contained in Amartya Sen, *On Economic Equality* (Oxford, England: Clarendon Press, 1973), pp. 6–15.

12. These ideas are put forward in Hollis Chenery et al., *Redistribution with Growth* (note 1), pp. 38–43.

13. Gunnar Myrdal, *Economic Theory and Underdeveloped Regions* (London: Duckworth, 1957), p. 123.

14. See Fishlow, "Brazilian Size Distribution" (note 6), pp. 391–402; Carlos Geraldo Langoni, *Distribuição da Renda e Desenvolvimento Económico do Brazil* (Rio de Janeiro: Editora Expressão e Cultura, 1973); Ricardo Tolipan and Arthus Carlos Tinelli, eds., *A Controvérsia sobrea Distribução da Renda e Desenvolvimento* (Rio de Janeiro: Zahar Editores, 1975); and "The Distribution of Income in Brazil," World Bank Staff Working Paper, no. 356 (Washington, D.C., 1979).

15. This source is analyzed by Samuel A. Morley, *Changes in Employment and the Distribution of Income During the Brazilian "Miracle"* (Geneva: International Labor Organization, 1976), pp. 27–34.

16. Edmar Bacha, "Hierarquia e Remuneração Gerencial," in Tolipan and Tinelli, eds., *A Controvérsia* (note 14), p. 140.

17. Eduardo H. Suplicy, "As Crescentes Diferenças de Renda no País," *Folha de São Paulo*, 15 March 1976.

18. In the early 1960s Peter Townsend argued that "both 'poverty' and 'subsistence' are relative concepts and . . . they can only be defined in relation to the material and emotional resources available at a particular time to members either of a particular society or different societies" ("The Meaning of Poverty," *British Journal of Sociology* 13 [1962]: 210–27).

19. Fishlow finds that for the millions of Brazilians who belong to families below this official poverty line the differentiating characteristics of poverty are the following: little or no education; concentration in agricultural activities; location in rural areas; residence in the northeast; and larger than average number of children (see Fishlow, "Brazilian Size Distribution" [note 6], p. 397). A recent study by the World Bank finds that 27 percent of Brazilian families fell below the poverty line in the mid-1970s (at this stage in time the World Bank defines the poverty line as constituting a family income that is less than two minimum wages [see "Distribution of Income in Brazil" (note 14), p. 99]).

20. Reported in "Brazil: Human Resources Special Report," World Bank Staff Working Paper (Washington, D.C., 1979), pp. 28–31.

21. "Brazil: Human Resources," p. 61.

22. There is some controversy over how much this figure has fallen in recent years. For example, the World Bank finds that the proportion of Brazilian families earning one

minimum wage or less dropped from 47 percent in 1970 to 20 percent in 1976. However, as this compares census figures with PNAD figures, it is acknowledged to be a gross overestimation of the actual drop. See "Distribution of Income in Brazil" (note 14), p. 23.

23. *Latin America Economic Report,* 27 October 1978, p. 332.

24. *Latin America Economic Report,* 14 July 1978, p. 215.

25. Cândido Procópio Ferreira de Camargo et al., *São Paulo 1975: Crescimento e Pobreza* (São Paulo: Edições Loylola, 1976), pp. 79–147.

26. Camargo et al., *São Paulo 1976,* pp. 79–107.

27. *New York Times,* 13 September 1976.

28. Shelton H. Davis, *Victims of the Miracle* (Cambridge, England: Cambridge University Press, 1977), pp. xi–xii. This is by far the best account of the history and meaning of official policies toward the Amazon Indians.

29. Davis, *Victims of the Miracle,* p. 32.

30. See International Committee of the Red Cross, *Report of the ICRC Medical Mission to the Brazilian Amazon Region* (Geneva, 1970); and Aborigines Protection Society of London, *Tribes of the Amazon Basin in Brazil, 1972* (London, 1973).

31. *O Estado de São Paulo,* 6 January 1974. Quoted in Davis, *Victims of the Miracle* (note 28), p. 72.

32. The only role given to the Indian population in contemporary development plans is as a reserve labor force and producer of marketable commodities. See report of a speech made by the President of FUNAI, *Visão,* 26 April 1971, p. 26.

33. W. G. Runciman, *Relative Deprivation and Social Justice* (London: Routledge & Kegan Paul, 1966), p. 337.

34. Albert O. Hirschman and Michael Rothschild, "The Changing Tolerance for Income Inequality in the Course of Economic Development," *Quarterly Journal of Economics* 87, no. 4 (November 1973), p. 546.

35. Hirschman himself is not unaware of these impediments; see "The Changing Tolerance," p. 554.

36. See, for example, George Martins and José Carlos P. Peliano, "Os Migrantes nos Mercados de Trabalho Metropolitanos," mimeographed (Brasília, Human Resources Planning Project, 1977), pp. 143–92.

37. Langoni, *Distribuição da Renda,* p. 13.

38. John Wells, "Distribution of Earnings, Growth and the Structure of Demand in Brazil During the 1960s," *World Development* 2, no. 1 (January 1974):9–24.

39. See Celso Furtado, *Análise do "Modelo" Brasileiro* (Rio de Janeiro: Civilização Brasileiria, 1972); Francisco de Oliveira, "A Economia Brasileira: Crítica à Razao Dualista," in *Seleções Cebrap: Questionando a Economia Brasileira* (São Paulo: Editora Brasiliense, 1976), pp. 5–78; and Maria da Conceição Tavares, "Distribuição da Renda Acumulação e Padrões de Industrialização: Um Ensaio Preliminar," in Tolipan and Tinelli, eds., *A Controvérsia* (note 14), pp. 36–73.

40. John Wells, "Underconsumption, Market Size and Expenditure Patterns in Brazil," *Bulletin of the Society for Latin American Studies, University of Liverpool,* no. 4 (1976): 23–58.

41. I should like to stress that in much of Celso Furtado's work there is a rich awareness of the influence of historical and political factors on contemporary growth patterns. Indeed, I am heavily indebted to his writings for my own conceptual framework (see chapter 3). We part company merely over some recent formulations of the demand intensification thesis.

42. This is a term I borrow from Edmar Bacha, "Hierarquia" (note 16), p. 147.

43. Piero Sraffa, ed., *The Works and Correspondence of David Ricardo* (Cambridge, England: Cambridge University Press, 1962), p. ix.

9

Control of Labor

A sharp rise in the rate of growth of numbers has set in in most of the countries of the Third World, and, in almost all of them, employment has been growing over the last twenty years less rapidly than population. Agriculture fails to provide even the barest livelihood for new generations of would-be cultivators, while the number of jobs in regular industry and commerce expands slowly. A flow of dispossessed families has drifted into shanty towns and slums or on to the streets of cities living on a physical and social standard of existence at the limit of human endurance.

Joan Robinson

THE STRUCTURAL CONDITIONS of late development provide a framework within which governments in the Third World have been able to co-opt and repress organized labor. Of particular significance are the demographic and employment properties of twentieth-century industrialization. With rapid rates of population growth and low rates of labor absorption into industry, the industrial work force becomes a privileged minority group within the population, and the majority of the populace are excluded from high productivity and high-paying occupations. This presence of a large surplus labor force opens the way for systematic manipulation of the industrial working class by governments.

The Brazilian population has grown at a rapid and accelerating pace during the twentieth century. In the year 1900 there were 17 million Brazilians; today there are 120 million. The most rapid rates of growth have been in the recent period (for example, between 1960 and 1970 population growth rates averaged 2.9 percent per year) and have resulted from a dramatic fall in the death rate juxtaposed with an unchanged (and high) birth rate.

This population "explosion" so typical of the Third World is in marked contrast to the histories of the presently rich industrial nations (see discussion in chapter 2). In their takeoff phase, the early developers of Western Europe and North America had a population growth rate that was generally less than half the rate now existing in Brazil or other poor nations. Moreover, the decline of the death rate in industrialized countries was gradual and linked to the development process itself; through such factors as improved diet, better housing, and sanitation, the life-span of the average person gradually lengthened. In other words, death rates in advanced nations declined as part of the general improvement in standards of living. They were accompanied by educational advances that permitted changes in social attitudes toward birth control. Consequently birth rates began to fall before death rates reached their lowest point, and population growth rates never reached modern proportions. Today mortality rates are falling in poor countries, not because of higher living standards for the mass of the population, but because scientific techniques of death control have been transferred from rich countries. In short, modern medical and public health advances have stimulated declines in mortality, independent of the indigenous social reality; and, as a result, birth rates remain high. In many poor nations a large segment of the populace has been excluded from modern industrial growth, and many individuals have neither the education nor the incentive to lower their birth rates. For a landless laborer in India or Brazil, it might make excellent sense to have a large family since children represent the prime source of security in old age.

As a result of these demographic trends, the current and prospective growth of the labor force in Brazil (or in India or Nigeria) is really massive by the standards of recent world history. For example, taking into consideration current rates of population growth and labor-force participation patterns, one can expect a 30 percent growth in the numbers wanting employment between 1980 and 1990 in Brazil; the figure for a typical developed country is approximately 10 percent.

Employment problems in Brazil (and in the developing world more generally) can best be thought of in terms of low-labor utilization and low earnings rather than in terms of unemployment per se, which is the conventional conception of such problems in advanced nations.[1] There are huge statistical complications involved in measuring open unemployment (let alone underemployment and disguised unemployment) in most developing countries, and it is doubtful that the concept is at all useful in these contexts.[2] For example, the official unemployment rate in Brazil has hovered around the 3 percent mark for several years.[3] This bears no relation to the actual number of people who are without decently paid and regular employment. In an economy such as Brazil's which has no effective system of unemployment insurance for workers outside the organized industrial sector, somebody looking for a job has to find some activity to keep himself from starving—even if this means watching cars or selling cigarettes on the street corner. This person is then deemed to be employed in the official statistics no matter how low his income is or how sporadic his productive activity.

In short, if one is interested in social welfare, "The ultimate object of policy is not just to provide more jobs, but to provide work which is socially productive and yields enough income for a reasonable standard of living." [4]

To assess adequately the implication of employment rates for living standards in Brazil it is necessary to turn to the type rather than to the number of jobs available in the economy. Table 18 traces the evolution of employment in Brazil by sector between 1940 and 1976. As one would expect, with the advent of industrialization and urbanization the agricultural sector has declined in relative terms. However, I should like to stress that there has been growth in absolute terms, and today there are still fourteen million Brazilians employed in agriculture. Given the extremely low-income levels prevailing in the rural economy (see discussion in chapter 8), agriculture still constitutes a huge reservoir of surplus labor, keeping down wages and salaries in the urban sector. Between 1960 and 1976 there was, for the first time, an absolute decline in the agricultural labor force in the most industrialized state (São Paulo); but, because of an improved transportation system, manufacturing and construction firms have been able to tap the labor surplus of less prosperous regions of the country—in particular, the northeast.

Employment in the secondary sector (especially in manufacturing) represents, in the clearest sense, the absorption of labor into high productivity and high-paying jobs. It is evident from table 17 that although employment in the secondary sector has grown in the modern period (somewhat faster in the 1940–50 and 1960–70 periods than in the 1950–60 decade), absolute levels of employment in this critical sector are still quite low, representing less than one-quarter of total employment. This compares quite badly with other countries.[5] The reasons behind these low levels of employment in the secondary sector should be quite clear from chapter 7. Import-substituting industrialization via the multinational firm has been extremely capital-intensive. Brazil has imported the products and technologies of rich countries and thus failed to provide mass employment in her rapidly expanding industrial economy.

The employment performance of the tertiary sector has been more impressive; indeed, in recent years this sector has employed roughly twice as many people as industry. However, the tertiary sector encompasses many residual categories of "marginal" jobs that serve the function of keeping body and soul together when nothing better is available. It includes the street vendors, the shoeshine boys, and the parking attendants whom one "hires" so that one's car will not be stripped of its removable parts—in other words, people who have not found full-time jobs in the modern sector.[6] The fact that recent growth rates in tertiary employment have varied inversely with rates of growth in industrial employment would seem to confirm that workers enter the service sector when they cannot find jobs in industry. The growth of employment in this sector therefore cannot be seen as evidence of labor absorption into high productivity and high-paying jobs.

In summary, despite significant gains in industrial employment since the 1940s, Brazil is a long way from absorbing the bulk of its work force into modern sector jobs. The population explosion and rapid urbanization combine to produce a situation where rates of growth within the urban population averaged 4.7 percent per year in the 1940–76 period. During this same time span, jobs in manufacturing expanded at a rate of 3.7 percent per year, and in the secondary sector as a whole at 4.2 percent per year.[7] Thus, an increasing proportion of city dwellers are in marginal low-paying occupations, swelling that already considerable reservoir of surplus labor in the countryside.

These critical facts, which are embedded in the structural characteristics of late development, help us understand how successive Brazilian regimes have successfully controlled labor. Labor unions (which represent the skilled, urban working class and have a combined membership of less than 3 million) [8] have been coaxed into conformity through various co-optation devices, and they have been intimidated through repression. These control mechanisms have worked because they are based on the threat posed by a reserve army of the underemployed. Whatever the conditions of employment in the modern sector, they are bound to be better than life as a shoeshine boy or a landless laborer.

The Evolution of Labor Control Mechanisms

As we know from earlier chapters of this book, pre-1930 Brazil was a rural society where large landholders dominated the political landscape and held social mobilization to a minimum. Industry was relatively unimportant during this era, and factory owners were able to contain the demands of their work force through the use of physical force. Washington Luiz, president of Brazil in the late 1920s, summed up the official attitude when he stated that "the social question is a matter for the Police."[9] In this early period the only workers' associations recognized in law were mutual aid and cooperative societies, organizations that would not create conflict between workers and employers.

In the post-1930 world it became clear that Brazil's long-run economic and political viability depended upon sustained domestic industrialization and a much more interventionist role for the state. As part of these changes, the corporatist institution builders of the *Estado Novo* (1937–45) attempted to secure state control over the new industrial working class by strictly regulating the economic, social, and political activities of labor. Following typical corporatist lines (discussed in chapter 6), the guiding principles of labor legislation in Brazil during this period came to be: a differentiation between trade unionism and socialism, leaving Brazilian labor organizations "professional, corporative and Christian";[10] the separation of the labor movement from political parties; and the careful structuring of unions in order to make them instruments of social integration in the nation-building process, rather than divisive agents of class conflict.

During the *Estado Novo* three types of institutions grew up to contain labor within the corporatist framework. They were the *sindicatos* or trade unions, the labor courts, and the social security system.[11] These structures have undergone modification over the course of the last forty years, but in a fundamental sense they have survived to this day as the basic framework within which the Brazilian state co-opts and controls the working class. During the period of relatively open political competition (1946–64), many of the repressive features of the system fell into disuse, while the post-1964 era of military rule has seen a massive reactivation of the control mechanisms of the corporatist labor system.

The CLT (Consolidação das Leis do Trabalho) of 1943 codified much of the labor legislation of the 1930s and provides the organizational framework of the modern system. The CLT set up a hierarchical union structure which facilitates state control. At the bottom are the *sindicatos*, local unions that represent workers in *municípios* (the smallest units of local government). The *sindicatos* are linked at the state level in federations that in turn are linked at the national level in given district, thus precluding competing nonofficial organizations with grievances, economic demands, and welfare services, while the federations and confederations operate in the administrative and political spheres.

This organizational framework includes several features that are important in furthering state control of the unions. For instance, legally recognized *sindicatos* have the right to exclusive representation within a given district, thus precluding competing nonofficial organizations with more radical programs. In a similar vein, the three-tiered structure and the lack of a peak organization—such as the CGT (Confederacion General del Trabajo) in Argentina—hinders the articulation of working-class demands, because the system lacks the capacity to produce a united labor response to repressive government action. The CLT also established a labor court system to deal with conflicts between employers and employees. These courts reflect a corporatist view of society, and their mandate is to resolve labor disputes in such a manner that no class or personal interests prevail over the public good.[12]

A final critical element in labor legislation is the social security system which was created by the CLT and by its own separate body of law. The founding principle of this system was the establishment of social harmony through the provision of numerous social welfare services to the working class. These programs were originally designed to be maintained by equal contributions from workers, employers, and the federal government. However, despite these initial intentions, for long periods of time the system has been inadequate, and the brunt of the cost of the programs has been borne by workers whose contributions take the form of compulsory payroll deductions that are unavoidable. Over the years the government has paid only a fraction of its statutory contribution; and prior to 1964 many employers failed to pay theirs.

The social security system has therefore proved to be both inequitable (with a disproportionate share of its costs falling on workers) and inadequate (the shortfall in government and employer contributions has meant that workers have received substandard health care and retirement benefits). Recent research demonstrates that, far from promoting social justice, the social security system has reinforced inequality in Brazil.[13]

Brazilian labor legislation has therefore carefully circumscribed the legitimate activities of workers' organizations; and the main function of the labor code has been to maintain a tight rein over the working class. This bears a close resemblance to the *Carta del Lavoro* of fascist Italy and is extremely different from the labor legislation of North America and Britain.[14] In particular, the corporatist structures of Brazil are intensely hostile to the existence of independent intermediary bodies; labor organizations remain under the strict tutelage of the state.

So far I have been describing the framework of a labor control system which has been in existence since the 1930s. However, the dramatic changes in political structures since World War II have had some effect on workers' organizations, particularly in determining how tightly or loosely corporatist controls over labor have been applied.

The 1946–64 era of democratic rule witnessed two periods when labor organizations sought to play a more independent political role: the 1953–54 period, when workers mobilized to strengthen the position of their political leaders; and the 1963–64 period, when labor began to demand genuine participation in the political process. This latter period saw the freeing of labor leaders from governmental controls and the participation of the labor Left in a national debate over basic reform in Brazil's economic and social structures. This loosening up was particularly pronounced during the tenure in office of Almino Afonso, the populist labor minister of Goulart.[15]

An avenue to independent political leverage for the labor leaders of the early 1960s was the social security system, which provided valuable types of patronage that union officers were able to convert into political power. First of all, since the institutes of the social security system employed 15 percent of all federal civil servants, they were a potent source of jobs for political supporters. Second, the chronic shortfall in revenues meant that there were never enough resources to go around—a situation that encouraged union officials to distribute or withhold benefits according to their own, often political, criteria.

All of this activity died away after 1964. Accusing Goulart of "deliberately bolshevizing" the nation, the new military regime used the full potential of the corporate institutions to demobilize the working class. The long-standing direct and indirect controls established by the

CLT were enforced, and these were complemented by new legislation designed to make the corporatist system work better, both as an agent of social control and as an instrument of accumulation. The generals urgently needed to suppress wages as part of their drive toward stabilization (see discussion in chapters 3, 4, and 5). To do this they needed to tighten their grip on the working class.

Leadership Controls

Intervention or threat of intervention has been the military regime's most potent weapon in dealing with recalcitrant labor leaders. Intervention involves state seizure of union headquarters and union funds, and the replacement of elected union officials with government appointees. One of the first acts of the Castello Branco administration (the first government of the military regime) was to intervene and purge the leadership of the most militant union bodies; indeed, 67 percent of the confederations were intervened at this time. The government also moved to institute more rigorous screening of union officials. New appointees were made to submit a declaration of obedience to the federal authorities, and the political police scrutinized all candidates for union positions.

These repressive controls over union leadership have been complemented by a carefully controlled system of co-optation designed to reward progovernment labor leaders. Within the union structure, material rewards are now deliberately and strictly limited. According to law, a union officer can receive a salary only if his position forces him to be absent from his regular job, and the union salary cannot exceed that which he received on the job. Hardly the route to riches! However, having barred the union structure as an avenue of upward mobility, the government has provided a series of substitute paths that are very useful in enticing union officers to cooperate with government policy. The most important of these is the position of labor judge (*vogel*) in the lower-level labor courts. These jobs are highly prized because of the minimal duties they entail and the high salaries they command (for example, in the São Paulo courts, labor judges receive thirteen times the minimum salary, and this is for part-time work). The federal government effectively controls access to these posts and tends to appoint passive individuals who support official policy. No wonder labor judges in post-1964 Brazil have not been militant advocates of working-class interests!

In addition to these repressive and co-optive leadership controls, the military regime has taken an active interest in the training and socialization of new cadres of labor leaders. For example, the regional office of the Ministry of Labor in São Paulo offers practical courses in union bookkeeping, labor law, and such uplifting topics as "Moral and Civil Education and the National Reality." [16] In a complementary effort the American Institute of Free Labor Development runs an intensive course in United States style business unionism. This institute is a blatantly anticommunist organization funded by the United States government with the express purpose of heading off labor radicalism in Brazil. Both of these training organizations have helped to produce a breed of labor leaders capable of collaborating with the military regime in its economic and social policies. [17]

It would be wrong to get the impression that government control over union leaders has stopped at intervention or in the training of an antiradical cadre of union organizers; arrest, interrogation, and torture have been used systematically to intimidate the more militant union leaders. This was particularly true in the 1968–73 period of violent repression described in chapter 4. In 1972 Amnesty International documented more than one thousand cases of torture in Brazil, and many left-wing labor leaders were on this list.

Organizational Controls

An important type of control over Brazilian labor unions rests on the fact that the government is responsible for the provision of the major portion of the revenue of these organizations, and access to this money is determined by whether a union is going to use it for government-approved activities.

The two major sources of funds are the trade union tax (*contri-*

buição sindical) and union membership dues. The trade union tax is collected from all workers, whether they are union members or not, in the local union's jurisdiction, and is equal to one day's wage per year. In addition to this tax, a worker must pay monthly dues to qualify as a union member. A third source of finance, which has emerged in the last few years, is a special discount taken from the workers' paycheck during the first month of the annual wage increase. As with the tax, the unions are dependent upon the government to gain this source of revenue and have to justify the discount each year in their annual court appearance—a powerful control device!

This financial structure ensures that approximately 60 percent of union revenues is directly controlled by the government, and it provides policy makers with a major lever for channeling union activities into nonmilitant activities. For example, Article 592 of the labor law specifies the following approved uses of the union tax: job placement agencies; maternity, medical, dental, and hospitalization assistance; credit and consumer cooperatives; professional and vocational training schools; vacation facilities; funeral aid; and so forth. The law states explicitly that tax revenues cannot be used for strike benefits or other militant activities.[18]

The normal sanction for unions who become too militant is the removal of their elected leaders through intervention. However, the government has another weapon in reserve. It can cancel the official registration of the disruptive labor organization, rendering it a legal nonentity. As official recognition is a prerequisite for use of the labor courts, for dealings with government agencies, and for negotiation of wage contracts, the loss of legal status means organizational death.

A major change initiated by the military regime has been the restructuring of the social security system, thereby preventing labor leaders from using these immense resources to subvert their membership. In 1966 a new law combined nearly all the institutes into one single National Social Welfare Institute (INPS), a mammoth organization whose budget today is second only to that of the federal government. In important policy shifts, new legislation reduced the government's contribution to a mere 5 percent of INPS revenues (thus shifting more of the burden to workers and employers) and replaced the old tripartite system of control (workers, employers, government) by a government-appointed director. The net results of these changes are: a social security system that has become less burdensome to government and more burdensome to workers; and an institutional structure under the tight control of a government that increasingly uses the immense resources of the system to further its own growth goals rather than the welfare of the working class. This all adds up to a rather depressing picture in the sphere of social justice.

Worker Controls

In the post-1964 period the military government has significantly increased its control over individual workers by enhancing the costs associated with protest behavior. The job security provisions of the labor law have been significantly weakened, making protesting workers much more susceptible to employer retaliation; and new restrictive regulations have attempted to decrease the use of the strike as a bargaining tool.

One of the most valuable rights of labor in the pre-1964 period had been job stability or tenure, which had effectively protected a worker from being fired once he or she had put in ten years of service with an employer. Foreign investors in particular objected strongly to this tenure law for reasons of efficiency: for example, it made it extremely difficult to cut down the work force in times of recession; and in the absence of the sanction of dismissal, it was difficult to enforce discipline on the job. The Castello Branco government in its efforts to promote growth and increase labor discipline decided to get rid of this right to job security. In 1966 a new law abolished tenure, except for those employees who had already attained it. Tenure was replaced by a severance pay fund, the FGTS (Fundo de Garantia do Tempo de Servico). This new system requires employers to establish a bank account in the name of each employee and each month to deposit in it 8 percent of each employee's wage. A worker may withdraw this money only in the event of some specific circumstance—such as dismissal, retirement, or marriage.

This elimination of job security has had several effects on the well-being and on the militancy of workers. It has heightened personal economic insecurity by encouraging high rates of turnover (in 1970, for example, 35 percent of the work force in São Paulo had put in less than one year in a current job).[19] It has also discouraged complaints about the conditions of work. For example, grievances initiated by workers against employers in the labor court system dropped dramatically (from 39 percent to 17 percent of total grievances) in the 1966–75 period. A final effect of the loss of tenure has been a cheapening of labor. Mericle demonstrates that over a seven-year period the paycheck of a tenured worker continuously employed by the same firm would have risen 17 percent over that of a newly hired worker.[20] No wonder industrialists were in favor of abolishing the tenure law!

Brazilian governments have always had extensive legal power to regulate strike activity; the labor law, for example, has always specified that workers cannot strike without the previous authorization of the labor courts. Since 1964 these regulations have been tightened. Under the military regime courts have restricted the use of strikes to enforcing either overdue salary payments or the payment of court-established wage adjustments. In these rare instances where strikes are allowed, the behavior of strikers is strictly regulated. In other words, the military has attempted to outlaw the use of strikes as a method of extracting concessions from employers. This weakening of the strike as a legitimate bargaining tool—and the heavy penalties attached to illegal strike activities—produced a dramatic decline in the incidence of strikes. There were 154 strikes in 1962, 302 in 1963, but only 25 in 1965. In the early 1970s the number of strikes dropped to zero. In 1978 and through most of 1979 there was an upsurge in illegal strike activity (see discussion in chapters 3 and 4) as workers tested the limits of the new political opening. However, all the repressive legislation remains in place; and in late 1979, with the new inflationary pressures of the Brazilian economy, the Brazilian government seemed ready once more to clamp down on strike activity.

Labor Controls in Action

In most eras and contexts, wage increases have been an important and conspicuous focus of working-class protest. During the 1930–64 period in Brazil this was especially true, as hours, working conditions, and fringe benefits were regulated in detail by the labor law and thus taken outside the bargaining process. Post-1964 policies in the sphere of wage setting, and trends in the level of real wages, are therefore sensitive indicators of the effectiveness of labor control in contemporary Brazil.

The Brazilian state influences wages in two ways: it sets the minimum wage for all wage and salaried workers, and it is heavily represented in the labor courts which grant annual wage increases to trade union members. Prior to 1964 labor protest played an important role in both procedures. For example, the minimum wage was adjusted at irregular intervals, primarily in response to working-class pressure, in the form of wage campaigns or strikes. The post-1964 regime has made several changes in wage-setting procedures so as to remove the issue from the realm of negotiation. The minimum wage is now adjusted at yearly intervals through an automatic adjustment device. The essence of this indexation procedure is a government formula that bases the wage increase on the value of real wages in the twenty-four months previous to the increase, on the anticipated inflation for the upcoming twelve months, and on national productivity figures. This formula is binding as a minimum; and for workers who have neither scarcity value nor bargaining power (that is, unskilled and semiskilled labor), it tends to be the maximum. Indeed, the government can ensure adherence to these guidelines through another avenue of control—the CIP (Conselho Interministerial de Preços). This agency fixes prices through a pricing formula that incorporates the officially decreed level of wage increases. The result is that employers and labor courts have minimal discretion over the size of the wage increase. In essence, wage decisions are no longer made through a collective bargaining process between employers and employees; instead, they are made in the Ministry of Finance.[21]

This transformation of the wage-setting procedure has considerably weakened the position of the working class. The new rules of the game make it extremely easy for the military regime to manipulate wage levels in the name of larger policy goals. For example, when it is convenient for inflation-control reasons to depress wage levels, the government formula merely underestimates the previous or the anticipated inflation figure. In the 1964–67 period and again in 1976–79, this formula provided a problem-free way of depressing the real wage, which, in its turn, was an important component of the stabilization packages of these years. Labor unions have little retaliatory power: in order to question a specific wage adjustment, the union cannot challenge a single employer via the labor courts; it has to take on the entire national wage policy. This is a challenge that the co-opted labor movement of post-1964 Brazil has been singularly unprepared to meet.

Labor's Response

Despite the panoply of repressive mechanisms at both the individual and the organizational level, the era of military rule has not been without labor unrest. In April 1968, for example, there was a major wildcat strike of metal workers in Contagem, Minas Gerais.[22] Fifteen thousand workers came out in protest against official wage policies and demanded immediate pay raises. The military police eventually occupied the city and crushed the strike with brute force.

The boom years of the early seventies gave certain segments of the labor force a scarcity value, and some workers fought for and gained economic concessions. The classic cases were at Volkswagen, Mercedes-Benz, Chrysler, and Villares Elevators where employees refused to work overtime until they had been granted wage hikes of 9–10 percent; they won these particular battles.

With the recession of 1974 and 1975 there was a tightening of the job market and a return to hard-line policies. The oil crisis which fueled domestic inflation and triggered immense balance-of-payments problems reduced employment levels, thus eroding the bargaining position of labor. Repression and intimidation became once more the order of the day. For example, in February of 1975 military and police authorities in São Paulo arrested a large number of union leaders.[23] Indeed, the commander of the Second Army, General Ednardo d'Avila Melo, became carried away in his enthusiasm to root out "red fascists." Several labor leaders died under torture (including the celebrated activist Manuel Fiel Filho); and in the ensuing scandal General Ednardo was dismissed by President Geisel, but his successor promptly vowed to continue the war against labor subversives.

More recently some categories of workers have fought for and obtained some material concessions. In October 1978 engineering workers in Rio de Janeiro won a 49 percent pay increase as a result of strike action.[24] The following month 200,000 engineering workers in São Paulo came out on strike, at least some of them successfully (the firm of Krupp and Mannesmann offered workers at the Betim plant an increase of 18 percent over the cost of living).[25] And, in the spring of 1979, teachers, nurses, bus drivers, civil servants, and junior hospital doctors staged successful strikes for higher pay.[26]

Significant as these isolated cases are, one should not exaggerate the strength of labor protest in the recent period. The new Figuieredo administration has made few across-the-board concessions. The minimum wage adjustment of May 1979 was 45.4 percent, which failed to make up for the erosion of living standards over the previous twelve months.[27] In addition, the new labor legislation, which is currently in draft form, retains all the important repressive measures introduced by previous military governments.[28] For example, it provides that leaders of illegal strikes be prosecuted under the harsh national security laws.

For the most part, the labor movement has been effectively cowed. Intervention and imprisonment have eradicated most militant union activity, and the majority of Brazilian workers have lost the ability to oppose repressive governmental actions. A few privileged subsectors of the labor force (those workers who possess scarce skills and therefore can command some market-derived bargaining power) have been able to extract concessions, but the overall trend in living standards, detailed in chapter 8, tells its own story. Organized labor has lost much of its power in the wage-setting arena; and it has been semi-skilled and unskilled labor, which has a chronically weak bargaining position in this labor surplus economy, that has failed most conspicuously to gain material rewards from the spectacular growth rates of recent years.

NOTES

1. D. Turnham, *The Employment Problem in Less Developed Countries* (Paris: Organization for Economic Cooperation and Development, 1971), p. 16.

2. See discussion in International Labor Organization, *Towards Full Employment: A Programme for Colombia* (Geneva, 1970), pp. 15–29.

3. Unemployment per se is not recorded in Brazil; instead, there is a category of persons listed as being "without remuneration." This category includes those unemployed and actively seeking jobs and those working in an unpaid capacity—that is, on the family farm.

4. International Labor Organization, *Towards Full Employment* (note 2), p. 15.

5. Argentina, Mexico, Spain, and Greece, as well as the advanced industrial nations, all have a larger proportion of their labor force employed in industry than has Brazil. See Helga Hoffman, *Desemprego e Subemprego no Brasil* (São Paulo: Editora Ática, 1977), p. 48. See S. Kuznets, *Economic Growth of Nations* (Cambridge, Mass.: Harvard University Press, 1971), for an analysis of international trends in employment creation.

6. See discussion in Raul Prebisch, *Change and Development: Latin America's Great Task* (Washington, D.C.: Inter-American Development Bank, 1970), pp. 28–33; and John Friedman and Flora Sullivan, "The Absorption of Labour in the Urban Economy: The Case of Developing Countries," *Economic Development and Cultural Change* 22, no. 3 (April 1974):385–414.

7. See discussion of this point in Hoffman, *Desemprego e Subemprego* (note 5), pp. 39–52.

8. In 1973, 2.7 million workers—or approximately 5 percent of the labor force—belonged to *sindicatos* in Brazil. See Kenneth Paul Erickson, *The Brazilian Corporative State and Working-Class Politics* (Berkeley: University of California Press, 1977), p. 31. This book constitutes a comprehensive and valuable account of organized labor in Brazil.

9. Erickson, *The Brazilian Corporative State*, p. 13.

10. Francisco José de Oliveira Vianna, *Problemas de Organização e Problemas de Direção* (Rio de Janeiro: José Olympio, 1952), p. 170. Vianna, an advisor to Vargas, was one of the prime intellectual influences during this period.

11. The corporatist labor control system is carefully described in Kenneth S. Mericle, "Corporatist Control of the Working Class: Authoritarian Brazil Since 1964," in James M. Malloy, ed., *Authoritarianism and Corporatism in Latin America* (Pittsburgh, Pa.: University of Pittsburgh Press, 1977), pp. 303–39.

12. Erickson, *The Brazilian Corporative State* (note 7), p. 32.

13. See James M. Malloy, "A Política de Previdência Social no Brasil: Participação e Paternalismo," *Revista Dados*, no. 13 (1976):93–115; and James M. Malloy, "The Evolution of Social Security Policy in Brazil: Policy Making and Income Distribution," paper presented at the 1975 Annual Meeting of the American Political Science Association, San Francisco.

14. See discussion in Evaristo de Morães Filho, *O Problema do Sindicato Unico no Brasil* (Rio de Janeiro: Editora a Noite, 1952), pp. 243–44.

15. The significance of Almino Afonso is discussed in Erickson, *The Brazilian Corporative State* (note 7), p. 77.

16. *O Estado de São Paulo*, 21 June 1972.

17. These union leaders are often referred to as the *pelegos*, a derogatory term for union leaders who cooperate with the Ministry of Labor. The word literally denotes the sheepskin blanket that is placed between saddle and horse to ease the burden of the rider on the horse.

18. The "bread and butter" orientation of Brazilian unions is documented in J. A. Rodrigues, *Sindicato e Desenvolvimento no Brasil* (São Paulo: Difusão Européia do Livro,

1968); and Juarez Rubens Brandão Lopes, *Sociedade Industrial no Brasil* (São Paulo; Difusão Européia do Livro, 1971).

19. Erickson, *The Brazilian Corporative State* (note 7), p. 166.

20. Kenneth S. Mericle, "Conflict Regulation in the Brazilian Industrial Relations System," Ph.D. dissertation (University of Wisconsin, 1974), pp. 280–85.

21. The wage control mechanisms epitomize what Leff has called "the myth of the 'technical solution' in Brazilian politics" (Nathaniel H. Leff, *Economic Policy-Making and Development in Brazil, 1947–1964* [New York: John Wiley, 1968], pp. 32–34). In mid-1979 a new system of wage adjustment was proposed. According to this scheme, workers will be allowed a small annual increase to be negotiated directly with employers. On top of this there will be a half-yearly cost of living increase to be fixed by the government. Only low-paid workers will have raises of more than the cost of living. This new proposal might decrease inequality among organized labor but will not affect that 40 percent of the labor force that is not officially registered. See discussion in *Latin America Economic Report*, 28 September 1979, p. 304.

22. See account in Francisco C. Weffort, *Participação e Conflito Industrial: Contagem e Osasco, 1968*, Caderno CEBRAP, no. 5 (São Paulo: Centro Brasileiro de Análise e Planejamento, 1972).

23. *Latin American Political Report*, March 1975.

24. *Latin America Economic Report*, 27 October 1978, p. 329.

25. *Latin America Economic Report*, 3 November 1978, p. 337.

26. *Latin America Political Report*, 4 May 1979, p. 134.

27. *Latin America Political Report*, 4 May 1979, p. 134.

28. *Latin America Economic Report*, 18 May 1979, p. 152.

CHAPTER

10

Conclusions

Cumulative and Multiple Causation

By now it should be clear that there are no simple or single answers to why Brazilian development has required poverty and repression. As I stated in chapter 1, economic factors constitute necessary but not sufficient causal links between growth and equity. Understanding the organic connection between economic growth and various types of social and political rights in Brazil involves a consideration of the historical evolution of economic structures, of the political and ideological frameworks of each successive phase, and of the international capitalist system that has both constrained and molded domestic choices. Figure 1 plays out the spiral of cumulative and multiple interaction among these various factors.[1]

In the economic sphere four centuries of primary production for export conditioned the terms and the shape of modern development. This historical experience meant that Brazil was a late industrializer with all the attendant symptoms of that condition—an interventionist illiberal state, a huge technological gap, the massive presence of foreign capital, and extremely fast rates of population growth. These factors triggered rapid growth but had a profoundly negative effect on social welfare.

In the political sphere the presence of cumulative momentum is equally pronounced. The modernizers of the post-1930 period built upon and co-opted the previously existing "colonial" social structures and thereby ensured that modern development was designed by and for an elite. For example, the rural oligarchy lost its political dominance but

FIGURE 1
The Spiral of Cumulative and Multiple Causation

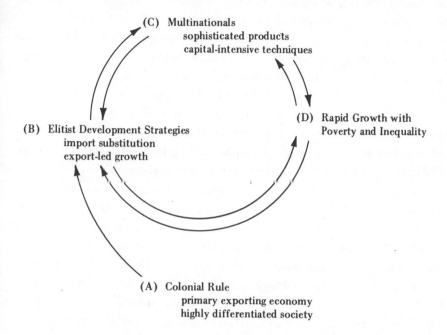

retained its claim to agricultural price supports and to the maintenance of existing land tenure arrangements. Brazil, quite simply, never had a revolution, and the move from primary production to domestic industrialization was accomplished through accretion and compromise rather than through radical changes in power relationships.

These types of cumulative momentum are powerful contributors to massive poverty and political repression in contemporary Brazil. For example, late development has meant that modern industrialization has been capital-intensive and has failed to provide enough jobs for the rapidly expanding population. Similarly, entrenched rural oligarchy, a legacy of the colonial era, has meant the preservation of an extremely skewed distribution of income in the countryside, which remains the breeding ground for the worst kinds of Brazilian poverty.

I would also like to stress the interactive nature of these processes. We are in a world of multiple causation where economic, political, internal, and external factors all interact and feed on one another so as to produce inequitable patterns of economic development. Let me illustrate this process of multiple causation by playing out the role of the multinational corporation in the industrialization of Brazil.

In the radical literature multinationals are often put forward as the bête noire, solely or directly responsible for the ills of underdeveloped nations.[2] However, while it is true that the product mix and employment propensities of multinational firms tend to confirm and exaggerate inequality in poor countries, it is wrong to imagine that multinational corporations *cause* poverty. We are in an interactive arena where changing one factor (in this case controlling or even eliminating foreign capital) would be fruitless without radical change in other spheres, such as domestic power structures and industrialization strategies. We must remember that multinationals entered Brazil, not in a self-conscious attempt to "warp" national development, but in response to the industrialization policies of successive Brazilian governments.

But this is not the full story. Complex as this interaction is between domestic industrialization strategies and multinational corporations, one has to probe deeper. The factors determining the choice and the viability of particular policies revolve around previously existing economic structures and political frameworks. This takes us back to the historical factors and cumulative momentum. The primary exporting phase of Brazilian development created a highly differentiated social structure. The wealth generated by international trade was appropriated by a planter-exporter elite which used it to buy imported luxury goods. When Brazil began to industrialize, the new modernizing regime primarily wanted to grow, and the easiest and most expedient route to rapid industrial growth was to internalize the existing, elite demand. This led to an import-substitution strategy that encouraged multinational corporations to produce "rich country goods" within the Brazilian domestic economy.

Thus, an elitist power structure inherited from an earlier epoch promotes an industrialization strategy that benefits a privileged group within the population. Succeeding cycles of industrial growth rigidify and exacerbate this process, as the imperatives of maintaining growth conditions (in particular inflation and balance-of-payments issues) require that segments of the industrial work force as well as the rural mass be excluded from the fruits of economic progress and from the political arena.

Particularly important in this respect is the need to control inflation. Import-substituting industrialization via the multinational firm in a populist political arena is a high-cost and inflationary process, involving, as we saw in chapter 5, supply bottlenecks, above-normal profit margins, and deficit financing. Brazil's resulting chronic inflation and balance-of-payments difficulties were resolved (in 1964) by military dictatorship and a ruthless set of stabilization measures. These included the reduction of real wage levels, a tightening of domestic sources of credit, budget cutting, and a concerted attempt to increase the rate of effective taxation, and were—as such programs always are—extremely unpopular, necessitating the suspension of a variety of political freedoms.

In short, massive poverty and political repression are consequences of rapid growth in this underdeveloped nation, but their manifestations are extremely complex and reach back into the past. One conclusion seems clear. There are no simple remedies and no easy way to point a finger and accuse a single actor of being the evil genius responsible for the human costs of Brazilian development.

Social and Political Trade-offs

In this matter of costs, it is important to distinguish between social and political trade-offs in the Brazilian development experience. As I stated in chapter 1, the social and political costs of growth are not identical, and in this nation, the prospects for political freedom are somewhat brighter than are those for social justice.

As I have shown, massive poverty and increasing inequality are deeply embedded in Brazilian history. Uneven and unequal development became entrenched during a colonial, primary exporting era, and this mode of development was built upon and exaggerated by the industrialization strategies of the modern period. Changing such an entrenched pattern of inequitable growth would involve a profound restructuring of the economy and of society.

Let us assume a Brazilian government wished to initiate a development plan that had as its goals the elimination of the worst kinds of poverty and a reduction in income inequalities. At a minimum, this would imply two things: in the rural sector, a thoroughgoing land reform that would distribute land to landless peasants; and in the urban sector, labor-intensive industrialization to create a much more rapid rate of employment creation in the modern sector.

The current Brazilian regime would not and could not foster such a program, as the Brazilian power elite (and the international capitalist system in general) has a great deal of vested interest in maintaining the status quo. Large-scale land reform, for instance, has to mean the expropriation of a powerful landlord class; and to achieve this, there has to be a radical shift in the domestic balance of power.[3] Here is an excellent example of the way in which the economic self-interest of ruling groups flies in the face of social justice.

In the sphere of industrialization policies the trade-offs at work are equally stark. Take the role of the multinational corporations operating in Brazil. These firms are rational economic actors and as such would be quite willing to experiment with more labor-intensive production techniques if they had a sufficiently compelling incentive to do so. But they do not, as there are severe barriers in the spheres of both production and consumption.

As we learned in chapter 7, 98 percent of all industrial research and development has been undertaken in advanced countries and is geared to the factor endowments of these rich nations. It therefore makes sense for a multinational corporation to capitalize on this accumulated vested interest and to transfer well-tried, rich country products with their sophisticated, capital-intensive technologies to the Third World. Although this type of industrialization has many negative social welfare repercussions for the host country, it is often adopted because this profit-maximizing behavior on the part of firms coincides with the needs and desires of the domestic elite. However, if the Brazilian government were to step in and provide a massive subsidy for research and development in labor-intensive technologies (or change factor prices so as to make labor cheap relative to capital), industrialization strategies could begin to change.

But an even stickier problem will have to be faced before labor-intensive industrialization can be achieved in Brazil, for who will buy the goods produced by these new labor-intensive industries? We know from previous chapters that multinational corporations moved into Brazil during the modern period in order to satisfy elite demand for a specific set of sophisticated goods. Clearly, without some significant income redistribution, it will prove difficult to change the demand profile and thereby the product mix and production technologies of multinational firms. At the present time income is so highly concentrated in Brazil—the top 10 percent of the population appropriates 50 percent of national income—that the elite market is capable of reproducing the demand characteristics of mass markets in rich countries. This means that at present effective demand in Brazil is for precisely that group of sophisticated products already manufactured by multinational firms, and little incentive is emanating from consumers to change the products or the technology. If income were redistributed so that a significant demand for goods in Brazil was generated by the bulk of the population clustered closely to the national average income (approximately US$1,000 per year), demand would tend to be for a range of wage goods—such as textiles, footwear, furniture, and utensils—which are characterized by intermediate technologies and labor-intensive production techniques. In turn, such large-scale employment creation would serve to reinforce the egalitarian aspects of the initial redistribution.

To sum up this complex picture. A crucial cause of unequal development in Brazil is that vicious circle of wealth set up by capital-intensive industrial structures producing sophisticated consumer goods for an elite market. One way to break out of this circle and increase employment and income levels for a majority of the population would be by massively subsidizing the development of a more appropriate technology, one that would, among other things, be more labor-intensive. However, this would not be enough. Such a reorientation toward an intermediate technology and a labor-intensive industrial structure would make sense only if there were substantial income redistribution that permitted the emergence of a large market for wage goods.

And this brings us to the crux of the matter. No Brazilian government enjoying the support of the contemporary power elite can make a significant dent on the social welfare problem, for a radical improvement in the condition of the poor would seriously threaten the very existence of this elite. First, such improvement would actually destroy individual segments of this elite: land reform would demolish the landlord class, while intermediate technology would weaken the position of those domestic elites attached to foreign capital. Second, by disturbing class relations and disrupting growth, such reform would threaten the collective well-being of the ruling classes.

Land reform, for example, obviously hurts landlords. But precisely because it gives land and food-producing capability to peasants, and thus allows the rural masses to consume more, there is less left over for the urban population (which now has to import food) or for cash crop exports. The end result can be severe balance-of-payments difficulties and a new constraint on growth, a state of affairs that harms the capitalist class.

Similarly, the introduction of labor-intensive technologies would weaken that segment of the Brazilian elite employed by foreign capital. national firms could now compete better in fields where foreign capital had less of a "head start." With less sophisticated goods and less complicated production and marketing techniques, the manufacturing sector would be less dependent on the types of technological and financial advantages enjoyed by the multinationals.

But the introduction of labor-intensive industries would do more than weaken that segment of the Brazilian elite employed by foreign capital. Such a policy shift would also involve income redistribution, a move that would be immensely threatening to the entire ruling class. At the very least, redistribution would mean a narrowing of income differentials (a trend that elite classes have always resisted because of the loss of status involved) and a shift to the Left in the balance of political power. Redistribution would also mean a larger, more prosperous, and more demanding work force. Wage hikes would send production costs up, strikes would destroy labor discipline, and profits would plummet. This would culminate in the disappearance of a surplus available for investment, and in a dramatic slowdown in rates of economic growth.[4]

Another serious consequence of the introduction of labor-intensive industries and the weakening of the position of multinational firms in Brazil would be the effect on the external account. Brazil desperately needs the goodwill of the international financial community to maintain healthy inflows of foreign capital to shore up its precarious balance of payments. As we saw in chapter 3, Brazil is in debt to the tune of US$52 billion. Such a level of indebtedness is compatible with domestic growth only if foreign investors continue to see this nation as having a good investment climate, which has to mean "business as usual" for multinational firms.

Thus, given the power structure and the development trajectory of this late-developing nation, there is a remorseless logic at work which makes poverty and inequality a *necessary* consequence of economic growth. And this logic holds true whatever the personal preferences of political leaders. Over the last decade, individual Brazilian politicians have vacillated over the "social question." Delfim Netto, for example, the finance minister during the years of the miracle and the current minister of planning, has not been overly concerned with Brazil's poor performance in the area of social justice. In 1973 he declared that at the present time all redistributional policies would succeed in doing would be "to divide up the misery more equally." [5] President Geisel, on the other hand, seemed genuinely concerned with improving the standard of living of Brazilian workers and repeatedly attempted to raise wages. But as we saw in chapter 4, his well-meaning initiatives were often blunted by economic constraints, and, even where they succeeded, they only benefited the relatively affluent. The fact is that the causes of poverty and inequality in Brazil are so deeply enmeshed in the social, political, and economic structures of this late-developing nation, that very little can be accomplished through marginal adjustments by enlightened leaders. Significant improvement requires a radical change in the political reality. As Fagen has put it, "There are massive and deeply rooted impediments to intranational equity in the South. . . . their removal implies 'revolutionary' changes in existing national and international structures." [6]

The Political Trade-off

In the sphere of political rights and civil liberties the scope for marginal improvements is greater. As the history of Brazil illustrates, for considerable periods of time it has proved possible to award the usual political and civil rights to privileged groups within the population, which has generally meant the articulate urban classes. This was particularly true during the populist phase of easy import-substituting industrialization, before severe economic constraints (primarily inflation and balance-of-payments problems), and threats from a militant Left, made democratic politics an unaffordable luxury. As stated elsewhere in this book, stabilization entails extremely unpopular policies, which, in the case of Brazil, could only be carried out by a repressive authoritarian regime that was both willing and able to suspend many political rights and civil liberties. The elite classes rallied behind such repressive measures, because they saw them as the only method of avoiding a socialist revolution.

The more extreme forms of political repression in the period since

1964 should therefore be viewed as temporary—a function of stringent stabilization policies and a very scared ruling class. Sustained and significant wage suppression did mean the tightening of controls over trade unions, the imprisonment (without trial) of the more active labor leaders, and at least some press censorship. In the same vein, increasing the price of basic food staples and of public transportation, and raising personal income taxes—although essential steps in controlling inflation via a balanced budget—were incompatible with electoral politics. However, the depth and the brutality of the repression in the late sixties and early seventies (widespread and systematic torture, death squads, violent crackdowns on students and labor, and across-the-board press censorship) owed at least something to the nervousness of a new and fragile military regime that saw subversion and socialist revolution around every corner. Such paranoia could not be sustained into the middle and late 1970s.

In general, the need for draconian stabilization measures has proven to be intermittent. For example, between 1964 and 1967 the Brazilian military regime did manage to tame inflation, and in 1974, at the crest of the economic miracle, when domestic growth was exuberant and the international outlook suggested continued high growth rates in the future, the Geisel government began to experiment with various types of political reform. This particular liberalization drive was blunted by the 1974–75 oil-induced world recession; and subsequent attempts to open up the political system have been further hindered (but not squashed) by new waves of domestic inflation and renewed balance-of-payments pressures. However, the 1974–75 recession was much less serious than the 1964 economic crisis, and the political reaction to the recession was tempered by a more restrained and secure ruling class. Memories of the chaos of the 1961–64 period have faded, and there is much less over-reaction to economic problems. The Geisel political reforms did not go as far as was promised, but in 1979 the Brazilian political system is more open than it was a decade ago. The military government has less arbitrary power, there is much less press censorship, at least some strikes are tolerated, torture seems on the wane, and political exiles are returning from abroad.

Recent trends underline the points that capitalist growth is a cyclical phenomenon, and that Brazil has, and will, enter periods when its political options are less constrained by the imperatives of economic growth. The 1964 developmental crisis was extremely severe and provoked a series of repressive policies which were rendered more extreme by a nervous and fearful ruling class. The 1974–75 recession was less serious, and political reactions were muted because of the absence of a militant Left. Brazil has weathered the oil shocks and world stagflation rather well and seems set on a new course of steady, if not spectacular growth. My prediction for the next decade is for a rather modest bundle of political freedoms that will ebb and flow within the narrow range of possibilities set by the economic circumstances of this country. At no time will these circumstances allow complete freedom of expression or fully independent labor unions, but neither will they force a return to the repressive extremes of the 1968–73 period. Brazil is now prosperous and secure enough to allow its elite classes some political and cultural space. This brings us to the question of the significance of enhanced political freedom in an underdeveloped country such as Brazil.

It should be clear from earlier chapters of this book that even during the "golden age of Brazilian democracy" (1946–64) political rights and civil liberties did not amount to much for perhaps 60 percent of the population. The rural mass and the marginal urban dwellers were largely excluded from the political process by the literacy requirement (an adult had to be able to read and write before he or she could vote), and had very little effective right to civil or individual liberties. Oppression is endemic in any society where there are great extremes between the rich and the poor, and millions of hungry people are teetering on the edge of existence. Writing in 1977, Capuano stated that "for the poor masses, whom no one sees and no one misses when they disappear, the torture and brutality of the police remains an unchanged and seemingly unchangeable reality." [7] He could have been writing at any point in the modern history of Brazil. A minimally decent material basis for life is necessary before more subtle forms of human rights attain any meaning. For example, freedom of the press has to be supremely irrelevant to the mass of the people living in a country where only 3 percent of the population reads newspapers.[8]

The classic link between political freedom and social justice lies of course in the right to form trade unions, and the pressure these organizations are then able to exert on employers and governments to raise living standards for workers. Indeed, the formation of independent labor organizations in nineteenth-century Europe was an important factor in the successful struggle for higher wages for the lower classes. In Brazil (and in most underdeveloped countries) this kind of political freedom cannot address the social question. Trade unions have grown up as government-sponsored interest groups with but limited ability to protect the economic interests of the industrial working class. At best, these unions serve only the labor aristocracy in most late-developing nations; they can play no part in protecting the life chances of the rural mass or of the marginal urban workers.

However, despite these qualifications, political freedoms and civil liberties are important rights for the elite classes. The fact that the majority of the Brazilian people have always lived in degrading circumstances and have often been treated brutally does not excuse or justify the fact that since 1964 there has been widespread violation of political and civil freedoms among the groups for whom these rights matter. The recent opening of the political system, however partial, should be welcome.

The Policy Alternatives

In 1973, the late Senator Hubert Humphrey declared that evidence of increased poverty and heightened repression in the Third World had caused a "veritable intellectual revolt against the long held view that growth alone is the answer that will trickle benefits to the poor majority." [9] He believed that policy makers and theorists should get to work on tackling the problems of misery and oppression directly. It is difficult to find fault with these admirable sentiments, but unfortunately this "intellectual revolt" is far from universal.

In several chapters of this book I have demonstrated how values and beliefs have informed the theory and the practice of economic development. We saw how conservative, laissez faire, schools of thought perceived direct foreign investment as an unmitigated blessing for underdeveloped countries, while Marxist theorists saw the same phenomenon as but the most recent episode in capitalist exploitation; and how right-wing theorists have blamed increasing inequality on market mechanisms, while radical schools of thought have laid the same facts at the feet of a military regime. In other words, social scientists and politicians are likely to interpret the same facts in antagonistic ways because they hold extremely different opinions as to what constitutes the "right," the "fair," or the "desirable" path to the modern world. However, despite this inevitable lack of consensus about what should constitute economic development, the ugly discoveries of the 1970s, described in chapter 1, have served to crystallize three major policy perspectives. The juxtaposition of rapid growth with deepening poverty and violent repression in the Third World has forced theorists and planners to be more self-conscious about their goals and their priorities.

On one extreme of the political spectrum is a conservative, hard-line perspective. Right-wing politicians and many orthodox neoclassical economists have continued to uphold the faith in the overriding importance of market mechanisms and economic efficiency. Only through increases in GNP, they argue, will there be anything significant to distribute. Policy efforts in underdeveloped nations should therefore be directed to getting prices right and maximizing growth rates. Eventually there will be "spread and trickle down effects among groups and across nations." [10] This school of thought warns against the dangers of tackling poverty and inequality directly, since this impedes the accumulation effort.[11] As Ian Little has put it, accelerating economic growth and "increasing the demand for unskilled labor is the best way to help the poor in most countries." [12] Needless to say, this right-wing perspective has little patience for the reformist zeal of the New International Economic Order.[13] Given its faith in free markets, it sees the route to rapid growth and maximum world welfare as one requiring less, rather than more, intervention in economic affairs. Brazilian policy makers in the post-1964 period have generally followed this hard-line approach to growth, as have many of those nations listed in table 1. However, in Brazil at least, enthusiasm for free markets and private enterprise has been tempered by the realities of late development. As we saw in chapter 6, twentieth-century conditions have required a large state presence in the Brazilian development effort.

In the middle of the political spectrum is a reformist or liberal perspective. The central message of this school is that it should be possible to initiate policies that will ameliorate the condition of the poor and oppressed within existing institutional and political structures. The proposed reforms of these liberal theorists and policy makers are far-reaching and encompass the restructuring of international financial and trading relationships, as well as the introduction of progressive social reforms within the domestic economies of the Third World. But in the international sphere few of these suggestions have yet got off the ground; and within the underdeveloped world, the economic performance of middle-of-the-road reformist regimes has been rather dismal.

India is often seen as the embodiment of the "soft" reformist approach to development. With low rates of profit in public enterprises, huge subsidies paid to big farmers, and large wage increases awarded to urban workers, there is little surplus left over to help the poor. "It is the paucity of the surplus and the consequent fall in the rate of public investment which largely explains why in recent years India has had as miserable performance in overall growth as in mitigation of poverty." [14] However, despite these depressing results in the economic and social welfare spheres, India has retained a surprisingly rich and resiliant form of democracy. Rights to political participation and to civil and individual liberties flourished in the 1947–75 period. And in 1976 India reaffirmed its commitment to political freedom by ousting the autocratic regime of Indira Gandhi. However, democracy "Western-style" has cost India much in the way of economic efficiency, and it is debatable whether the 500 million Indians who live at subsistence levels in the countryside have benefited much from political and civil freedom.

Peru is another example of reformist policies in the Third World. Between 1968 and 1975 the Velasco regime constituted a "nationalist reforming regime," [15] which, while not committed "to a full-fledged 'transition to socialism,'" [16] had as its aim "the establishment of a more just society." [17] However, by refusing to move to the left, the military failed to mobilize mass support through major redistributional policies.[18] At the same time, the regime lost the confidence and support of local capitalists and alienated foreign interests. The result: stagnation, balance-of-payment crises, and a worsening of the situation of the poor.

Both right-wing and reformist policy perspectives have attempted to hang on to some of the optimism of the 1950s and 1960s, and both deal with development options within a market framework. However, on the Left, a more radical line of reasoning is intensely pessimistic about the possibility for basic human rights within capitalist development.

The radical perspective denies that there ever could be a peaceful transition to a better life for the majority of the population in the Third World. Cataclysmic revolutionary change is seen as a necessary condition for social justice. This school of thought draws on Marxian theory which perceives capitalist development as encompassing an ever-widening gap between the classes.[19] Conflicts, disequilibrium, and recurring breaks in the process of development will culminate in socialist revolution.

Socialist revolutions tend to be equalizing, since they involve the confiscation of property and the ousting of a ruling class. However, revolutions generally mean violence, destruction, and the disruption of production. This not only implies considerable human suffering but also triggers a decline in the output of an economy. Consequently, a population may suffer more, at least for a number of years, than it would under some highly unequal capitalist alternative. J. L. Enos, for example, finds that it takes sixteen years for the social benefits of an "expropriation and assimilation" socialist strategy to overtake an "impoverishment with growth" capitalist strategy.[20] In addition, a whole range of individual, political, and civil rights normally proves incompatible with the mass mobilization and mass discipline needed for socialist development.

The conservative (capitalist) and the radical (socialist) routes to the modern world constitute the starkest alternatives. Both would seem to have distinct advantages over reformist solutions to twentieth-century development. Conservative growth strategies offer rapid growth with at least some political freedom, while socialist transformation offers a significant measure of social justice. Middle-of-the-road growth strategies run the risk of achieving neither growth nor equity. I now want to play out the policy options represented by the polar cases by comparing Brazil with China.

A Comparative Perspective

The Brazilian case is now thoroughly familiar to us. This capitalist nation has experienced extremely high rates of growth over the last three decades, but such economic dynamism has been bought at a high price. In the social sphere, a third of all Brazilian families have been excluded from the modernization process, and they remain in a state of abject poverty. In the political sphere, the recent period has been characterized by military dictatorship, periodic violent repression, and a restricted range of political rights for elite groups.

China represents a very different image. This nation has undergone massive socialist transformation in the period since 1949. Growth has been rather erratic, but through such devices as food rationing and large-scale land reform, the vast majority of Chinese people now have reasonable access to such basic rights as food, shelter, educational and health facilities, and security in old age.[21] There remain flaws in the social welfare system. For example, there are large disparities between standards of living in the countryside and in the town, and between rich and poor provinces; but this socialist regime has managed to set a floor below which no Chinese can sink. "Mao did not eliminate poverty in China but . . . to his eternal credit within a generation he reduced the incidence of destitution in a land where wretched poverty had been the accepted lot of the lower classes for three thousand years." [22]

The drive toward these social goals has meant mass mobilization and the conscious restriction of individual, civil, and political freedoms, especially among that 4–5 percent of the population drawn from "landlords, rich peasants, counterrevolutionaries, bad elements and anticommunist rightists." [23] Whether one is talking about the killing of thousands of reactionaries in the cultural revolution or the forced move of young people to the countryside, individual rights and liberties, in the sense we know them in advanced democracies, are absent in modern China. Social justice for one billion Chinese has entailed considerable political repression.

This fact has provoked much critical comment from Western liberal thinkers. In Leys's eloquent words:

You have to accept the truth: in the People's Republic today, the whisper of the wind in the pines is a reactionary and subversive music, looking at the moon is a feudal left-over toward which one should adopt a clear and strong class position, a taste for being alone is an individualistic, petty bourgeois, maybe worse, counter-revolutionary tendency.[24]

However much one may deplore the restriction of individual freedoms in modern China, it is important to recognize that such oppression does not stem from arbitrary cruelty on the part of the regime, but is part of the drive toward socialist transformation and a more just society. Until recently the Chinese leadership has consistently placed "collective betterment ahead of respect for individual claims against society or the state." [25]

Thus, there are important contrasts between the Brazilian and the Chinese routes to economic development. In the sphere of social welfare, the mass of the people derive little benefit from a capitalist orientation to development, while they are the prime beneficiaries of socialist strategies. On the political front, the contrast is less dramatic. China and at least some other socialist Third World nations (Chile under Allende was a short-lived exception) have explicitly denied the importance of individual political freedoms. Capitalist underdeveloped countries, on the other hand, maintain certain realms of private freedom. "The ethos of the market, the class affinities of intellectuals and bureaucrats, the importance of sustaining ties to the liberal west, all tend towards preserving, by and large, greater space for cultural freedom and creativity" [26] in the capitalist Third World.

However, one should not overdraw the significance of these private freedoms. As stated earlier on in this chapter, the very depth of poverty in capitalist underdeveloped nations, particularly the high ratio of poor to rich, means that brutality and oppression is a necessary part of the social fabric. Individual liberties, insofar as they exist, tend to be luxuries enjoyed by an elite group.

Finally, there are contrasts in the growth sphere. Brazil has achieved considerably more growth than China in the postwar years largely through reliance on foreign capital and advanced technology (annual growth rates have been roughly twice as fast).[27] It is conceivable that Brazil's "larger pie" will eventually foster a slight improvement in living standards for middle groups within the population, while China's disappointing growth performance will further constrain developmental choices (see, for example, the current turning toward Western technology and market incentives and away from social considerations in Chinese economic planning). All of which is to say that the level of economic achievement is capable of enlarging or constraining choice, and that the trade-off picture should not be seen in too static a way.

It should be clear by now that neither capitalism nor socialism is reponsible for the presence of costs in the growth process, but the values of each system do impart a distinct pattern to the developmental outcome. Socialism is better adapted to the realization of fundamental social welfare goals, while capitalism has performed better in the growth sphere and has produced a limited degree of political freedom.

How one judges these results depends on personal value judgments. In particular, it depends on how one rates the fulfillment of basic needs for the majority against political freedom for a minority. It also depends on one's image of the future. Fifty years down the line, a more prosperous Brazil with an impressive array of individual freedoms for the elite classes, and at least some trickle-down of the fruits of growth to middle segements of the population, may present a more attractive image than a stagnant and politically repressive China.

One conclusion is unambiguous. There are no easy routes to the modern world; the choices involved are extremely painful and will confront nations well into the future. In 1932 John Maynard Keynes stated that

the economic problem, the problem of want and poverty and the economic struggle between nations and classes, is nothing but . . . a transitory muddle. . . . [T]he day is not far off when the economic problem will take a back seat where it belongs, and the arena of the heart and the mind will be occupied, or reoccupied by our real problems—the problems of life and of human relations, of creation and behavior and religion.[28]

He was wrong.

NOTES

1. In developing my concept of cumulative causation, I owe much to the work of Gunnar Myrdal; see *Rich Lands and Poor* (New York: Harper & Brothers, 1957), pp. 11–23.

2. A point of view put forward by Richard J. Barnet and Ronald E. Muller, in *Global Reach* (New York: Simon & Schuster, 1974), pp. 123–213.

3. Chile under Allende is an extremely good example of a case in which land reform radicalized the political situation and created a situation where the landlord class became actively involved in trying to overthrow Allende. See discussion in David F. Cusack, *Revolution and Reaction: The Internal Dynamics of Conflict and Confrontation in Chile*, vol. 14, no. 3, Monograph series in World Affairs (University of Denver Graduate School of International Studies, 1977), pp. 39–45. See also Brian Loveman, *Struggle in the Countryside: Politics and Rural Labor in Chile 1919–1973* (Bloomington, Ind.: Indiana University Press, 1976), pp. 303–34.

4. Some of these interactions are discussed in F. Stewart and P. Streeten, "Conflicts between Output and Employment Objectives in Developing Countries," *Oxford Economic Papers* 23, no. 2 (July 1971): 145–69.

5. See Carlos Geraldo Langoni, *Distribuição da Renda e Desenvolvimento Econômico do Brasil* (Rio de Janeiro: Editora Expressão e Cultura, 1973), p. 13.

6. Richard Fagen, "Equity in the South in the Context of North–South Relations," in Albert Fishlow et al., *Rich and Poor Nations in the World Economy* (New York: McGraw-Hill, 1978), p. 172.

7. *New York Times*, 1 September 1977.

8. The daily circulation of newspapers throughout Brazil is a little more than 4 million (Amnesty International, "Brazil: Background Paper," 7 June 1978, p. 5).

9. Statement by Senator Hubert Humphrey introducing the 1973 foreign aid bill in the United States Congress; cited in Pan A. Yotopoulos and Jeffrey B. Nugent, *Economics of Development: Empirical Investigations* (New York: Harper & Row, 1976), p. 430.

10. Yotopoulos and Nugent, *Economics of Development*, p. 9.

11. Ranis goes so far as to assert that "every time a mixed economy intervenes on behalf of the poor the poor find themselves worse off" ("Growth and Redistribution: Tradeoffs or Complements," Discussion Paper No. 245 (New Haven, Conn.: Yale University Economic Growth Center, May 1976), p. 24.

12. Ian Little, "Book Review of Adelman and Morris (1973) and Chenery et al. (1974)," *Journal of Development Economics* 3 (1976) :104.

13. The New International Economic Order was the name given to the economic reforms proposed in 1974 by the United Nations General Assembly. Since that time Third World nations have been engaged in a series of protracted negotiations with the industrial nations about such issues as commodity prices and access to the markets of the industrial countries for manufactured goods. Little progress has as yet been made. See discussion in D. A. Avramovic, "Developing/Developed Country Negotiations: Recent Experience and Prospects," mimeographed (Geneva, Independent Commission on International Development Issues, 1978).

14. Pranab K. Bhardan, "India," in Chenery et al., *Redistribution with Growth* (London: Oxford University Press, 1974), p. 261.

15. E. V. K. Fitzgerald, *The State and Economic Development in Peru since 1968* (Cambridge, England: Cambridge University Press, 1976), p. 1.

16. Fitzgerald, *The State*, p. 1.

17. Fitzgerald, *The State* (note 15), p. 6.

18. Rosemary Thorp and Geoffrey Bertram, *Peru 1890–1977: Growth and Policy in an Open Economy* (New York: Columbia University Press, 1978), p. 319.

19. See Paul Baran, *The Political Economy of Growth* (New York: Monthly Review Press, 1973), p. 1.

20. J. L. Enos, "Thoughts upon Reading Redistribution with Growth" (Oxford, England: Magdalen College, February 1976), p. 20.

21. These are discussed by Martin King Whyte, "Inequality and Stratification in China," *China Quarterly*, no. 64 (December 1975) : 684–712.

22. Nick Eberstadt, "China: How Much Success?" *New York Review of Books*, 3 May 1979.

23. Susan L. Shirk, "Human Rights: What About China?" *Foreign Policy*, no. 29 (Winter 1977–78) :118.

24. Simon Leys, *Chinese Shadows* (Harmondsworth, England: Penguin Books, 1978), p. 25. For another indictment of the political and cultural costs of socialism in China, see Chen Jo-Hsi, *The Execution of Mayor Yin and Other Stories from the Great Proletarian Cultural Revolution* (Bloomington, Ind.: Indiana University Press, 1978).

25. Shirk, "Human Rights" (note 23), p. 40. Mao, in a famous statement, declared: "Of all things in the world, people are the most precious." This statement reflects the priorities of his regime. See Mao Tse-Tung, *Selected Works* (Peking: Foreign Language Press, 1961), p. 454.

26. Richard Falk, "Comparative Protection of Human Rights in Capitalist and Social-

ist Third World Countries," paper delivered at the 1978 annual meeting of the American Political Science Association (New York, September 1978), p. 9.

27.   See Alexander Eckstein, *China's Economic Development* (Ann Arbor, Mich.: University of Michigan Press, 1975), pp. 9–55, for a discussion of Chinese growth rates between 1952 and 1970. Most estimates suggest that the Chinese economy grew, on average, at approximately 4.25 percent per year during this time. This is slighly more than half the Brazilian growth rate (see table 2).

28.   John Maynard Keynes, *Essays in Persuasion* (New York: Harcourt, Brace, 1932), p. vii.

Appendix Tables

TABLE 1

Some Examples of Successful but Oppressive Growth Strategies in the Capitalist Third World

Country*	Average Annual Growth of GNP 1970-77[1]	Proportion of National Income Captured by the Top 20% of the Population[2]	Violation of Political and Civil Rights (1976)[3]
Ecuador	10.5	74%	Authoritarian rule, self-censorship of press, political prisoners, illegal arrests
Ivory Coast	10.3	57%	One-party state, state-controlled press, political prisoners
Iran	10.2	55%	Authoritarian rule, press censorship, political prisoners and executions, widespread torture
South Korea	9.9	45%	Authoritarian rule, press censorship, political prisoners
Brazil	9.8	62%	Authoritarian rule, political prisoners, state-controlled elections, torture
Dominican Republic	8.4	58%	Political prisoners, illegal arrests and detentions
Indonesia	7.8	n.a.†	Authoritarian rule, political prisoners, press censorship
Nigeria	7.8	61%	Authoritarian rule, summary trials and executions
Turkey	7.4	61%	Political prisoners, illegal arrests, torture
Paraguay	7.0	n.a.	Authoritarian rule, most civil and political freedoms suspended, widespread torture
Thailand	6.7	46%	Authoritarian rule, self-censorship of press, political prisoners
Philippines	6.4	55%	Martial law, political prisoners, press censorship, torture
Guatemala	6.0	53%	Political murder, illegal arrests and detentions, torture
Nicaragua	5.9	n.a.	Authoritarian rule, most civil and political freedoms suspended, press censorship, torture
Mexico	5.5	64%	One-party state, some arbitrary arrests and detentions

*I have excluded those countries, such as Saudi Arabia, that have achieved high growth rates during the 1970s through an overwhelming dependence on oil. I have also excluded Chile, because during the early 1970s, the period under consideration, growth rates were low. There was a military coup in 1973, and since that date Chile has followed a successful and oppressive growth strategy similar to those countries listed in table 1.
†Not available.

[1] Source: *Statistical Yearbook 1978* (New York: United Nations), pp. 732-39. The growth rates for Iran and Turkey are for the 1970-76 period, and for Nigeria they are for the 1970-75 period.

[2] Source: Montek S. Ahluwalia, "Inequality, Poverty and Development," *Journal of Development Economics* 3 (1975): 341; Hollis Chenery et al., eds., *Redistribution with Growth* (Oxford University Press, 1974), pp. 8-9; and Irma Adelman and Cynthia Taft Morris, *Economic Growth and Social Equity in Developing Countries* (Stanford, California: Stanford University Press, 1973), p. 152. South Korea has a relatively equal distribution of income. This is due partially to large-scale land reform carried out by the occupying forces at the end of Word War II—a circumstance that is hard for other Third World nations to replicate. See B. Renaud, "Economic Growth and Income Inequality in Korea; World Bank Staff Working Paper, no. 240, Washington, D.C., February 1976.

[3] Compiled from *Human Rights Reports*, Committee on Foreign Relations, United States Senate, 95th Congress, 1st Session (Washington, D.C.: United States Government Printing Office, March 1977); and *Human Rights Conditions in Selected Countries and the U.S. Response, Committee on International Relations*

TABLE 2
Brazilian Growth Rates, 1921-78

| | Real Output Growth Rate (%) | | |
Year	GDP	Agri-culture	In-dustry
1921-30	3.7	3.4	3.3
1931-40	4.6	4.3	5.2
1940-47	5.1	3.9	6.5
1948-56	6.4	3.9	8.8
1957-61	8.3	5.8	10.7
1962-67	3.5	3.9	3.5
1968-73	11.5	4.7	13.2
1974-78	7.5	n.a.[†]	n.a.[†]
1979*	7.1	5.5	7.8

SOURCE: Fundação Getulio Vargas, *Conjunctura Economica*, various issues.
*Estimated.
[†]Not available.

TABLE 3
Industrial Growth Rates during the Years of the "Miracle"

	1967-70	1971	1972	1973	1974
Nonmetal minerals	17.3	11.1	13.7	16.4	15.1
Metal products	14.4	5.6	12.1	6.3	4.3
Machinery	22.7	3.6	} 18.9	} 27.8	} 11.6
Electronics	13.4	21.3			
Transport equipment	32.6	19.0	22.5	27.6	19.1
Paper and paper products	9.1	6.3	7.0	10.1	3.5
Rubber products	15.3	11.8	13.0	12.4	10.8
Chemicals	15.6	13.6	16.3	22.3	8.5
Textiles	7.4	8.8	} 4.1	} 8.4	} -2.8
Clothing, shoes, etc.	1.7	-1.8			
Food products	8.3	3.6	} 13.3	} 9.6	} 4.4
Beverages	8.2	4.8			
Tobacco	9.6	5.7			
Total Manufacturing	14.2	11.6	13.6	15.8	7.1
Construction	14.4	8.4	13.0	15.4	11.2
Public utilities	12.2	n.a.	11.1	12.5	12.0

SOURCE: Fundação Getulio Vargas, *Conjunctura Econômica*, various issues.

TABLE 4
Brazilian Trade, 1964-78
(US$ millions)

	Exports		Imports		
	Total	Manu- factured Goods	Total	Petro- leum	Capital Goods
1964	1,430	89	1,086	180	300
1968	1,881	75	1,855	204	704
1970	2,739	365	2,507	236	1,074
1972	3,991	899	4,232	409	1,750
1974	7,951	2,263	12,643	2,962	3,119
1976	10,128	2,776	12,347	3,846	3,556
1978	12,650	5,083	13,674	4,485	2,870

SOURCE: Fundaçâo Getulio Vargas, Conjuntura Econômica, various issues.

TABLE 5
Growth of the Brazilian Debt and
International Reserves, 1964-79

	Debt Outstanding End of Year	International Reserves
1964	2,502	244
1966	2,956	421
1968	3,780	257
1970	5,295	1,187
1972	9,521	4,183
1974	17,166	5,269
1976	25,985	6,544
1978	43,510	11,895
1979*	52,000	9,000

SOURCE: Banco Central do Brasil, Boletim, various issues.
*Estimated.

TABLE 6

Items From the Brazilian Balance of Payments, 1964-78

	1964	1966	1968	1970	1972	1974	1976	1978
Current Account	−140	54	−508	−562	−1,489	−7,122	−6,133	−5,927
Trade Balance (f.o.b.)	344	438	26	232	−244	−4,690	−2,219	−1,024
Services (net)	−259	−463	−556	−815	−1,250	−2,433	−3,919	−4,975
Capital Movements (net)	82	124	541	1,015	3,492	6,254	6,866	9,439

SOURCE: Banco Central do Brasil, *Boletim*, various issues.

TABLE 7
Brazilian Rates of Inflation, 1948-78

Year	Rate of Inflation (% per year)
1948-61	17.6
1962-64	70.6
1965-73	27.3
1974-78	36.6
1979*	80.0

SOURCE: Fundação Getulio Vargas, *Conjunctura Economica*, various issues. GDP implicit deflator.
*Estimated.

TABLE 8
Changes in Ownership among Large Brazilian Firms, 1973-78

	Private National (%)	Multi-national (%)	State (%)
Largest 500			
1973	43.1	41.1	15.8
1976	34.6	40.8	24.6
1978	35.9	35.4	28.7
Largest 25			
1973	6.1	61.0	32.9
1976	7.2	54.9	37.9
1978	5.4	40.8	53.8

SOURCE: "Melhores e Maiores," *Exame* (Edição especial, September 1979), p. 128. These figures refer to the sales of the 500 largest and the 25 largest firms in Brazil.

TABLE 9

The Role of Private National, Multinational, and State Firms in the Various Sectors of the Brazilian Economy, 1978

	Private National (%)	Multi-national (%)	State (%)
Predominantly National			
Civil construction	100.0	–	–
Communications	100.0	–	–
Supermarkets	98.3	1.7	–
Furniture	97.4	2.6	–
Clothing, shoes	96.9	3.1	–
Retail business	90.0	10.0	–
Heavy construction	88.7	8.5	2.8
Printing and publishing	73.8	26.2	–
Food	66.6	33.4	–
Pulp and paper	59.9	32.9	7.2
Nonmetallic minerals	58.0	42.0	–
Predominantly Foreign			
Wholesale business	41.4	42.2	16.4
Machinery	41.5	48.8	9.7
Transportation equipment	37.7	53.6	8.7
Heavy vehicles	45.2	54.8	–
Petroleum distribution	11.0	60.8	28.2
Electronics	33.6	66.4	–
Textiles	31.8	68.2	–
Cleaning products	27.2	72.8	–
Plastics and rubber	21.5	76.1	2.4
Beverages and tobacco	23.6	76.4	–
Pharmaceuticals	15.6	84.4	–
Office equipment	13.8	86.2	–
Automobiles	0.6	99.4	–
Predominantly State			
Public services	–	–	100.0
Chemicals and petrochemicals	5.0	15.8	79.2
Steel	27.1	7.9	65.0
Minerals	29.5	12.0	58.5
Transportation	49.6	–	50.4

SOURCE: "Melhores e Maiores," *Exame* (Edição especial, September 1979), p. 125. These figures refer to the sales of the twenty largest firms in each sector.

TABLE 10
Direct Private Investment in Brazil, 1929-78

(1) United States Direct Private Investment in Brazil

	US$ Book Value at Year End		
Year	Total	Manu-facturing	Manufacturing as Percentage of Total
1929	194	46	24%
1940	240	70	29%
1946	323	125	39%
1950	644	285	44%
1957	835	378	45%
1961	1,000	543	54%
1964	994	673	68%
1967	1,326	891	67%
1972	2,490	1,745	70%
1974	3,760	2,578	68%
1977	5,956	3,935	66%
1978	7,170	4,684	65%

(2) Direct Foreign Investment in Brazil by Country of Origin

	Percentage Distribution by Country of Origin				
Year	United States	West Germany	France	United Kingdom	Japan
1961	43%	9%	4%	4%	4%
1969	48%	10%	2%	6%	3%
1975	33%	12%	4%	6%	12%
1977	31%	14%	4%	5%	11%
1978	29%	15%	4%	5%	10%

SOURCE: (1) *Survey of Current Business,* August issue, various years.

(2) Banco Central do Brasil, *Boletim,* various issues.

TABLE 11
The Financial Impact of Multinational Corporations in Brazil, 1965-75

US$ millions

Multinational Corporation	(1) Total Capital Brought into Brazil (including years before 1965)	(2) Reinvestment (1965-75)	(3) Profits and Dividends Remitted Abroad (1965-75)	(4) Remittances Abroad in Payment for Technology	(5) Total Remittances Abroad (3 + 4)	(6) Surplus Generated in Brazil (2 + 3 + 4)	(7) Ratio of Surplus Generated in Brazil to Capital Brought into Brazil
Volkswagen	119.5	72.8	70.6	208.5	279.1	351.9	2:9
Rhodia	14.3	108.7	39.9	20.7	60.6	169.3	11:8
Exxon	1.8	67.7	44.5	n.a.	44.5	112.2	62:3
Pirelli	28.7	37.8	45.1	19.8	64.9	102.7	3:6
Phillips	9.9	51.2	5.0	9.4	14.4	65.6	6:6
Firestone	4.1	44.5	48.1	2.1	50.2	94.7	23:1
General Electric	13.9	32.2	19.4	4.3	23.7	55.9	4:0
Souza Cruz	2.5	129.5	81.3	1.0	82.3	211.8	84:7
Johnson & Johnson	0.7	34.0	17.0	5.7	22.7	56.7	81:0
Anderson Clayton	1.4	28.2	16.8	n.a.	16.8	45.0	82:1
Brazilian Light	102.0	86.4	114.7	0.6	115.3	201.7	1:9
Total	298.8	693.0	502.4	272.1	774.5	1,467.7	

SOURCE: Brazilian-American Chamber of Commerce, *News Bulletin* 6, no. 75 (1976): 3. Figures cited in this source were obtained from the Central Bank of Brazil.

TABLE 12

The Distribution of Income in a Number of Underdeveloped and Developed Countries

Underdeveloped Countries	Per Capita Group (1970 US$)	Income Shares				
		Bottom 20%	Second Quintile	Third Quintile	Fourth Quintile	Top 20%
Ecuador	313	2.5	3.9	5.6	14.5	73.5
Kenya	153	3.8	6.2	8.5	13.5	68.0
Mexico	697	4.0	6.5	9.5	16.0	64.0
Brazil	457	3.1	6.9	10.8	17.0	62.2
Turkey	322	3.0	6.5	11.1	18.8	60.6
Ivory Coast	328	3.9	6.2	11.8	20.9	57.2
Philippines	224	3.9	7.9	12.5	20.3	55.4
Developed Countries						
West Germany	3,209	5.9	10.4	15.6	22.5	45.6
Japan	1,713	4.6	11.3	16.8	23.4	43.8
Sweden	4,452	5.4	9.9	17.6	24.6	42.5
United Kingdom	2,414	6.0	12.8	18.2	23.8	39.2
United States	5,244	6.7	13.0	17.4	24.1	38.8
Australia	2,632	6.6	13.5	17.8	23.4	38.7

SOURCE: Compiled from Montek S. Ahluwalia, "Inequality, Poverty and Development," *Journal of Development Economics* 34 (1976): 340-41.

TABLE 13

The Brazilian Distribution of Income, 1960-76

Income Groups (Percentile)	Relative Income Levels (Percentage of total income)				Absolute Income Levels (Average annual income for each income group, 1970 US$)*			
	1960†	1970†	1976	Change 1960/76	1960†	1970†	1976†	Change 1960/76
10−	1.0	1.2	1.0	−47%	102	91	138	35%
10	2.0	2.2	2.2	+10%	112	167	303	170%
10	3.0	2.9	2.7	−10%	167	211	373	123%
10	4.1	3.7	3.2	−31%	243	271	451	86%
10	6.1	4.9	4.4	−28%	339	357	616	82%
10	7.5	6.0	5.1	−32%	420	446	712	70%
10	9.0	7.3	6.7	−26%	498	535	937	88%
10	11.3	9.9	9.8	−13%	626	728	1,375	120%
10	15.2	15.2	14.5	−5%	845	1,119	2,037	141%
10+	39.5	46.7	50.4	+27%	2,197	3,441	7,057	221%
5+	28.3	34.1	37.9	+34%	3,138	5,032	10,604	238%
1+	11.0	14.7	17.4	+46%	6,631	10,818	24,328	267%

SOURCE: Compiled from *Indicadores Sociais* (Rio de Janeiro: Instituto Brasileiro de Geografia o Estatística, 1979), pp. 63-64.

*In 1970 the dollar was worth 4.6 cruzeiros.

†The 1960 and 1970 figures are obtained from the demographic census; the 1976 figures are obtained from the household expenditure survey PNAD (Pesquisa Nacional por Amostra de Domicilios). Both sets of figures refer to the economically active population. A variety of statistical problems is encountered in trying to compare these two sources; see discussion in "The Distribution of Income in Brazil," World Bank Staff Working Paper no. 356 (Washington, D.C., 1979), pp. 7-37. However, no one disputes the general trend toward increased inequality shown up by this table.

TABLE 14
Infant Mortality in Brazil, 1960-70

Year	Deaths per Thousand Live Births in Babies Less Than One Year Old*
1960	105.2
1965	101.1
1966	98.0
1967	105.9
1968	89.6
1969	91.2
1970	108.7

SOURCE: *Indicadores Sociais* (Rio de Janeiro: Instituto Brasileiro de Geografia e Estatística, 1979), p. 128.
*The figures on infant mortality refer to the Brazilian cities of Manans, São Luis, Terezina, Fortaleza, Natal, João Pessoa, Recife, Maceio, Aracaju, Salvador, Belo Horizonte, Vitória, Rio de Janeiro, Curitiba, Porto Alegre, Goiania e Brasilia.

TABLE 15
Evolution of the Minimum Wage in Brazil, 1964-78

	1970 Cruzeiros*					
	Rio de Janeiro		São Paulo		Porto Alegre	
Year	Real Value of the Monthly Wage	Annual Variation	Real Value of the Monthly Wage	Annual Variation	Real Value of the Monthly Wage	Annual Variation
1964	216		225		191	
1965	209	−2.8	215	−4.7	175	−8.7
1966	182	−12.8	191	−11.1	165	−5.3
1967	185	1.6	184	−3.3	162	−2.1
1968	169	−8.6	184	0	164	0.8
1969	181	6.6	175	−5.0	162	−1.3
1970	176	−3.3	176	0.9	161	−0.5
1971	177	0.2	175	−0.5	163	1.6
1972	181	2.7	178	1.3	164	0.3
1973	188	3.9	181	1.5	163	−0.6
1974	178	−5.7	174	−3.9	154	−5.5
1975	190	6.7	184	5.8	162	5.1
1976	187	−1.6	190	3.1	168	3.6
1977	187	0.3	194	2.6	168	0.3
1978	191	2.3	199	2.5	173	2.5

SOURCE: *Indicadores Sociais* (Rio de Janeiro: Instituto Brasileiro de Geografia e Estatística, 1979), p. 56.
*In 1970 the dollar was worth 4.6 *cruzeiros.*

TABLE 16

Standards of Living for the Average Working Class Family in São Paulo, 1958 and 1969

	1958	1969
Household members	4.5	4.9
Number employed	1.0	2.0
Monthly income (in current prices)	Cr$10.2	Cr$512.1
Real income (prices of 1958)	Cr$10.2	Cr$9.2
Monthly earnings of head of household	Cr$8.5	Cr$361.0
Real income (prices of 1958)	Cr$8.5	Cr$5.4

SOURCE: Cândido Procópio Ferreira de Camargo et al., *São Paulo 1975: Cresimento e Pobreza* (São Paulo: Edições Loyola; 1976), p. 67.

TABLE 17

Structure of Consumption in a Typical Working-Class Household, São Paulo, 1958 and 1970 (% per year)

Type of Expense	Percentage of Monthly Budget	
	1958	1970
Food	64.3	51.0
Clothing	14.2	10.6
Health Care	5.7	4.7
Domestic Cleanliness	4.3	2.2
Domestic Appliances	4.3	8.5
Transport (mainly second-hand automobiles)	2.9	11.5
Personal Hygiene	2.1	1.6
Education and Culture	1.4	4.6
Smoking	0.7	5.3

SOURCE: Cândido Procópio Ferreira de Camargo et al., *São Paulo 1975: Cresimento e Pobreza* (São Paulo: Edições Loyola; 1976), p. 75.

TABLE 18
Growth of the Brazilian Population and Labor Force, 1940-76

	Number of People in 1976	Percentage in 1976	Average Annual Growth Rates			
			1940/50	1950/60	1960/70	1970/76
Population						
Total	105.8	100%	2.3	3.1	2.9	2.8
Urban	62.1	58%	3.8	5.3	5.1	4.4
Labor Force						
Primary	14.3	36%	0.5	1.7	0.7	0.7
Secondary	9.1	23%	4.4	2.4	5.9	3.8
Tertiary	16.3	41%	2.5	5.3	4.0	5.8

SOURCE: Compiled from Helga Hoffman, *Desemprego e Subemprego no Brasil* (São Paulo: Editora Ática, 1977), pp. 44-47; and *Indicadores Sociais* (Rio de Janeiro: Instituto Brasileiro de Geografia e Estatística, 1979), pp. 30-32.

INDEX

(Numbers in bold face refer to specific tables. All tables follow page 221.)

Action for National Liberation (ALN), 77
Adelman, Irma, 163–64
Advertising, 139, 147–49, 173–74
Afonso, Almino Monteiro Alvares, 191
Africa, 6, 21, 25
Agências Folhas, 81
Agriculture, 22, 31, 33; in the Amazon basin, 172–73; cash crop, 60, 93, 126–27, 129, 207; decline of, 187; and export price fluctuations, 95; and food supply flexibility, 93; and inflation, 90–91; labor force in, 23–25; and national priorities, 129; 1921–79 growth rates in, **2**; public sector importance to, 125–26
Alcohol, 172
Allende, Salvadore, 217
Alliance for Progress, 5
Aluminum, 171
Amarizi region, 170
Amazonas, 172
Amazon basin, 3, 171–72
Amazonian Indians, 171–73
American Chamber of Commerce, 140
American Institute of Free Labor Development, 193
American Revolution, 23
Amnesty, 79
Amnesty International, 193
Anderson Clayton, **11**
Angola, 52
Appalachia, 9
APS (Aborigines Protection Society), 172
ARENA (Aliança Renovadora Nacional), 77, 79–80
Argentina, 3, 47, 89, 164, 190
Aristotle, 108–9, 163
Asia, 6–7, 21
Australia, **12**
Automobile industry, 98–99, 122; multinational domination of, 135, 143, 150

Bacha, Edmar, 111, 167
Bahia, 115
Balance-of-payments problems, 42–56, 142; and exchange rate policies, 39, 95; and growth conditions, 204–5; and land reform, 207–8; 1969–78, **6**
Ball, George W., 135

Bank of Brazil, 126
Banks, 77, 91, 123. *See also* Credit
Barnet, Richard J., 147
Barros, José Roberto Mendonça de, 128
Belo Horizonte, 82
Beltrão, Helio, 116–17
Bergsman, Joel, 95
Betim, 199
Beverages industry, **3**, **9**
B. F. Goodrich, 145
Billboards, 148
Birth control, 186
Birth rates, 185–86
BNDE (national development bank), 50, 126
Boa Vista, 172
Branco, Castello, 70, 74–76, 192, 195
Brasilia, 39
Brazil: causes of poverty and repression in, 203–18 (*see also* Poverty; Repression); chronic inflation in, 92–103 (*see also* Inflation); colonial and oligarchic rule in, 59–61; control of organized labor in, 185–200 (*see also* Labor; Unions); correlates of growth strategies in, **1**; destruction of Indian tribes in, 171–73; direct private investment in, **10**; economic history of, 31–56; export-led growth in, 45–49, 128, 143; impact of multinationals on, 144–56, 165–75, **11** (*see also* Multinational corporations); import-substituting industrialization of, 36–40 (*see also* Import-substituting industrialization); incentive structures and investment patterns in, 37–40; income distribution in, 31–32, 35–36, **12**, **13** (*see also* Income distribution); industrialization of, 36–40, 63–67, 203–4 (*see also* Industrialization); infant mortality in, **14** (*see also* Infant mortality); influence of foreign capital on, 135–36, 140–44; manufacturing in, 110–22, 187–88 (*see also* Manufacturing; military rule in, 67–83; minimum wage in, **15**; 1978 role of large firms in, **9**; 1969–78 balance of payments in, **6**; 1921–79 growth rates in, **2**; population growth in, 202, **18** (*see also* Population growth); populist period in, 62–67, 74, 99–100, 102, 209; poverty and inequality in, 163–64, 166–72, 176–82; primary export economy in, 32–36; recent economic growth in, 49–56; role of the state in, 105–6, 127–31 (*see*